TORN
ASUNDER

TORN ASUNDER

RECOVERING FROM
EXTRAMARITAL AFFAIRS

DAVE CARDER

MOODY PRESS

CHICAGO

ISBN: 0-8024-7748-8

13 15 17 19 20 18 16 14

Printed in the United States of America

To my wife, Ronnie,
who, for over twenty-five years
across our family life cycle
(now including four adolescents),
in the midst of her own
educational and career achievements,
has always been involved in
creating that special world
within our marriage that
has made my life so rich

CONTENTS

Section 1: Understanding Extramarital Affairs

The "perfect match" □ "success" at work □ things heat up
□ the revelation □ a new beginning □ steps forward and
backward □ digging for answers □ cast of characters □
about sin and guilt □ regarding divorce □ who this
book is for □ to spouses who are "alone" □ to adult
children of parental affairs □ to those who are thinking
of having an affair

Three types of affairs □ the one-night stand (Class I affair)
□ the entangled affair (Class II affair) □ sexual addiction (Class III affair)

Four styles of Class II affairs □ the intimacy-avoidance affair
(the windshield wiper syndrome) □ the conflict-avoid-
ance affair (the dial tone syndrome) □ the empty nest
affair (the midlife crisis) □ the out-the-door affair
("finally it's my turn")

Cultural myth 1 (for men): "only women can/should nurture" □ cultural myth 2 (for women): "I need a man to
be happy" □ spiritual myth 1: performance orientation
□ spiritual myth 2: dependency orientation □ marital
styles □ the spouse as parent □ the child as spouse

FOREWORD

One does not have to be a pastor or counselor to realize that marital infidelity has now become endemic in our country. In a recent letter to Ann Landers, a man who signed himself as "No Male Chauvinist, Just Observant in the East" asked the columnist's opinion on his observation that an increasing number of wives cheat on their husbands. She replied, "If you had asked me that 20 years ago, I would have said, 'No, I don't agree.' Today, however, I would have to say you are right. The reason, of course, is that many more women are out there in the workplace. They have more visibility, more mobility, more temptations and greater economic independence. Is the trend toward infidelity going to change? I don't see how. Cheating on spouses is now an equal-opportunity sport."*

Such an attempt at humor only underscores how tragic the situation is. It also illustrates how successfully our pagan, amoral media has eroded moral boundaries and eased us into not only *accepting* but almost *expecting* adultery as a part of married life.

But the greater tragedy is how infidelity has infected even the church and affected the lives of Christian couples. Pastoral coun-

---

* December 15, 1991. Permission granted by Ann Landers and Creators Syndicate.

selors spend a disproportionate amount of time trying to help restore marriages badly disrupted by infidelity. However, there are many more couples who are ashamed to seek outside help and who try to put the pieces together by themselves. Either way, in spite of the high level of spiritual commitment, the results are not always successful. The rising divorce rate among Christians is evidence of that sad fact.

Dave Carder has given us a comprehensive and practical guide for dealing with extramarital affairs. It is *comprehensive* because it carefully sorts out the different kinds of affairs. It does not fall into the error of lumping all infidelity together and giving oversimplistic spiritual answers. Without this understanding and diagnosis of what has really happened, the "after-recovery prescription," though pious-sounding and well-intentioned, will not bring permanent healing and restoration. It is *practical* because it deals with the daily, gut-level issues both partners face. The heart of the matter is the long, hard task of rebuilding the bridge of trust, and then learning to once again walk on it, to renew that intimacy which is the essence of marriage.

This book, better than any other I know, provides the down-to-earth "how-to's" to bring that healing about.

David A. Seamands
Professor of Pastoral Ministry
Asbury Theological Seminary

PREFACE

Remember when you were a kid, lying on the grass in your front yard and gazing at clouds drifting by? Most of us used to daydream about what we'd be "when we grew up." Butchers, bakers, and candlestick-makers; the possibilities seemed endless, and such they were.

I did my share of daydreaming, too. But I never dreamed I'd become a specialist in adultery! Yet here I am, after more than twenty years of full-time Christian ministry, with a counseling ministry that tends to specialize in, of all things, helping people recover from affairs. From time to time I shake my head in amazement—it still surprises me.

But don't get me wrong—I'm thankful that the Lord has steered me this way. There's a lot of carnage out there. Adultery and divorce rates among the evangelical population are nearly the same as for the general population in this country, and that's a lot of broken hearts, broken lives, broken homes, and broken careers. I know; I've seen them—and more often than I'd like, I've seen them in thoroughly Christian circles.

Shortly after I came to know Christ, as a freshman in high school, our family started attending a little Bible church. We were all new Christians—my parents and siblings also received Christ about that time—and we eagerly drank in the solid Bible teaching we received there. It was a wonderful start to our spiritual walk, but within a couple of years we were shocked when the pastor (whose wife had recently died) ran off with the wife of the chairman of the board of elders.

After I finished high school, I went off to Bible college, where I thought I might be immune from such shockers. Wrong! During my first year there, I was floored to learn that many of my single classmates were sexually active. Additionally, adultery was revealed among some of the staff of the school. So much for pure and holy Bible schools.

After graduation I took my first pastorate on the staff of a large independent church, where I stayed for fourteen years. The specter of infidelity continued to haunt me as I watched our senior pastor leave town by cover of night with a single-parent mom he had been counseling, abandoning his wife of twenty-five years and family of three. I was devastated. Here was my first boss in the ministry, the man to whom I looked for leadership and guidance and modeling, acting out the sexual and moral antithesis of his lifelong message.

The immediate reaction to the senior pastor's affair at the church office was to change the way business was conducted: only open doors in the counseling offices, all same-sex counseling, staff restricted to daytime office hours. Such rule changes seemed to me to be superficial Band-Aids™ at best. I also resented—as did many of my colleagues—the implication that we might get involved in an affair just because our senior pastor did.

Yet the upset the changes in regulations caused was not near the effect this final example of infidelity exacted on my personal psyche. It took some serious processing on my part to get over it. But when the dust settled I vowed that I was going to find out how adultery happens and how to prevent it and how to help those who fall into it.

I continued my graduate studies and found, as I counseled with pastors and their wives, missionary couples, and others, that indeed there were shared threads of experience among them all. There is a pattern, and I've tried to put whatever wisdom I've acquired over many years of studying the subject and counseling individuals and couples into these pages. I have worked in tandem with my friend and coauthor Duncan Jaenicke, and I believe there is valuable material between these covers. I pray that God's Spirit might use it in your life and the lives of your loved ones. The Lord knows we need some help in this area!

ACKNOWLEDGMENTS

Dave wishes to thank Duncan for all his work in making this information helpful and meaningful. Thanks go as well to Pat Lampman, Ph.D., who helped shape this book from its inception, and to David Stoop, Ph.D., Clinical Director for the Minirth-Meier Clinic West's Behavioral Day Treatment Program, for that enlightening conversation we had about the split in personality of those involved in affairs.

A special thanks goes to Buck Buchanan, Gary Richmond, and John Coulombe, my coworkers in the Care and Concern team at First Evangelical Free in Fullerton; to Paul Sailhamer, our senior associate at First Evangelical Free, for working with me on a number of these situations and helping to shape my thinking about recovery from infidelity; and to Chuck Swindoll, my senior pastor, whose preaching and encouragement has meant a lot to me over the years.

To my fellow counselors Earl Henslin, Psy.D., John Townsend, Ph.D., and Henry Cloud, Ph.D., goes a special appreciation for their contribution to my thinking on this subject.

Thanks go to those two dozen or so couples across the country who experienced an affair in their marriage, survived, and early on provided valuable insights and suggestions for this project; to Emily Brown, author of *Patterns of Infidelity and Their Treatment*, whose workshop refined my thinking and helped me actually to experience through role-play the pain and conflict of the infidel; and, finally, to Annie Finkemeier for her tireless hours at the MacIntosh keyboard.

Duncan wishes to thank his wife, Priscilla, faithful friend and gentle editor, for her loyal support and helpful feedback during this project. Thanks are also due Bethany, Grace, Kris, Anne, Larry, Joanie, Gary, and Sue for their faithful prayers, friendship, and support. To Dave, for inviting me along on this most challenging and edifying of journeys: Dave, you're the greatest. And most of all, thanks go to the Lord for putting this book together, honoring both Dave and me in allowing us to share these truths in His name. May He mightily use these pages to bless multitudes.

A LETTER FROM
"THE OTHER WOMAN"

Author's note: The following is an adaptation of a letter I received from a woman who, through the grapevine, got hold of an early draft of the manuscript that became this book. She had been romantically involved with a pastor in her church and asked to speak to others out of her pain in the hope that they wouldn't get sucked into the trap she did.

I believe her story is a good way to get us thinking about this important and painful subject. And, since in most of this book we deal primarily with the straying mate and his/her spouse, it might be good to have a brief word from "the other woman." After all, it takes three to make a love triangle and, unfortunately, that's what is happening in many marriages today. The stuff of soap operas is invading the Christian marriage with far too much regularity.

So sit back and hang on to your hat. Allow me to introduce you to "the other woman."

My husband and I married young, when I found out I was pregnant with his child. We were typical middle-class teenagers— we had just gone too far with our passions a few times, and we got pregnant. It happened to a lot of kids we knew.

So we got married. We loved each other and, besides, I reasoned to myself, if it didn't work out, I could always get a divorce and start again. My mother had done that; plenty of my girlfriends had too, and I didn't think it was a bad plan.

But then a few months before our wedding, I trusted Christ personally and became a Christian. My husband became a believer shortly after our wedding. As I grew in my faith and started reading the Bible, I found that divorce is not an easily exercised option in God's eyes. But that didn't worry me too much since our marriage seemed off to a good start.

Ten years reeled off the calendar as we had three children and established a typical home for them.

In my fervor to be the super-Christian wife and mother, I began to dominate many of the functions in our family, taking complete care of the car, bills, planning, scheduling, home repairs, and so on, while my husband, Tyler, got more and more passive in the face of my hyperactivity. His job entailed ten- to twelve-hour days, and he flexed his energy muscles there instead of at home. And why shouldn't he? I was doing everything anyway.

In my flurry of activity I didn't even notice that Tyler and I were growing more and more distant. I didn't see us traveling in separate orbits. I didn't even know that many of my needs weren't being met—I just kept chasing my tail each day, falling into bed exhausted, trying to get enough energy up to run the treadmill the next day.

At church I began to get involved in the youth ministry and had some success there. The ministry was growing, lots of kids were getting saved and growing in their faith, and it was highly satisfying to me.

In that ministry I worked closely with the youth pastor, a man I'll call Tim. I found myself enjoying Tim's company more and more. I felt alive around him. He looked into my eyes when we spoke and gave me his full attention. He noticed when I wore my hair differently or wore a new outfit. We would talk and talk for hours about our goals in the ministry, better strategies for reaching out, and so on.

As I write this, my eyes are filled with tears because it's all in ashes now. All the lofty goals, the dreams of ministry to young people, the joys and successes of that time are dashed upon the rocks. Tim has withdrawn from the ministry in shame and disgrace, and the church has suffered tremendously from the revelation that one of the pastors was sleeping with one of his volunteer staff members: me.

I remember the first time I felt my heart begin bonding to Tim's. I shared some of the pain in my life with him, especially in the family I grew up in. Tim listened intently and compassionately, and when I had poured out my heart, said to me, "I don't want anyone to hurt you ever again. I want to protect you." Those words electrified me, as buried emotions welled up in my heart.

I couldn't get those words out of my mind for days. Tim would protect me—that thought felt good to my wounded soul. By the way I was acting at home—playing the take-charge "tough guy" role of super-mom and super-wife—my husband had no idea that I needed to be protected or that I even wanted that. I was sending him all the wrong signals.

Another attraction Tim had for me was his leadership. When I would tell him of a problem I was having, he would listen fully, then suggest a strategy to overcome it. In contrast, Tyler would listen partially and then respond, "Whatever you think is best."

As my relationship with Tim heated up, I found my view of my husband changing. In hindsight I can see that Satan was getting his hooks into us and that we were seeking to justify our illicit feelings toward each other, but Tim and I started to list all the faults our respective spouses had. Instead of tolerating Tyler's failings and normal shortcomings, I constantly harped on them—to Tim and in turn to Tyler by nagging him and complaining.

Tim and I tried to stop our ever-accelerating relationship, since we could see it was headed in the wrong direction, but we didn't take drastic enough measures. We tried becoming accountable to another person, but it didn't work. Our passions soon blinded us to our reason, and we fell into each other's arms with abandon.

Somewhere along the way, we made an unconscious decision to live our lives completely by our emotions. I knew what would happen if we were ever caught—his career would probably crash and burn, and my marriage might go up in flames—but we both were convinced we'd never be discovered.

Then it happened. Tim's spouse caught us red-handed. She gave us until the end of the week to decide what our course of action would be. Tyler was out of town that week on business, and I was petrified with fear and indecision.

Strangely enough, Tim's wife was of the opinion that I should *not* tell my husband—I think she and Tim were afraid of his losing the pastorate. They thought we could seal off this unfortunate chapter in our lives and go on. I liked that idea, as I dreaded facing Tyler.

Tim and I talked by phone that week, and we decided that was our best option. We prayed together over the phone and said good-bye. In my heart, I really didn't believe that Tim wouldn't call me again. Wishful thinking, I guess.

But a week went by, and he didn't call. I saw them in church that Sunday, arm in arm and laughing together with another couple. His wife was radiant, and Tim was obviously enjoying himself too. I was crushed. I couldn't help myself—I just burst out crying right then and there.

I was deeply hurt. I felt as if Tim had used me, and now that it was over, his wife was number one in his life. In my state of distraught emotionality, I couldn't stop thinking that just a few short days earlier I had been the most important woman in his life. Now she was back in "my" place, and it was over. I felt used. Worthless. Discarded.

At church in those moments of my despair, Tyler was, of course, puzzled, and we hurried home. I was totally undone—a basket case. Tyler wanted to know what I was so upset about, and I thought it would be more than I could handle to tell him right then.

But he persisted, and I thought it'd be worse if I continued the charade, so I blurted out my whole ugly story.

Tyler was floored. It was a long while before he could believe that my story was true. He walked around in a daze for weeks.

In the meantime, I was totally depressed and even considered suicide. Satan had a foothold in my life through my sinful actions, and he continually accused me: "How could you give yourself so freely to someone like Tim? He was so weak in his sin, too—and him a pastor! See, he never really loved you; he's dumped you and gone back to his wife. You're a fool."

Needless to say, Tyler soon called Tim's boss, our senior pastor, and the result was Tim's resignation. The church board knew, but they tried to keep it from the congregation, terming the reasons "personal." Personal indeed! Thinking that they could keep the secret was wishful thinking on their part.

Soon my friends began calling me to see if what they had heard was really true. Many of them unwittingly hurt me even further, and I still wonder why they thought it necessary to admonish me, a person who had sat under Bible teaching for years, that my actions were sinful. Didn't they know that I *knew* what I'd done was wrong? I knew that all too well and wanted to end my life some days because of it.

The net result of my so-called friends' reminding me of my failure was that I wanted my true friend Tim all the more. I felt as if nobody understood me except Tim. Tyler was trying to understand me, but he was pretty upset and it wasn't easy. Besides, we had put quite a bit of water under the bridge by not communicating at a deep level, so that relationship didn't provide much relief. I craved unconditional love and acceptance but found practically none.

Several months went by with no contact from Tim. He seemed to be settling back into his marriage, a distinct contrast from my situation. I continued to feel cut adrift, exposed, and ashamed.

Then one day, while Tyler was at work, Tim called me. He told me how much he missed me and how much he still loved me. He had only waited so long to call me, he said, because he wanted to wait until the dust settled a bit. He had taken a job in a fast-food restaurant, and his wife was starting to relax about monitoring him. He asked if we could see each other that afternoon. We got together all right.

In my state of burnout, I sucked up Tim's renewed affections like a dry sponge. The flames of our affair immediately burst into a conflagration like a spark landing on dry kindling.

We carried on that way for months, with neither of our spouses suspecting. Tim told me that his love for me was so important that he'd risk anything. Even losing his ministry had been worth it, he said.

I felt more loved than ever and eagerly reentered my fantasy world: I began dreaming again of marrying Tim someday. Surely our spouses would find other people to remarry, I reasoned foolishly. In our renewed affair, my pain was temporarily salved, and I began to emerge from the emotional dumps.

Then we got caught again.

I felt like an alcoholic addicted to booze. Except my liquor was Tim.

Tyler leaped into action this time. He insisted that we change our phone number to an unlisted one and that we change churches. I agreed to the changes; we both knew it was my last chance to reform—it was now or never. Tyler and I really began to communicate now.

We had many late-night tearful sessions. I remember one night where I really "came clean" with him regarding my weak resolve and self-control. In tears I literally screamed to him, "Help me! I don't know how to stop! I'm weak, and I don't even know what's right anymore. I'm blinded and can only see what I'm feeling right now. Please, Tyler, help me stop!" I wept and wept in Tyler's arms that night. It was a turning point for us.

Tyler and I entered counseling and today are slowly but steadily recovering. God is teaching me some important lessons, such as leaning on Him and on finding my identity in Him, rather than on any man, whether my husband or a lover. Of course, my husband is my primary person to lean on, but even he is not my sole support. If he listens to my troubles less intently than another man might, that's all right. My chief goal is to walk with God and with Tyler, letting my husband know of my needs but not desperately seeking to have them met in another man.

One of the ideas that helped push me back toward staying in my marriage was the reality factor. I read a very helpful book, *The Divorce Decision,*[1] that spoke of the harsh realities of a broken marriage. Staggering financial costs, angry stepchildren, visitation hassles, ex-spouse headaches, blended families, haunting guilt, depression, and the like really do follow when you decide to divorce your spouse and go off with your partner. When I looked that squarely in the face, it sobered me up. I began to give up the fantasy world I dreamed of where Tim and I would go off and live happily ever after.

I could go on and on about the lessons I've learned from my behavior but will close by encouraging you, the reader, to delve into the material in this book. I pray that it will be a source of wisdom and blessing for you. It is helpful and practical for those who have experienced infidelity. But more than that, it's a word to the wise for every married couple.

NOTE

1. Gary Richmond, *The Divorce Decision* (Waco, Tex.: Word, 1988).

SECTION 1:
UNDERSTANDING EXTRAMARITAL AFFAIRS

1

"What God Hath Joined Together": In Pursuit of Healing for Shattered Marriages

Infidelity is woven throughout the fabric of our culture. From television shows such as "NYPD Blue," "Melrose Place," and "Sisters," to the pages of our daily newspapers, infidelity is all too common—and is being glamorized to our youth.

For example, it's a well-established political fact that the Kennedy clan—starting with family patriarch Joseph Patrick Kennedy and his long-suffering wife, Rose, on down through sons Bobby, John (JFK), and Edward (Ted)—has been plagued by this usually secret behavior pattern. Marilyn Monroe[1] and others[2] have openly admitted to liaisons with the former president and his brother Bobby. "Womanizing was a family tradition," says Kennedy biographer and Northwestern University professor Garry Wills. "The family game of 'chasing' is part of the self that was built up by all three imitators [sons] of their magnetic father. Passing women around and boasting of it was a Kennedy achievement."[3]

Our national conscience is being seared to the point where we're not even shocked when we hear such things. For example, when this book went to press, an author was making the rounds of national TV talk shows (Donahue, Sally Jessy Raphael, Larry King) talking about his latest book, *How to Cheat on Your Wife and Not Get Caught*. Sound like a hoax? No, he's serious, promising in his promotional materials to teach readers "how to lie successfully," "how to have the edge over a clever or suspicious wife," "how to avoid feeling guilty," and "how to outfox your wife's detective."[4]

What's more, statistical studies back up the headlines. In the general population some reports suggest an astounding 50–65 percent of husbands and an equally shocking 45–55 percent of wives have had extramarital affairs by the time they are forty.[5] Statistics within the Christian community are more difficult to come by, due to the shame placed upon such behavior by those circles. But a study of pastors sponsored by *Christianity Today* found that 23 percent of the 300 pastors who responded admitted to some form of sexually inappropriate behavior with someone other than their wives while in the ministry; 12 percent admitted to extramarital intercourse; 18 percent confessed to other forms of sexual contact (such as passionate kissing or fondling); only 4 percent said they were found out.[6]

True, the percentages among Christians are lower than those among the general population, but there is probably a large degree of underreporting among the clergy, due to the stigma attached to such behavior. Regardless of the fact that the numbers may be too low to reflect reality, they are still far too high for Christian leaders. And the sad thing is that among their parishioners the incidence of infidelity is probably close to the general population's. And that's far too high for those who carry the name of Christ.

BEN AND LYNN'S PAIN

It has been well said that people and the Word of God are the only two things worth investing one's time in. And it's people's stories that I'll be sharing—with names and certain circumstances changed, of course—in this book. As you and I walk alongside the various people we meet in these pages, we'll share their pain and try to learn something about this most devastating of marital events, the extramarital affair.

As we get started, I want to share the story of Ben and Lynn. It epitomizes so many aspects of this painful subject that it'll get us off on the right foot. Later in the book we'll take a more in-depth look at their story.

THE "PERFECT MATCH"

Ben grew up in a warm, affectionate family, with lots of hugs and nurturing from Mom and lots of special times with Dad, smiling and sharing hobbies. Ben had Dad's aptitude for drama and theater. It was natural for him to follow in Dad's footsteps, and numerous individuals began to talk about his abilities superseding those of his well-known father, who had done quite a bit of community theater in their area. Dad had founded a Christian radio ministry and was not threatened by that talk—he always encouraged Ben to pursue his interests. Mom and Dad were supportive emotionally and financially all along the way.

Lynn, on the other hand, lost her father to illness at the age of six. Mom and the two girls bonded together in their little family and continued on. There wasn't a lot of time to feel sorry for yourself—Mom worked long hard hours, and the two girls did all the household chores including cooking. They did all right, though no one had time to relax, be frivolous, or have fun. Everybody became very efficient, and the place ran like a well-oiled machine.

Ben and Lynn met in college and became quick friends and dates. Ben loved Lynn and the smooth way things always ran when she was in charge. He had a tendency to be spontaneous; his mom said that was true of all good actors. Intuitively, he knew Lynn would be good for him with her organized ways.

Lynn found in Ben that warm gregarious masculinity that she had been missing most of her life. He provided the fun and security, and she provided the efficiency and productivity. Together they seemed a natural.

Graduate school for Ben (in broadcasting like his father) followed marriage, and three children came along. Lynn handled it all in stride. Ben moved into his father's organization as a producer/director and was doing extremely well.

It seemed there was no end to what needed to be done at home, and they were all constantly on the run. The kids were constantly traveling to and from games, lessons, and school. Going to a private school meant the kids' best friends didn't live in the neighborhood, and that meant additional driving. Changing clothes, putting on makeup, grabbing lunch—all were done in the car on an everyday basis.

Ben and Lynn would joke about it occasionally and lament with other couples caught in the seemingly endless round of activity. But nothing ever changed. As he lay in bed watching the late news one night, Ben glanced down the hall at Lynn carrying the folded clothes to each of the kids' bedrooms. She was a great mother, but somewhere along the line, Ben felt as if they had got off track. But how could he complain? He knew Lynn was exhausted after each day.

Their marriage looked good, even perfect. But Ben's doubts and sense of emptiness didn't disappear. At first he tried to put such thoughts aside. When that didn't work, he tried to talk with Lynn, but there never seemed to be time. She was always in high gear, cooking, cleaning, and helping with homework.

"Success" at Work

Gradually, Ben became more and more involved in his new position, and his concerns about their busyness and lack of communication waned. The new position was demanding, but Ben rose to the occasion and won the admiration of his colleagues both inside and outside the studio.

Several members of the broadcast team were openly complimentary of Ben's efforts, and he found himself thriving on their recognition. His assistant producer, Whitney, especially seemed to admire his work. She was warm and fun-loving but also extremely efficient and productive. When it was one hour until air time, she could really make things happen.

Ben naturally admired that combination of talents in Whitney. She was married but had no children. She brought humor to an otherwise rather serious process. Most of the team took themselves seriously, but she was humble. Though capable, she didn't seem to be overly enthralled with herself.

They started catching meals together in groups after broadcasts. Once only the two of them and another woman could make it, and they all had fun. They talked and laughed about some of their families' recent experiences, and it was refreshing for Ben.

As he drove home, he thought about how long it had been since he had spent that kind of time with Lynn. He vowed to change that and asked her to set aside time for a date that weekend or the next. But after several last-minute cancellations for orthodontist appointments and school conferences, he gave up trying to break into Lynn's jam-packed schedule.

Things Heat Up

Soon Ben and Whitney were eating together after the broadcast more often than not. After shutting down the studio, she would stop by his office briefly to say thanks for his capable leadership. In addition, they often saw each other socially with a variety of other couples. At times, Ben felt a little uncomfortable with her obvious admiration, but her marriage appeared secure and he dismissed his concerns.

That is, until one night after the broadcast when she stopped by to say her usual thanks. He couldn't believe the sudden rush of emotion he felt. He wanted her to linger longer, but she left quickly. On the way home he felt confused. He wished he could talk about it with Lynn, but he knew that was out of the question. *That's all Lynn needs—to hear her husband is falling for another woman.* So he put it out of his head.

To keep himself from falling for Whitney, Ben tried to put some distance between them. Apparently he was successful, because after a taping several months later, Whitney stopped by and asked if she could talk to him. He knew he should have said no, but the hurt in her voice appealed to his sense of fairness. He knew he needed to tell her why he was avoiding her.

As she sat down, Ben didn't even wait for her to bring up the subject. He blurted out that he thought he was falling in love with her and therefore needed to stay away. She shared mutual feelings of affection for him. Over the next several months it became a full-blown love relationship.

After about eight or nine months, Ben began thinking about getting out of the affair. He was concerned with Whitney's spontaneous comments around other people—they were starting to raise eyebrows. She was becoming increasingly careless about how she acted around him, and he could sense that she really didn't care who found out about their relationship. He tried to talk to her about it, but their time together always was so short and intense that he couldn't seem to get the point across.

So far, no one knew, even though Lynn had quizzed him about Whitney's behavior. The pressure was building, and he was having to increase his deceptions. Where was he? When would he be back? Why this expense? He hated lying to Lynn, but by now it had become a way of life. Whitney was worth it to Ben, or so he thought.

When she started talking about their leaving their mates and getting married, he was frightened. He couldn't do that to his reputation, his kids, his wife, his parents, his career. That *was* too much to give up for Whitney, no matter how much he loved her. Whitney started actually making plans to leave her husband, and Ben realized that their relationship meant even more to her than it did to him. He was feeling increasingly trapped but still couldn't bring himself to end it.

Now Whitney was talking dates—an actual departure time and how they would plan their wedding. Ben became more nervous and upset. Still nobody knew about the affair. He had had some close calls but had always managed to weasel out of them. But to give it up or to go away—neither seemed necessary. *Why can't Whitney just leave it like it is?* he mused, bothered by her insistence on escalating the intensity.

Such questions generated anger and accusations from Whitney. She claimed that he really didn't love her and was backing out. He sensed a threat of blackmail. With his high profile in the radio ministry, she'd have leverage against him. She demanded more and more of his time. His anxiety was sky-high.

At home Lynn's sexual overtures turned him off. All he wanted was to be left alone. But when he was with Whitney, it was special. It sort of made up for all the pain at home.

Finally after one of his agonizing mental back-and-forth sessions, Ben decided once and for all that maintaining the deception wasn't worth it. He knew he had to break it off.

After their next broadcast, Whitney, probably sensing his turmoil, pressed him for an actual runaway time. Even though he had prepared to end the affair, when she mentioned the actual departure, it appealed to him. *What an escape! No more having to maintain the facade.* Ben heard himself saying yes to all her plans, but in his head he knew he had to go home and tell Lynn the truth. It was now or never.

THE REVELATION

Lynn went berserk, as he expected. She immediately called Ben's boss, the executive producer. Until the producer and his wife arrived, Lynn stayed in the bedroom alone sobbing.

Lynn heard the doorbell, and she came out as they walked in. It was like a torrent from a broken dam. She swore at Ben repeatedly, called him every name she could think of, asked questions about the affair, but started swearing at him again before he had a chance to answer. The torrent of swearing, name calling, crying, and raging finally began to subside after a couple of hours.

The producer's wife was shocked and overwhelmed. The producer himself was concerned about the ministry since Ben was so highly identified as the son of the founder and Whitney was known in the industry as working with him. He asked a lot of detailed questions that reflected his own sense of betrayal and his feeling stupid for having the wool pulled over his eyes.

Lynn learned some facts from listening to Ben talk to the producer. When Ben cried from time to time, she found herself alternating between pitying Ben and getting even angrier at him—*What a hypocrite he is*, she kept repeating to herself.

When she heard that Ben and Whitney had been planning to leave town that weekend together, she ran to the phone in the bedroom and called Whitney's husband. She wanted to kill both of them and even told Ben he ought to leave with Whitney and get out of her life. At first she screamed at him to leave the house, then she changed her mind.

Finally the producer and his wife were ready to go—but before leaving, the producer summarily fired Ben right on the spot, telling him to have his desk cleaned out before the next round of tapings. There was no appeal, no consulting with the board of directors, no suggestion of therapy to help Ben recover from his shattered moral condition and be restored to his ministry or even to his wife. Ben was so ashamed at that point that he just agreed to disappear quietly. He didn't know of any other option.

Two weeks later, they pulled out of town, Ben driving the U-Haul and Lynn in the van with a trailer and two of the kids. A 1,500-mile trip lay ahead. They were moving in with his parents in Florida. They had nowhere else to go.

A NEW BEGINNING

The questions from his parents ruined their arrival. Money was scarce, so Lynn jumped at the chance to take a long-term substitute teaching position. It was her first outside job in ten years. A humiliating departure, a cross-country move, a job dismissal for Ben, a new career for Lynn, new schools for the kids, financial uncertainty, and the loss of their friends, home, and all that was secure—all in just three weeks!

Lynn hadn't even had time to think about it. The surprise of Ben's revelation left her exhausted, bewildered, and barely functioning. No one at the new location knew about the affair, but both of them worried that their secret would follow them.

Things started to look up. A tour bus driving job shuttling the hordes of tourists to and from the theme parks in central Florida opened up for Ben—hardly a respectable position for someone with a master's degree and national media experience, but at least it was something to keep the wolf from the door and to keep him busy and not depressed, he hoped. He also got involved in a discipleship/accountability program with one of the pastors at their new church. Together Ben and Lynn started seeing a counselor in central Florida.

In their initial session, the marriage therapist asked them to review the story. That started the anger and obsession all over again.

Lynn couldn't stop herself, so Ben left the room until she got control. When Ben came in for his time alone, however, she panicked. The whole thing had been such a secret before that she couldn't stand any more secrets or "secret sessions," even though it was with a counselor.

When the counselor suggested to Lynn that she didn't absolutely need her husband in order to survive as a person, she agreed. After all, she had grown up in a single-parent home and had made it just fine.

But when it was suggested by the counselor that the infidelity was really a joint problem and not just Ben's problem, the roof came off with more name calling and a lot of justifications about her behavior as a wife, his lousy deception, and so on and so on.

The balance of the sessions was spent helping Lynn see that only as she "owned" her part in the affair would she have any influence upon the reconciliation. At that point, she wasn't sure she even wanted reconciliation. She felt attached to no one except the children.

Lynn needed to slow down and focus on how she had distanced herself in the marriage. That distancing had encouraged Ben to get involved with another woman. Gradually, she recognized that she was mothering her children in the same way her widowed mother had. Lynn did everything; she acted as though she were a single mom, even though she was married to Ben.

Ben had thus been left to fend for himself emotionally. For Lynn, there was always something to do and plenty of little ones to hug. Somewhere along the way, Ben had "died," stepping out of their lives little by little. When her suspicions grew and the accusations started, she went into denial about her emotional distancing and just started doing more. She figured that if she just kept chasing from one thing to another, she wouldn't feel the pain. She didn't have time to enjoy the reasons she chose Ben in the first place—the sweet, fun-loving spirit that she had seen so little of as a child.

Teaching allowed Lynn to live in another world for most of the day. However, coming home from work to the children, in-laws, two bedrooms, and two baths quickly brought back the harsh reality. The time between 4:00 and 10:00 P.M. seemed to rekindle all Lynn's anger and anguish daily.

But several things began to happen. Lynn couldn't stay up washing the dishes because it wasn't her home. Second, she went to bed all stirred up—which forced her to talk to Ben. Third, they had to keep their voices low, so as not to disturb the children or his parents. That made listening easier for Ben. They had many nights of little sleep and lots of tears, but the forced intimate communication began to leave its healing mark on their relationship.

It also helped Lynn to see why Ben's parents had been so happy to have her marry their only son. From their point of view, Lynn's efficiency and organization was just what Ben needed to be free to pursue his career. Lynn would take care of everything, so Ben could be successful.

At first, she resented that insight. She also resented her mother-in-law's daily practice of hugging Ben. *How can she do that when her son has created all of this havoc and heartache?* she mused bitterly. As she observed Ben's family more closely, she began to put together the clues to what Ben was missing in their marriage. Even with all his parents' faults, at least Ben received emotional and physical nurturance from them, which was more than he got, she sadly conceded, from their relationship.

Meanwhile Ben had a lot of time to think while driving the tour bus, and he got in some valuable reading while waiting for his passengers to reboard. He gained numerous insights as to why he had had the affair and was gradually learning to verbalize his needs to Lynn more effectively.

STEPS FORWARD AND BACKWARD

About that time, Ben's former radio ministry asked a couple from the board of directors who were to be in their area on business to meet with Ben and Lynn and bring a report back. At first Ben and Lynn were encouraged; at least someone remembered them back home and seemed to care. That particular couple had been very supportive back home; the wife had even volunteered to Lynn that her husband had had a "one-night stand" early in their marriage— and they had survived it, so she and Ben could too.

When they got together with the visiting couple, however, it was obvious that the other couple had never worked through their own affair. They very legalistically and judgmentally presented a long list of things that the "evil infidel," Ben, should be doing, and they completely ignored the marriage setting.

That visit set Ben and Lynn's progress back several steps. It is generally true that if another couple who hasn't processed their own affair tries to step in, it generally hurts more than helps. As you'll see throughout this book, full and proper processing of any infidelity is absolutely crucial.

For Ben the meeting stirred up unresolved issues of the affair, bringing back memories of the environment where the affair took place. He wanted to go back home and defend himself, and he was frustrated that everyone seemed to be overlooking all of his achievements and contributions to focus on his "indiscretion." He knew they were talking about him as the initiator of the affair and that Lynn was seen as the hero for not leaving him in the wake of revelation. He was being made out the bad guy.

Needless to say, Ben had to work through that anger and all of the stages of his own grieving process. He realized that though he couldn't make it different in the eyes of people back home, he could work to make the marriage better for Lynn and himself, regardless of what others thought.

DIGGING FOR ANSWERS

It was shortly after that that the counselor asked Ben to pursue his family's history of affairs and asked Lynn to focus on the males who had abandoned her through death (Dad), through her marriage (her big brother had gotten mad and distanced himself from her), and now through an affair (Ben). Such history was critical to the attitude about men she conveyed to her daughters. In addition, each received a reading assignment: for Lynn, *Back from Betrayal: Surviving His Affairs;* for Ben, *Sex in the Forbidden Zone: When Men in Power—Therapists, Doctors, Clergy, Teachers, and Others—Betray Women's Trust.*[7]

When Ben went in search of his family history, his father was surprisingly candid. He related his own temptations with infidelity, which helped explain why Dad had counseled his son, after the revelation of Ben's affair, just to go on as though nothing had happened. It was the "water under the bridge" approach: it's done, you can't change it, so don't address the issues. That conversation was revolutionary for Ben—he began to understand the influences that had been at work in him.

Finally Ben and his family moved to their own apartment. That provided Ben with a sense of identity and represented measurable progress that they were getting back on track. Lynn breathed a sigh of relief because she did not have to live with her mother-in-law anymore. In addition, her job was turning out to be a positive experience.

Now, seven months into recovery, both Ben and Lynn were feeling as if they were going to make it. It was now safe for Ben to start grieving his losses (a process we'll examine in subsequent chapters), a process that provoked a lot of sadness in Ben. Lynn was able to comfort him when he was hurting, and she even found herself encouraging him that it was all going to work out for good.

During this time they returned to their old college campus. What a nostalgic review of happier times! It was a reassuring reminder that they were on the right track. Their therapist began leading them through the trust-building and intimacy-creating exercises that we will expand upon in chapters 10 and 11. It was not easy for them, since they had had so much practice distancing themselves from one another, but they slowly began to get in touch with each other.

Lynn had difficulty seeing a loving touch as anything but a prelude to sex. Ben learned to be gentle and patient with her, and things improved. Ben explained that he was especially vulnerable to compliments from other women, and Lynn realized that she had hardly ever stated her admiration of him verbally. All those years with hardly any verbal affirmation had taken their toll on Ben.

After a full year of marriage therapy, Lynn is still teaching and Ben is getting itchy to get back into radio. They are not finished with their recovery, but they are progressing. They are together because they want to be, not because they had no other options. They are simply enjoying each other, not waiting to see who will last the longest this time around. They are together in total honesty; they know there is nothing left to hide.

Recently they chose to tell some close friends what they had learned over the past year about their affair and their relationship. It was a scary moment for Ben and Lynn, but the couple's affirmation made their risk worthwhile. It is probably just a matter of time before other couples in the midst of processing their own affairs will begin to seek out Ben and Lynn's assistance. Then they will be able to pass along the healing they have received.

SOME WORDS OF ORIENTATION

CAST OF CHARACTERS

Affairs can go both ways. That is an important point that we should get straight at the outset of this book. *Husbands can cheat on wives, and wives can be unfaithful to husbands.* Though that may seem somewhat obvious, it's important to make that clear at the beginning.

There are three key identifiers that we'll use throughout these pages to refer to the cast of characters.

Infidel: This is the mate who strays and gets involved in an illicit relationship outside the bonds of marriage.

Spouse: This the mate who is cheated upon, the one who does not stray.

Partner: This is the person with whom the infidel gets involved.

For reasons of clarity and consistency in this book, I've chosen to refer to the infidel as "he" and to the spouse as "she." Accordingly, the partner will most often be referred to as "she." (This book does not address the scenario where the male gets involved in a homosexual affair, although many similarities do hold for that pattern.) By choosing a convention of referring to infidels in the masculine and spouses in the feminine, I'm not saying that only men cheat on their wives—in this day of role reversals and sexual freedom, there's plenty of the reverse happening. (Young wives today are actually having affairs at a faster rate than same-aged men.)

Thus in the pages that follow, you can feel free to replace my male infidel with a female one in your mind, if it better applies to your situation.

ABOUT SIN AND GUILT

As you read this book, you may get the idea that I don't think it's appropriate to call infidelity sin or to call adultery just what it is: adultery.

Nothing could be further from the truth! God has condemned this behavior, and I assume that readers agree it is wrong. However, what is most needed upon the revelation of an affair is compassion and understanding, not condemnation. That the infidel has betrayed the spouse is obvious; how to repair and rebuild the marriage is not.

REGARDING DIVORCE

This book is not a treatise about God's will regarding divorce and remarriage. That is a long and involved subject, and not one I wish to elaborate on here. My approach here is:

1. God hates divorce (Malachi 2:16), and so does every person who has been through it.
2. God's goal for cases of infidelity is forgiveness and reconciliation.

3. However, due to the spouse's own background, history of abandonment or abuse, fear of processing the tough issues, and so on, infidelity might make a marriage irreconcilable. Thus, even though all possible efforts to avoid divorce should be made, adultery is a biblical ground for divorce (Matthew 19:1–12). It is important to understand that many people will simply run from their problems and choose this option. But the purpose of this book is to show them another way.

4. Divorce is never a healthy way to resolve problems in the marriage. It might appear to be the best escape to one who is suffering, but it never is. The victims of adultery should make the effort to work through the recovery process outlined in this book, even if a divorce does occur. Processing the unfinished business (unresolved issues) of a finished marriage is crucial. Failure to do so generates high risk for future marital and relational failure.

WHO IS THIS BOOK FOR?

This book is intended, in one sense, for all married people. We all know that infidelity can be a danger for all of us, given our fallen human nature. But primarily it's written for those who have been touched by infidelity already—whether their marriage is currently in trouble or has been split by it in the past. It's for those who are now divorced or separated, to help them understand what happened in their marriage. And it's for those who, as professional counselors or close friends, want to help those stricken by this most lethal of marital problems.

Ideally this book will address the needs of those couples who, following the revelation of the affair, want help in putting their shattered marriage back together. I decided to write this book for those of you who have no one to help you in the recovery process. This subject is so sensitive and complex that most couples will need (or desperately want) some outside assistance. As one couple declared, "We never would have made it without counseling! I'm almost sure we would have given up or not known the path to follow." Unfortunately, trained counselors are not always available, so I have tried to be very specific and direct and to lay out the material in a clear, self-help fashion. It has been organized according to the optimum process of recovery.

For those of you who are fortunate enough to be in a good

therapy program, this book will assist you as a guidebook. You will find it reassuring and helpful as a way to check your progress.

For those of you who have not yet told anyone about your secret affair—whether it was in the past or is currently in progress—this book will provide you with the courage to disclose the affair and to get on with recovery. You'll find that to not confess will only lead to further destruction of your life and reputation.

It Ain't Easy

As any couple in this process knows, picking up the pieces of your marriage is not easy, quick, predictable, rational, or linear; people involved in infidelity rarely act rationally. Affairs do strange things to people. A sense of normalcy is lost. New boundaries have to be established.

If you happen to come across this book after some time has passed in your reconciliation process, you might be somewhat discouraged by the distance you have yet to go. If that's your feeling, view this as a marker along the road. You may indeed have some distance to go, but don't be discouraged because this is no easy journey. Several of the couples I've counseled through affair recovery affirm the idea that if the topic is still painful for one or both of you to talk about, then you have probably not talked about it enough. There are plenty of places to jump in. Make the bad experience bear good results by reading this material together.

Most of the time, the processes described in this book will appear clear, easy, and straightforward. In other places, your feelings will say that nothing could be further from the truth. Repairing the damage done to the marriage is exceedingly messy and doesn't always follow a simple path. But don't be deterred. Stay with it. If you do, you will make it through this terrible storm.

To those of you who have recently discovered your spouse's affair, now is *not* the time to decide whether to reconcile your marriage. You're experiencing too much anger and hurt. You will eventually go through much of what I describe here, whether the marriage stays together or not. So get started on processing; you can decide whether you are going to stay later.

This book addresses many volatile subjects. It deals with fragile and unstable components of both parties' psyches and their relationship. There is plenty of ammunition here with which you may either hurt your mate or help him/her (and yourself) heal. The choice of how to use it is up to you.

To Spouses Who Are "Alone"

If you want to put your marriage back together but your mate doesn't, or your infidel remarried after you divorced years ago, you will find help and relief here. There are ways to encourage a stubborn spouse or infidel to budge, which we'll discuss in chapters 7 and 10. For those who are already divorced, this book will offer a way for you to work through your pain, a way to do "retroactive therapy" in your own heart.

Perhaps in your situation the infidel has returned to the marriage and stopped seeing the partner but refuses to process the affair. In this case, the infidel often pretends that the problem is solved because the marriage has stayed intact. But if nothing is altered, the marriage will undoubtedly maintain the same patterns that fueled the affair in the first place. If that's your situation, you will receive encouragement and direction from this material.

A couple of suggestions are in order for those of you who are going it alone.

1. Don't use this book as a weapon or read it solely with the hopes of getting your spouse to read it. *You* apply it to your relationship. Your changed attitude will be message enough for him/her to notice that something significant is happening. If you have the opportunity to speak of the changes you are making, do so; but only speak for yourself—what you are doing, what you have learned, how you are feeling about what's going on inside of you and in the marriage. Leave your spouse out of it. He might not be ready yet. An appropriate statement might be, "I'm reading a great book about affair recovery that is changing my entire perception about what happened in our relationship. I knew I was part of the cause, but I never fully understood how I contributed to what happened." If he's interested, he'll let you know, especially after seeing real change in your life.
2. If your spouse has left the marriage permanently (for example, you are divorced, and he has remarried) but you think there has never been closure to the affair and its resulting damage, I would encourage you to read this material and pursue a discussion in a face-to-face meeting with your ex, in the presence of an appropriate third party.

To Those Who Offer Support to Friends

Whether you are a licensed professional, a pastor, or simply a friend attempting to support a couple working through their reconciliation, the following suggestions are offered:

1. *Watch out for your own stuff.* Most of us have beliefs, feelings, and experiences that prejudice us when we deal with other peoples' relationships—that's what I mean by "stuff." Never will your marriage be more vulnerable than when you are trying to assist a couple in their recovery from infidelity. You will find yourself working through the same issues with your own spouse. As I prepared this book, I was affected that way and counted it as healthy. We could all use stronger marriages.

2. *The survival of your friend's marital relationship is not dependent upon you.* In most cases, the couple you are working with chose to marry each other before you were in the picture. You didn't bring them together, and you can't keep them together. You must set the couple free to pursue their own course. At times you will want to take control of their recovery process, but you must refrain for their sake.

3. *They must never be able to draw you into their relationship* (a process technically called triangulation). If that happens, each will individually attempt to align you with his or her side. Remember, the infidelity was an inappropriate triangulation, and so is an attempt to overly involve yourself.

4. *Keep the two of them talking to each other.* Don't maintain secrets that one party shares with you hoping to align you with his or her side. Remember, infidelity was the worst secret that could afflict a marriage, and more secrecy doesn't help. At times your neutrality may appear brutal, especially since you're probably closer to one party than the other (e.g., your high school friend who got married). You will feel the urge to intervene and provide protection, but you need to resist it.

5. *If you are feeling more exhausted in the struggle than they are, you are inappropriately involved.* That is not to say that some of your time with them won't be exhausting, but you need to gauge your degree of involvement. You shouldn't work at it harder than they do.

6. *Keep in mind that the material in this book is the practical "how to," to assist in the forgiveness, reconciliation, and restoration of the marriage.* It should never be viewed as a

replacement for what God can do. As you seek to support your friends or counselees, be prayerful and stay close to God's Word. Forgiveness and reconciliation are always miracles. Only God can heal!

To Adult Children of Parental Affairs

Some of you reading this material are looking for clues to what happened in your own parents' marriage, which was split or shaken by infidelity. Children rarely address their parents' marital affairs until they are married themselves. Since you certainly want your marital relationship to be different from your parents' experience, keep reading. This is surely an appropriate time for you to get involved in this material.

You might find your perceptions to be quite different from those of your parents. I encourage you to talk with them after (and even while) reading this book. They are probably more willing to talk about their experience at this juncture than they were when you were young.

Be open to hearing both sides of the story. If the affair resulted in an end to your parents' marriage, this might be the first opportunity to bring closure to the wounds of long ago. Sit down with them individually and listen. Ask them questions in order to draw out their feelings about it and hear what lessons they've learned. Don't let the "secret business" be buried alive, only to crop up later. You are doing the right thing to explore it. Affairs do run in family trees, and they tend to continue unless the cycle is interrupted.

Adult children of parental affairs are at particular risk to repeat the pattern. The most important motivator of any affair is the deep desire to be nurtured and loved unconditionally. That includes many components, such as touch, attitude, playfulness, romance, sex, and appreciation. Some adult children of parental affairs have huge agendas, or needs, that could never be met by any spouse— and they bring them, like baggage, into the marriage. If that description fits you and you are married, don't put off working on this issue any longer.

To Those Who Are Thinking of Having an Affair

That heading is probably a shocker to a lot of Christians. Even to acknowledge that people would consciously think about having an affair seems somehow to validate having one. Not so. In our culture, almost everyone has thoughts about affairs. If one is not thinking of straying, he or she is fearing that the spouse will have one. It's time to stop denying the prevalence of affairs in the Christian community. We need to come out of the closet and address this problem in the light of day.

If you are

- thinking of having an affair with someone you know at work or in your social or church circle
- hoping that your spouse will suffer an auto accident, cancer, or other turn of fate, so that you can have a "legitimate" affair
- hoping your spouse will have an affair so that you can be free to be on your own
- wishing the children were gone so that you could get out of the marriage without hurting them
- thinking other "pre-infidelity" thoughts

—then you desperately need the material in this book. By entertaining such thoughts, you are simply hoping that your spouse will magically "get the message" of your dissatisfaction with the relationship. Feeling that you can't get the message across to your spouse any other way, you are thinking of having an affair to get free of the marriage. Such thinking is a ticking time bomb in your life, and you need to defuse it at once or suffer the consequences.

Do you feel ashamed, overwhelmed, unheard, and uncared for? You might possibly feel trapped, exhausted, numb, and in despair over the fact that you are aging, for example. Maybe you are disappointed and angry at your spouse's failure to meet your needs. You feel isolated—nothing seems to get through to your mate. In general, you feel "dead" and wonder if you have any passion left. Everything is a duty, a drag, and there are few "bright lights" in your life. Even though others would be surprised, even shocked, at your appraisal of your marriage, you assume it's true in theirs as well.

My encouragement is to stay in touch with your emotions. Affairs never solve the problems that cause them. They can't; by their very nature, affairs are artificial worlds in the midst of reality. In your head you know that, but you find much emotional satisfaction in fantasizing about a perfect relationship outside the bonds of marriage.

Could I suggest a better way to find satisfaction? Read this material. Let it soak down into your soul, your emotions, your heart. It's been tested in real life and represents many, many peoples' lives.

As you're reading, talk about the material with someone close—your spouse or a best friend. Hopefully, it will provoke interaction between you and your spouse that will lead to significant change and enhanced emotional benefit to both of you.

LOOKING AHEAD

In the next two chapters we'll start to sort out the chaos that surrounds any marriage where infidelity has crept in to do its dirty work. Not all affairs are alike, and finding out which of the three types has struck your relationship is the first important step toward recovery.

NOTES

1. David Kramer, "The Kennedy Complex: Why They Womanize," *McCall's*, August 1991, p. 44.

2. "Woman Says She Was JFK's Mob Liason," *Chicago Tribune*, October 7, 1991, sec. 1.

3. Kramer, "The Kennedy Complex," p. 45.

4. "How to Cheat on Your Wife—And Not Get Caught!" *Radio–TV Interview Report*, September 15, 1991, p. 34.

5. Grant L. Martin, "Relationship, Romance, and Sexual Addiction in Extramarital Affairs," *Journal of Psychology and Christianity* 8, no. 4 (Winter 1989): 5.

6. Raymond T. Brock and Horace C. Lukens, Jr., "Affair Prevention in the Ministry," *Journal of Psychology and Christianity* 8, no. 4 (Winter 1989): 44.

7. Jennifer Schneider, *Back from Betrayal: Recovering from His Affairs* (San Francisco: Harper & Row, 1989). Peter Rutter, *Sex in the Forbidden Zone: When Men in Power—Therapists, Doctors, Clergy, Teachers, and Others—Betray Women's Trust* (Los Angeles: J. P. Tarcher, 1989). For other helpful sources, see Appendix D.

2

SORTING OUT THE CHAOS: THE ONE-NIGHT STAND AND SEXUAL ADDICTION

Exhausted, Bill decided to return to his hotel for a brief nap prior to grabbing a bite to eat in preparation for the evening's seminar. Upon arriving in his room, he noticed the red message light flashing; his wife had been trying to reach him throughout the afternoon.

When he called, he found that Gwen was struggling again with their two adolescent children. *Nothing unusual,* he thought. *They aren't bad kids, but she always has a difficult time controlling them when I'm away.* He realized from her tone of voice that Gwen was both angry and hurt that he had to be gone again.

As he hung up the phone in discouragement, Bill reflected on how exciting it had been when he had taken this new job several years ago. The pay increase was phenomenal, the relocation in new quarters sounded attractive; but the side effects—family concerns, mainly—had been pretty negative.

He tried to fall asleep, but now his mind was racing and he couldn't. Finally, in frustration, he jumped off the bed and decided to go eat a little early—maybe that would make him feel better. Tonight's meeting was to be a big one, so he took a little extra care in dressing appropriately.

As he walked to the elevator, he thought that even the new clothes he wore tonight didn't perk up his spirits much. In fact, he found himself a little surprised that he wasn't looking forward to hearing Dr. Lowrey speak, an authority he usually enjoyed hearing greatly. But tonight, especially after that phone call, he just didn't feel up to it. Maybe some good food would help.

Due to the early hour, the restaurant was nearly empty. Maybe here in this peaceful spot he could find some rest from all the turmoil he was feeling inside.

Why did Gwen have to call and dump all that stuff on me anyway? He felt bad that she had to be home alone, but he also felt angry because they had decided to take the new career position together, both of them knowing a lot of travel would be involved. *Why can't she live up to her end of the bargain?*

He felt torn. And the more he thought about it, the more stirred up he got inside. Scanning the menu didn't help either. What normally would have been a fun part of his day—enjoying some good food—had suddenly turned flat. He read through the entire entree section twice before finally making a decision. Even as he repeated it to the waiter, he felt ambivalent about his choice. For a moment he toyed with the idea of changing his mind but resigned himself to the fact that nothing was going to taste really great tonight.

Only after the waiter departed his table did Bill notice the attractive woman sitting across the aisle and down one booth. She was busy making notations on some reports. Unaware of his glance, she remained engrossed in her work.

Wow, she looks so in control of what she's doing, so professional and, I have to admit, quite attractive. He couldn't help but notice that she wasn't wearing a wedding ring. She was quite a bit younger than he was. *Somebody's going to be lucky to have her as a wife someday.*

His mind drifted back to Gwen and how she used to appear so efficient and attractive when they first met. But family wear and tear had taken its toll. Then again, he mused, he wasn't all he used to be either. *Time marches on, I guess.*

He cast another glance at the woman and, as if by some magic cue, she looked up at the same time. The meeting of their eyes frightened him, and he immediately looked away.

In the moments that followed, Bill couldn't believe the sudden rush of emotion he felt. What could that confusing bundle of feelings be? He hadn't felt so anxious since he was in high school. He didn't even know this woman—he'd only seen her five minutes ago. Irrationally, he felt sure that she could see his heart pounding wildly in his chest.

Get a grip, Bill. Stop acting so foolish and juvenile.

He tried to change the focus of his thoughts. But he had no luck—over his coffee cup, he found himself glancing at her again. From then on, it was just a matter of time before their eyes connected.

She smiled, and he reciprocated. She started some innocent small talk across the empty aisle; they were both on business trips, both in sales.

Innocently, she asked whether he'd care to join her at her table. *Why not? It's nice to meet a fellow business traveler in a near-empty restaurant. The road gets lonely, and a little conversation might help. Maybe it'll perk me up for tonight's seminar.* He decided to not be rude by declining, and slipped into the booth across from her.

Amazingly, Bill found himself thoroughly enjoying the stranger's company. She often traveled on business and was married too. They had a little wine and a few laughs with their supper. Like cool water on parched ground, Bill soaked up her company and felt thoroughly refreshed by the time the checks came.

He knew it was almost time for him to leave for the seminar, but she invited him to her room for an after-dinner drink. He knew he shouldn't—that in fact he had probably gone too far already. For a brief instant he teetered on the knife's edge of indecision. But in his confused mind he didn't much care anymore about keeping the rules. *I haven't felt this alive and vibrant in years. I'll accept her offer, just this once. I'll miss the seminar, but I can always order the tape. This won't get out of hand.*

But it did get out of hand. A few hours later, all those alive and vibrant feelings were gone. He had lost all control in the intoxication of the moment.

As he rushed to dress and depart later that night, she was hurt that he was leaving so quickly and not spending the night; he was angry at himself and furious at her. He felt so full of turmoil that he thought he would explode. How he hated himself for what he had done.

Back in his room, Bill tried to go to sleep but couldn't. He tried to put her out of his mind but without success. He was disgusted with himself; he had totally blown this business trip in more ways than one. He decided he'd go home early, even though the conference wasn't closing down until Friday.

Yet even after he made the necessary ticket changes, he wished he hadn't. He didn't feel ready to face Gwen just yet. *Maybe I won't have to tell her—after all, what she doesn't know won't hurt her. No, that won't work—we've never kept secrets from each other.* He went around and around in his mind, unable to decide one way or the other.

He was in anguish the entire flight home. He tried in vain to do some paperwork on the plane to get his mind off the dilemma.

As Bill raised his tray table for touchdown, he decided he would have to work through his agony by himself. He couldn't dump his burden on Gwen and hope that her forgiveness would take away his guilt. He'd just keep it a secret and pretend it never happened. *Time heals all wounds, doesn't it?*

Gwen was thrilled to see him home early, and her reaction assured him that he'd made the right decision.

However, the months that followed weren't easy. The more he tried to put the attractive stranger out of his mind, the more she had a tendency to return. He often found himself hoping against all hope that he'd come across her on other business trips to the same city. He felt guilty for even wishing this but couldn't seem to shake the desire.

He found himself even hoping on several crazy occasions that maybe something tragic would accidently happen to his family that would set him free to go looking for her. He knew that was impossible, and he always felt terrible for entertaining such thoughts.

Bill had repented to God in silent prayer innumerable times, but still he couldn't find relief. The memory of the one-night affair produced a kind of regretful remorse at the back of his mind, always lurking just beyond reach of his consciousness. He knew he didn't have to fear being found out—strangers coming together on a first name basis in a city far away from home in a lonely moment—it happened all the time.

Yet why did he feel so bad about it? Why couldn't he forget it, if it was such a small thing?

As time passed, it seemed that even God Himself was intent on reminding him of his failure. Several of his colleagues at work had come to him—as the Christian in the group—to seek his help for their own guilt over an affair. A man at church wanted to return to his spouse and asked Bill for advice on how to do it.

Thus Bill found himself giving counsel to his friends that he had not practiced himself. One of the lessons in his adult fellowship group at church focused on—of all things—affair-proofing your marriage. Another focused on total honesty in Christian marriage. The pastor even preached on infidelity for four weeks. It seemed to Bill that the whole world already knew his secret. His private agony seemed to stretch to the horizon.

Still and all, Bill decided to "tough it out" a little longer and just see if it wouldn't go away with the passage of time. He even decided to take up racquetball. The exercise proved helpful in relieving the inner tension for a while. But finally Bill knew he could run no longer from the guilt, the shame, and the self-reproach. He decided to share his shame with Gwen.

But how to do it? *This could be really touchy—I've got to pull it off right, or my marriage could explode.* His emotional turmoil didn't help as he tried to plan the revelation—his powers of concentration were flagging on many counts. His job performance was down, his supervisor was beginning to wonder what was bugging him, and he knew he was becoming depressed again.

Finally one night Gwen approached him sexually, and he found himself withdrawing from her. He didn't understand it himself, but the thought of sex with her was almost repulsive. Gwen's hurt expression signaled that he had overreacted without realizing it. He wanted to reach out and take her in his arms and sob out his story, but he couldn't bring himself to do it. It was a miserable evening for both of them.

Time passed, as months stretched into years. Bill didn't try again to bring it up—he just tried to bury his secret entirely. Their adolescent children grew up and eventually departed the nest. Things actually began to settle down in Bill and Gwen's home. They settled into a form of relationship that, while not exactly close and intimate, was at least workable.

Bill and Gwen had become busy people. There were always lots of projects for them to do together, and many of their friends actually thought they were close to each other. In conversation with one another, they talked about their projects and activities, but not about themselves. They were busy, active, always on the go, but rarely intimate in conversation—or in the marriage bed, for that matter.

Today their marriage is still together, but it's lackluster at best. They both disapprove of divorce, so they just muddle along with their unspoken secret lurking in the background. Bill has never "slipped" again, but he's basically miserable carrying around his loathsome secret. It gets terribly heavy sometimes, but he is either unable or unwilling to cast it off.

The tragedy is that Bill and Gwen will never be intimate unless they deal with their secret past. They'll never know one another's hurts and fears and anxious thoughts. They'll never know what it is to comfort one another. They'll only know efficiency, performance, and lots of activity—lots of running, running, running.

Do you identify with any of Bill and Gwen's story? Are you busily chasing your tail each day, never slowing down enough to relate closely with your mate? Or, if you are an infidel who hasn't shared his/her dark secret, are you getting tired of carrying around that burden? If so, you'll find help in these pages.

THREE TYPES OF AFFAIRS

If a couple wants to start over and repair the damage to their marriage, they must both understand exactly what they are dealing with. All affairs are not the same, and, as a result, different classes of affairs require different forms of treatment.

I divide affairs into three classes.

Class I Affairs:	The One-Night Stand
Class II Affairs:	The Entangled Affair
Class III Affairs:	Sexual Addiction

In Bill and Gwen's story we have seen a Class I affair. Known commonly as a "one-night stand," it occurs with too-frequent regularity, especially in our sex-saturated society. I chose to illustrate with a business trip because the new work force has more men and women traveling, often alone. The opportunities for immoral behavior have increased exponentially, it seems, in recent years.

This chapter briefly examines Class I and Class III affairs; then in the next chapter we'll take an in-depth look at the Class II affair. Book-wide, I'll focus almost exclusively on the latter type, the Class II affair, which I call the "entangled affair" because it always involves emotional and sexual entanglement. In the entangled affair, the man and woman have a relationship—often akin to the marriage relationship. The similarity to the marriage bond is part of the reason it's so dangerous: the infidel is finding needs met that he has been seeking to have met in his marriage for years, usually unsuccessfully.

The entangled affair is neither a one-night fling (Class I) nor an extended pattern of addictive behavior (Class III), both of which usually show only minimal relationship development. Put another way, the entangled affair is not a "temporary suspension of the rules" like a one-night stand, or a deep-rooted compulsion like sexual addiction. We'll get into the differences between the types of affairs later; suffice to say at this point that it's primarily the Class II affair that we'll be examining in this book.

Why the somewhat exclusive focus on Class II affairs? Simply put, the entangled, or Class II, affair is the most problematic and common form of infidelity, and one of the most stubborn to rehabilitate due to the extensive emotional involvement. In contrast to the Class II affair, the Class I affair is fairly easily remedied (though not an insignificant problem), and the Class III affair—sexual addiction—would fill an entire book of its own.

The following chart lists the three classes of affairs. In each specific situation there might be some overlap between the three classes, but overall the affair needs to be classified so that appropriate treatment can start.

Look over the chart carefully to get an idea of how each class differs from the others. This chart serves as a reference point for much of the discussion throughout the book, so study it carefully. It will help you sort out the chaos and focus on which type of affair has afflicted your marriage or the marriage of a friend or loved one.

	CLASS I One-Night Stand	CLASS II Entangled Affair	CLASS III Sexual Addiction
BIBLICAL ILLUSTRATION	David and Bathsheba (2 Samuel 11–12)	Samson and Delilah (Judges 16)	Eli's sons (1 Samuel 2:22)
DESCRIPTION	One-night stand	Long-term relationship	Multiple partners
DEVELOPMENT	Immediate	Gradual	Impulsive
EMOTIONAL INVOLVEMENT	None	Intense	None
SEXUAL ACTIVITY	Single experience; intense, lustful, passionate	Only much later in relationship—after friendship established	Immediate and repeated with multiple partners and increasingly distorted sexual activity
REMORSE / REPENTANCE	Usually immediate and intense	Initially none—initial grief is for lost relationship; later grief is possible	Only after acting-out episode; internal tension escalates until another episode is inevitable
RECOVERY	Can be immediate with forgiveness	Long-term process with marital therapy	Sobriety first; then individual therapy; marital therapy later

Three Types of Extramarital Affairs

Class I Affairs

The story of King David's lusting after Bathsheba, a beautiful woman he saw bathing, is a classic one-night stand. David wanted Bathsheba intensely, but afterward she was only one of many wives. He didn't have a long-term emotional relationship with her, so it was not a Class II affair in that respect. Infidels in a Class I affair merely "use" their partners for the short term, often dumping them shortly afterward with no regrets.

David's repentance pattern fits a Class I affair, too. When God's prophet Nathan confronted the king about his sin, David gave in rather quickly (2 Samuel 12), a pattern we usually see in Class I infidelities. Bold but simple confrontation will usually turn the infidel around, and, with brief therapy, that one-night fall can become his only-night fall.

But that is not to say this type of affair is harmless—a Class I affair that is not properly dealt with can set the stage for future sexual impropriety—leading possibly to Class II or even Class III affairs.

Keeping the one-night stand secret—as Bill did from Gwen— is the worst way to handle such a "fling." Whatever walls of secrecy a person builds will keep significant others, such as his wife, outside. That is never healthy, and the resulting loss of intimacy will encourage the need for emotional involvement with someone else, thus setting him or her up for another affair. Few of us are really good enough to fake it forever; most of us sense when something is troubling our spouse.

Marriage is all about honesty, and the spouse who strayed (even though "only once") absolutely needs to reveal his downfall and process it correctly; otherwise the secret amounts to a ticking time bomb. It will either explode dramatically one day or slowly do its damage, as in the case of Bill and Gwen, who wound up with a case of strangulated intimacy. Theirs was a slow death of relationship, as opposed to a Fourth-of-July breakup—though no less painful by any means.

The recovery process for one-night stands is very similar to that of the entangled affair, and positive outcomes are frequent when the entire process is applied. But often the infidel minimizes his "one little slip-up" and thus doesn't tell his spouse about it. If that's your case, you need to read chapter 12 on the secret affair. There's more involved here than one little slip!

CLASS II AFFAIRS

In the next chapter, we will look comprehensively at the Class II pattern of infidelity, so I won't give too many details here. Briefly, in the entangled affair, the infidel and partner have "got something going," to use the popular phrase. The affair develops slowly and gradually. They usually know each other quite well—often they work together or have some other frequent or long-standing basis for relationship.

The infidel usually feels as if he is in love with the partner. There's a lot of emotional turmoil in this type of affair: both the infidel and his partner are truly torn, as their feelings often rival those initially felt for their spouses. That's why it's so tough to turn their situation around.

Their illegitimate relationship is meeting a crucial relational need for them, which I call "the message of the affair" (we'll examine that in detail in chapter 8). Identifying that need (or needs) is a crucial step on the road to full and lasting recovery.

To use fishing parlance, in this type of affair "the hook's in deep." And it takes real soul surgery to get it out.

CLASS III AFFAIRS

Class III affairs amount to sexual addiction. As outlined in the previous chart, this type of infidelity has characteristics and dynamics totally different from those in Class I and II affairs. It would require an entire book to go into these dynamics (and several excellent ones have been written; see Appendix D), so we will only briefly compare this type to the other two. That way you can identify whether yours is a Class III affair or one of the other two types.

A helpful definition of an addiction is: "a pathological relationship to any mood-altering experience that has life-damaging consequences."[1] For the sexual addict, affairs definitely alter his mood; he needs illicit relationships like an alcoholic needs booze.

As a point of comparison, this mood-altering effect is true to a lesser degree in Class I and Class II affairs, but don't let that fool you; the characteristics in the other types don't line up with the Class III pattern. Remember, some characteristics may overlap between types, but taken in their totality, the symptoms will point to one pattern over another.

The infidel in the Class III affair will practice a number of the following behaviors:

The infidel usually has a string of relationships with multiple partners over time. He may have, as the old saying of sailors goes, "a woman in every port." (Business travel is the modern-day equivalent.) Considerable juggling is required to keep the partners unaware of each other and the spouse unaware of the many partners.

Sexual activity becomes increasingly more compulsive, with greater risk to himself. That might mean skipping out afternoons from work to indulge in sexual behavior or perverted forms of sexual expression, such as pornography, prostitution (both male and female), adult bookstores, erotic videos, pedophilia, and so on. The infidel may very well be caught by the police, be exposed to sexually transmitted diseases (STDs)—including AIDS, of course, but there are others too—or even be killed by other infections or by violence at the hands of others like him.

Emotional attachment, though present at first superficially, diminishes as time passes. The partner becomes more and more a mere "sex object" and less and less a person in the infidel's eyes. What may start out as a Class II affair may shift to a Class III when sex becomes the focal point of the relationship.

The partner is usually of a lesser socioeconomic status than the infidel. The common expression is "dating down" or "slumming." If the partner is of a "lower class" than the infidel, it is easier for the infidel to relegate her to a less-than-human state, reinforce his one-up position of power, and perpetuate his addiction.

Because the behavior is addictive, it usually requires the infidel to lie, cheat, and steal to get the relief he craves. Hence a sexual addict can never be treated in a conventional manner before he "gets off the drug," or gets sober. Until then, he will be extremely self-serving and say whatever it takes to get the necessary relief. There are no consistent moral rules in the addict's life, regardless of what he says. Spouses and therapists dealing with this pattern need to know they are dealing with a con artist; otherwise the desperate sex addict can lead them on innumerable wild goose chases. He will be to you whatever he thinks you want him to be, as long as he can maintain his addiction.

The infidel's behavior becomes a self-perpetuating cycle. The net result of the behavior is acceleration, because each "sexual fix" both meets his craving need temporarily and saps his strength. Thus the exhilaration-depression cycle accelerates until his life becomes literally out of control. This is why, for example, some of the nationally infamous televangelists of the late '80s and early '90s found it almost impossible to halt their sexual activities—they were (and some still are, at this writing) locked into a vicious merry-go-round that eventually destroyed them.

The self-perpetuating nature of the Class III affair is illustrated below:

No significant recovery can be accomplished (or even initiated) before the infidel has

- been "sober" from his behavior for several months;
- refused to replace the "lost" addiction with a new one (e.g., replacing sexual compulsions with substance abuse);
- made conscious efforts to recognize and change his belief system;
- submitted to structure and accountability in his daily schedule.

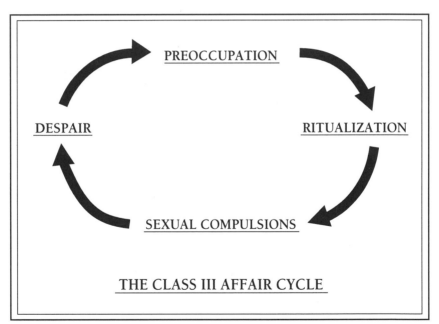

THE CLASS III AFFAIR CYCLE

From *Out of the Shadows* © by Patrick J. Carnes, Ph.D. Published by CompCare Publishers, Minneapolis, Minn. Used with permission.

When the Class III infidel gets into an accountability schedule in therapy and sobriety, he will at first be tremendously bored. Life before sobriety was so much more exciting! Even though he may acknowledge intellectually that the former pattern was self-destructive, his feelings will take a while to catch up. That boredom will be followed by depression, introspection, and eventually a return to the normal ebb and flow of feelings necessary to reestablish the emotional intimacy with his mate.

Unlike Class I and Class II affairs, this type absolutely requires the help of a professional therapist who is experienced in this specific area. It's different in many ways from the other two types and requires an entirely different approach.

LOOKING AHEAD

As you think about the three types of affairs defined, compared, and contrasted in this chapter, try to classify your situation. It may be difficult at first to sort out all the complicated emotions and twists of plot your particular situation entails, but if you keep at it, a theme will eventually emerge, and you'll tend toward one of the classifications. Remember that no two situations are exactly alike, but if you look for a preponderance of factors and characteristics, you'll be able to plug yours into the correct slot eventually. That way you'll have a better handle on how best to process the affair.

Having defined the various classes of infidelities, let's now look in depth at the entangled affair.

NOTE

1. John Bradshaw, *Healing the Shame That Binds You* (Deerfield Beach, Fla.: Health Communications, 1988), p. 15.

3

SORTING OUT THE CHAOS: THE ENTANGLED AFFAIR

Bob was in graduate school at night and working full-time; Becky was doing quite well in her career. Becky had enough going for her that she was able to hide her disappointment in Bob's overinvolvement in his work and studies. They had talked about this season in their lives beforehand, and both knew that it was going to be tough.

However, Becky just couldn't help feeling utterly unimportant to her mate—left out of Bob's daily life. She told herself, *Once school is over it'll get better. Better to go along now than to rock the boat. Bob has enough to worry about without a whining wife added.* So she tried to hang on and wait for the situation to improve.

Instead, it got worse. When graduate school was over, Bob began to study intensively for the certification required for his profession by the state. Licensing would take another two years of internship. When that began to sink in, Becky started to feel as if she were at the end of her rope. *Another two years? I don't know if I can last that long—I'm dying on the vine.*

She tried to discuss her feelings of desperation, isolation, and emotional fatigue with Bob, but there was so little time. So she shared her frustration and disappointment with her girlfriends at work. If Bob wouldn't listen, at least they would.

Apparently one of them mentioned it to Tom, her boss.

Tom called Becky into his office one afternoon and gently probed about how she and Bob were doing. He had noticed the

59

slide in Becky's production, he said kindly. Becky didn't intend to, but right then and there she broke down and wept. Tom seemed so kind and understanding—he even offered to take her out to supper that night while Bob was at school. Tearfully, she accepted.

She and her supervisor had already established a friendly relationship in their interactions at the office. At first she rationalized that there were no romantic feelings between them, that it was still just business. That carried her through several of their after-work dining experiences.

Soon their suppers together became a regular feature in Becky's needy life. Their times together made work more pleasant, and it gave her something to look forward to, instead of the lonely evenings to which she was accustomed. Bob never got home earlier than 10:00 and was usually so exhausted that he really didn't seem interested in hearing about her life that day.

As Becky and her boss got to know each other better, they began to really hit it off. Tom had other facets of his personality that she hadn't noticed before they began this new aspect of their relationship. Before long, they started exchanging little hugs upon separating after dinner. Though she felt guilty about it, Becky found herself thinking about Tom more and more. She valued their newly escalated relationship a lot—maybe too much. But she tried to put her worries out of her mind.

Tom apparently felt the same way Becky did. One night at dinner, he revealed his feelings for her, and she had to admit that she felt the same for him. That evening when they left the restaurant, they decided to go to his apartment, and there they lost all control. Becky hurried home late that night and luckily was able to arrive before Bob did.

When Becky and her boss went to his apartment a second time, she knew she had to quit seeing him outside the office. *We can just go back to our business relationship*, she thought. *After all, we had that for two years before it got out of control.* So they decided to call it off. They both felt guilty enough to agree readily to such a plan.

But it didn't last long. Two days later, Tom called her into his office to say he just couldn't end it that quickly. Through all those great dinner conversations, her friendship had become very meaningful to him. "Couldn't we just be friends?" he suggested. "We can talk during dinner and then just say good night."

Becky wanted to maintain their relationship just as badly as he did. So, mustering all her willpower, she agreed to try it.

But that night they ended up at his apartment once more. She was able to beat Bob home again; she had the timing down pat by now. The next morning at the office, Tom called her in and apologized for not holding up his end of the bargain and suggested that maybe they needed a break from each other for a week or two.

Becky by this time was thoroughly confused. Her feelings for Tom were becoming stronger every day. She admired him for being so considerate as to apologize and suggest the time apart. She agreed to the "trial separation," even though last night, while with him, things had been so perfect that she had entertained the idea that Tom was "the one" for her.

A week went by, and Becky found herself desperate just to talk to Tom. *This is almost like going through drug withdrawal,* she thought with some concern. Finally, she couldn't stand it anymore. She called him on the intercom and asked if she could see him in his office. She did have a reason: a special report had come across her desk that needed updating with figures to which only Tom had access. When he answered, she couldn't believe the rush of feeling she experienced upon simply hearing his voice.

During their conversation in his office, she could hardly control herself—she was barely able to get the statistics she needed without asking him out to dinner. Reflecting after work on that contact, she was shocked at her lack of control and stewed about it all night, losing precious sleep. *Why am I so obsessed with our relationship?*

By the next morning—dragging herself to work after a sleepless night—she knew she had to end it.

After work that day, she called Tom and said good-bye. He argued that his feelings were involved and that it wasn't fair to end it so quickly. Why couldn't they just stick with the plan for two weeks off and then reevaluate?

But Becky just hung up. She knew it wouldn't work; they had tried self-control, and it never worked. Tom tried to call her again on several occasions, but she was strong, holding on by the skin of her teeth to her resolution.

Then, rather suddenly, Tom was promoted to a new division and transferred to a new office across the country.

Becky was devastated, even though she had been the one to insist that they end their relationship. She almost called Tom before he shipped out to offer congratulations, but she talked herself out of it, albeit with great difficulty. She was miserable whenever she thought about him, which seemed to be most waking moments these days.

While Becky was struggling one morning, Tom called on the intercom and asked her out for one final dinner. She couldn't resist and heard herself saying yes with the condition that he not invite her over afterward. He agreed.

Their last evening together was filled with deeply felt mutual feelings being shared across the table. She bravely tried to bury her feelings of loss and disappointment, and at evening's end she watched him walk out of that restaurant—and out of her life—for the last time.

The loss of Tom—though she knew their relationship was wrong—left a tremendous hole in Becky's life. It took her months just to get over the numbness and disorientation at work and at home. Yet her husband, Bob, never caught on. That fact alone was mute testimony to the lack of communication in their marriage.

Bob was licensed just as everyone expected. However, his new career now consumed him. His practice prospered, so they began making plans to start their family.

Conception was difficult, so fertility testing ensued. After several months of testing, with still no results, they made plans to adopt. As often happens, they adopted and then promptly got pregnant.

Having one baby in hand and another on the way consumed Becky's energies. She now needed to be close to Bob more than ever. But they didn't know how to connect, since they had been running on separate tracks for so long.

She couldn't be honest about her needs, and he assumed everything was OK. Bob knew their marriage wasn't as much fun as it used to be, but after all there were now two small children in the family, and that explained it in his mind. Both he and Becky were always tired—but what could he expect, being new parents?

Now Becky became afraid of her own vulnerability. She was fed up with her distant marriage, yet she couldn't just divorce Bob. She needed the marriage now—she couldn't manage with two small children as a single parent—but she couldn't explain to him the struggles she was going through. She decided to get some counseling.

It took a long time to clarify what her needs were and whether she was willing to state them plainly to her husband. The agony of the concealed affair was crushing her with guilt.

Finally, Becky made up her mind to tell Bob about her affair with her boss. She was scared stiff of what might ensue, yet she knew it was the right thing to do. As long as the secret was between them, they'd never be able to be close.

Miraculously, Bob extended his love to his wife in a wonderful time of forgiveness and reconciliation.

A period of numbness ensued, followed by relief. Today they're still working on their marriage, and it's not perfect yet. But, for the first time, both of them report a newfound openness and closeness that neither had sensed was possible before. They feel a new confidence that their marriage is going to make it.

Key to their recovery was both parties acknowledging their share of responsibility for the affair. Becky acknowledged straying, but Bob admitted distancing himself. Only then were they able to make progress toward rebuilding the trust and intimacy so critical to success in marriage.

Bob and Becky's story is typical of the entangled affair (Class II). Chances are that if you've been involved in an affair, you see many parallels to your experience in their story.

But there are four marital variations on this theme.[1] They are:

1. Intimacy Avoiding
2. Conflict Avoiding
3. Empty Nest
4. Out the Door

If you recognize your infidelity as a Class II affair, read through the following descriptions and see if you can further identify the causative factors. If you can, it will be helpful to your recovery as a couple. The more specifically you categorize it, the more specific your recovery can be.

FOUR STYLES OF CLASS II AFFAIRS

It is important for the couple to agree on the class and kind of the affair. If the couple disagrees, the final determination needs to be made in light of the infidel's perception. After all, he/she is the one who initiated the illicit relationship. Often the spouse's perceptions are slightly skewed, due to relational dysfunction, so the infidel's perceptions have to receive priority if there's not total agreement on classification.

The exception is if the spouse senses that there might be a case of sexual addiction (Class III affair), with multiple or repeated sexual perversions. You haven't seen a case of denial until you've confronted a sexual addict! As we discussed in the previous chapter, irrational behavior or lying is common in any kind of addict.

Now let's look at the first style of entangled affair.

THE INTIMACY-AVOIDANCE AFFAIR (THE WINDSHIELD WIPER SYNDROME)

The first type of affair typically occurs in a marriage that avoids intimacy at all costs through constant bickering, criticism, and even open conflict. Do you know any couples like that? They would never separate ("Remember your vows" is their motto), but they maintain an agreed-upon distance between them. They're like a set of windshield wipers—always the same distance apart.

That distance is never discussed openly, but it is fully understood by both. What may look like a terrible marriage to most outsiders is actually reassuring to the partners. They feel safe because the relationship is so predictable.

They even test the system occasionally for no reason other than to see if it still works the way it did last time. Hurtful words are exchanged, and the responses verify that all systems are in order. Even though that is extremely painful to both parties, it is still a means to feel attached and important to one another.

Not only does the conflict keep the spouses the right distance apart, it also contributes to a sense of power in both parties. They trade "tit for tat" as they volley back and forth. This balance of power is so critical that if one spouse has an affair, the other partner will promptly have one too (to help the other "see what he/she did to me—now we're equal"). Again, it's tit for tat.

Besides maintaining distance and keeping the power balanced, the windshield wiper relationship will allow the two partners to carry out their family chores and assignments efficiently and without interference from each other. Note that when your car's windshield wipers clear the rain from your windshield, they don't clunk into each other (if they do, they're broken, and you promptly correct such close contact). Such a marriage relationship consists of two individuals who perform efficiently and predictably, stay the same distance apart, and even "cover" for one another, all the while seemingly held together (yet apart) by an invisible rod.

One young man I know was pained to hear his parents quarreling when he was a child. When he became an adolescent, he sometimes intervened, trying to protect his mother from what he thought were the ravages of his father. But to his utter amazement, his mother would turn on him and tell him to mind his own business—that she didn't need his help at all. In hindsight he realizes that she was saying in effect, "Leave us alone, this is our dance.

We're like two windshield wipers, furiously beating back and forth on the windshield, always the same distance apart. It's not really that bad."

The recovery process for this kind of marriage will be difficult, due to the need for equalization between the two. One partner's affair will unbalance the system so severely that the couple are both destabilized and fearful. Blame and open hostility are long-term habits in this marriage, so for both parties to accept responsibility is difficult. Recovery will require new habits that are foreign to the couple (such as sharing blame), but it can be done if they are willing to try something new.

If you always do what you've always done, you'll always get what you've always got. Turn that one over in your mind—it sounds inside-out, but it says a lot to those locked into a windshield-wiper pattern of relating. You need to try to do things differently.

THE CONFLICT-AVOIDANCE AFFAIR (THE DIAL TONE SYNDRONE)

Whereas the previous marital style resembles the windshield wipers on your automobile, this kind of relationship could best be described as the dial tone on your telephone. Like a dial tone, there is no variation; it is always predictable. That is initially reassuring, but it can be maddening when you listen to it for long periods of time. Just try holding the receiver to your ear for a while—you'll see what I mean!

Individuals in this relationship will either have separate roles, lifestyles, and interests, or one partner will run everything while the other partner becomes an obedient child. In the former case, the two mates have very rigid roles that don't mix well. Both know exactly what to do, and it does no good to argue for a different procedure. Everything is predictable—maddeningly so. There's no need to argue; "just do it," as the commercial says. Drudgery and lifelessness result.

In the latter case (one partner the parent, and the other the child), the powerful partner will often make the family look good, but it is a "peace at any price" and therefore decidedly unhealthy. It's a false peace, and the lack of bad times brings with it a lack of good times.

Amazingly, such conflict avoidance is common among Christians. The emphasis placed on looking good in many evangelical circles encourages couples to believe in a false serenity—they misinterpret the dial tone as smooth sailing. In fact many people use this kind of marriage as "a Christian example" for others to emulate, but it is missing a large ingredient of life—the ability to be human and honest with yourself, others, and God.

Both partners usually appear content with the dial-tone arrangement until one begins to feel an attraction for another person. Suddenly a whole new range of emotions becomes available to the infatuated one. A new awareness of being alive surfaces—the freedom from the dial tone is exhilarating; the transformation within is unbelievably wonderful. This kind of affair (and the empty nest affair that follows) generates the largest differences in the infidel's behavior.

The message of the affair, or what the infidel wants the spouse to know about himself (see chapter 8), in such a marriage is often extremely difficult for the spouse to hear. The message often indicates a marital deficit that the straying spouse is seeking to fulfill, and admitting any deficit is often an anathema to the dial-tone spouse. She usually believes she was doing everything perfectly to start with—so how could she possibly improve? In other words, if the dial tone is to be desired, why would she need to change?

Also, the spouse often thinks that to change would mean admitting, "I was making a mistake," and to acknowledge that would devastate the reputation she had worked so hard to build. Often this spouse has lots of support from the church family and finds it easy to maintain her reputation while holding the infidel fully accountable and refusing to accept any part of the responsibility. It's a tragic attitude that I see far too often, and it renders recovery practically impossible.

THE EMPTY NEST AFFAIR (THE MIDLIFE CRISIS)

How many times have you heard of a couple separating very close to their platinum or silver anniversary? Not only is eighteen to twenty-five years into the marriage a common adjustment time for all marriages, it is a common crisis time for the adult who has spent most, if not all, of his adult life providing for his children. By the time the "golden" years roll around, the kids are teens, going off to college, and doing other autonomous things. Such developments can really rock a marriage that revolves around the kids.

An individual who gets involved in this type of affair is typically the conscientious family man or the perfect mother. He/she has put in twenty years relating to the spouse not as a marital partner but as a parent. And when the kids leave, there's nothing left to talk about. All the unfinished business (unresolved issues) of their own family, all the stuff they've left undone in the marriage simply because there was always more to do than anyone had time for, comes crashing to the fore. Combine those factors with the unknowns of the future, and you have a situation where both spouses are vulnerable to the affection, attention, and nurturance of another partner.

The partner of this infidel man is almost always younger than his wife. The infidel is usually a generation older, with more power, prestige, and money than the partner. Those distinctions are important for the couple to explore as they work through the reason for the affair. They represent basic needs that have been put on hold while both spouses have consumed themselves with raising the children.

This type of affair is most often ended by the infidel. He finally "gets his head together" and realizes that his family is more important than his fling. The termination is completely unexpected by the partner.

Yet instead of revealing the affair to the spouse, the infidel reverts back to his well-established pattern of relating around the kids and not around the marriage relationship. "Keeping the peace" becomes all important, so he keeps his secret. Plus, he reasons, if he revealed it, his image as the all-American family man—or woman— would be shattered. The secret then festers.

THE OUT-THE-DOOR AFFAIR ("FINALLY IT'S MY TURN")

This type of affair is usually the outcome of a twenty-year train of thought based on some marker: either the kids' departure from the home or the end of a multiyear career (e.g., military, corporate, or governmental service). The affair is actually initiated years earlier in the mind of the infidel, and the marriage relationship is maintained and tolerated by the infidel on the basis of the future plan. When he finally does leave the spouse for the partner, the infidel will often say, "I've toyed with this idea for many years, and I finally decided to do it."

People who have never been tempted to be unfaithful tend to find this concept incredulous. But those who have been through it, or who know others who have, report no surprise at all. In hindsight, folks who experience it say that they should have seen it coming for years. The infidel certainly saw it coming—he planned it!

The plan to leave the spouse usually comes as a result of the spouse's refusal to change, adapt, communicate, or meet some key relational need in the marriage. The hurting spouse (the future infidel) may, to one degree or another, try to discuss his or her needs, but the mate either doesn't hear or doesn't understand.

After a time of arguing about the need, the infidel gives up and resigns himself to enduring until he can get out, and the spouse misinterprets that as resolution. The infidel tolerates the tension for many years on the basis of his decision to leave in the future, and the spouse interprets the lack of conflict as a sign that things are going fine. Again, the "smooth sailing" mirage is at work.

Many infidels try to make their abandonment of their spouse downright nice. They may plan years in advance to provide for the spouse when the time of departure finally does arrive. In fact, one of the interesting phenomena of this kind of affair is the contact the infidel will often make with a pastor or counselor in order to help the spouse in the ensuing transition and crisis. His thinking is that once he turns the care of the spouse over to someone else, he is free to walk out. His thoughts are, *This job is done. I spent twenty years of my life in this relationship, did what I was supposed to do, and now I'm out of here. I'm going to do what I've really wanted to do all these years while I'm still young enough to enjoy it.* It's a lot like the McDonald's slogan—he "deserves a break today." Or so he thinks.

After separating from the spouse, rarely does the infidel marry his partner. If he does, the new marriage rarely lasts beyond two years.[2] The partner simply serves as an aid to empower the infidel to leave the pain of his marriage. If no new marriage takes place or if the new union breaks up quickly, a long period of singleness usually ensues. He focuses on his own whims and avoids commitment and its entrapments—he's free now and he's going to stay that way, if he can help it.

Yet the new lifestyle rapidly becomes boring and empty. Having a nice new car and new boat just can't compare to having a soul mate to travel through life with. Besides, such annoyances as alimony, child support, and child care tend to burst the free and easy bachelor's bubble.

The injured spouse often can't understand what caused the infidel to leave her for the partner, since she views the partner as less appealing than herself.

But the central reason the infidel has the affair is to get out of the marriage. He doesn't want to live with the partner forever; he just wants out. Later he will use the socioeconomic differences between the partner and him as an excuse for dropping her once he is freed of his family responsibilities.

Sadly, marriages that suffer the out-the-door affair rarely reconcile. If the spouse chases after the infidel and begs him/her to return, the results are usually fruitless. In fact, such behavior will often cause the infidel to marry his partner, just to put some space between him and his former spouse. This is an escape that has been long in the planning. The infidel is usually "locked on" to his objective of freedom with a tenacity that would put a bulldog to shame. If interest in reconciliation is expressed by the infidel at all, it will only be after a minimum of two years of separation, when the fantasy bubble has begun to burst.

LOOKING AHEAD

In the past two chapters, we have looked at the three classes of affairs in an attempt to sort out some of the hysteria and chaos that usually accompany disclosure of infidelity. By this point you should be zeroing in on the exact characteristics of your particular situation.

Next we'll look at the tough question of Why? as it comes to bear on affairs. We'll look at the broad picture—environments that set us up to be predisposed toward unfaithfulness. We'll examine American cultural myths, spiritual belief patterns, and marital styles that work together to make cheating entirely too easy. In addition to our fallen sin nature, these influences have a powerful hold on us, our attitudes, and our behavior when it comes to infidelity.

NOTES

1. These four categories were first formulated by Emily Brown, in *Patterns of Infidelity and Their Treatment* (New York: Brunner/Mazel, 1991), pp. 28–48.

2. Ibid, p. 44.

4

CAUSES: ENVIRONMENTS THAT ALLOW AFFAIRS TO FLOURISH

Owen had long regarded himself as fortunate. His two brothers were still struggling—one was an alcoholic and part-time
cocaine user, the other had finally achieved sobriety from
alcohol but still had numerous affairs, with several marriages to tes-
tify of his failed attempts to control himself.

As a parent, Dad was OK, Owen recalled. *He was harsh at times,
but what could I expect when he was an alcoholic, abusive to Mom, and
a womanizer? Dad was the enforcer in our family, and Mom was the
nurturer, holding it all together when Dad stirred it up. Mom was the
one who healed our hurts and calmed our fears and comforted us in our
childhood accidents.*

Actually, Owen further reflected, Dad's mother had held her
family together, just as Owen's mother had. So Dad was just repeating what he had seen modeled in his family growing up.

Though Owen had never heard his father say it, he had a lingering suspicion that Dad thought he had been babied too much.
Sure, Mom had protected him a lot, but it didn't seem too much to
him. Dad's attitude seemed unfair to Owen, and it hurt to think
about it.

In junior high and high school, Owen got along very well with
the girls. He was witty, got decent grades, and didn't really feel comfortable hanging around the school jocks or the town toughs.
Although he certainly wasn't what you would have called a "party
animal," he had got too involved physically with a couple of girls in

high school and college. But he had never "gone all the way," until he met his wife.

They had "slipped" a couple of times on trips back home from college before they got married. They rationalized that they were as committed to each other as the day when they would walk down the aisle. They weren't Christians then, so they chalked it up to "sowing wild oats."

Shortly after the birth of their first child, Owen and his wife became interested in spiritual things. Now that they had a child to raise, they started looking for a church to attend and in the process came face-to-face with the gospel. They both put their trust in Christ. As they had approached everything else in life, they dived into Christianity with gusto.

Their adult Sunday school class talked about affair-proofing their marriage. Owen and his wife had a few questions about that, but they were too embarrassed to ask them in public, so they just went along as if they understood. They were both glad when that course was over; the next topic was a Bible study. That seemed a lot safer.

Owen's wife began teaching Sunday school, and over the course of time they began to make friends with several other young couples who were in their stage of life. His wife became especially close to another married woman who taught in the same Sunday school department. Together they planned a weekend getaway with their husbands.

That trip went so well that other trips soon followed, and the two couples became quite close. The weekends were always good experiences, and Al, the other husband, got along great with Owen.

The two men were very different. Al was both more muscular and more aggressive than Owen. Whereas Owen was a bit on the passive side (he called it being cooperative), Al would dive right in and take control of any situation. Al had worked his way up into management in a package delivery service, and his take-charge style worked well there. Al always seemed to dominate—both at work and on their social jaunts together—but he wasn't oppressive; he was gracious as well. Al's ideas worked well, and Owen looked forward to being around him, since he could just relax and let Al take the initiative.

Everything was going well until one Saturday evening when Owen got a phone call from Al's wife, who said that she needed to get together with him right away. Owen's wife wasn't home; she was going to run several errands, she said, as she had breezed out the door a few hours ago. Owen tried to put Al's wife off until she blurted it out: Owen's wife had run off with Al.

His head reeling, Owen almost passed out from the shock.

He hadn't even been quarreling with his wife. He had thought their marriage was fine. But in the aftermath of the disclosure of the affair, his wife angrily accused Owen of ignoring her needs and emotionally distancing himself from her.

She felt abandoned, she said, and had found a willing heart in Al. Instead of facing the probability of a lifetime of married unhappiness with Owen, she decided to take things into her own hands and pursue her relationship with Al. Even now, she was still on the knife's edge as she wavered between coming back to Owen and marrying Al, whose marriage was also in disarray.

Several months later Owen still struggled with his grief and anger, and there were times when he told himself that he was through trying to reconcile their relationship. On those days he just wanted to accept the inevitability of the divorce and call it quits. There were still days when he wanted to kill Al, but he was also beginning to acknowledge his part in the experience.

Through counseling, Owen was beginning to understand why the affair had occurred. It wasn't totally clear yet, but the outline was beginning to appear out of the fog. He was starting to see what he had brought into his family system and how the environment in their marriage had actually been a setup for an affair. In hindsight, he should have seen it coming, he ruefully acknowledged.

ENVIRONMENT 1: CULTURAL MYTHS

Although I think our culture is making progress toward reversing the following two myths, it is painfully slow. Some excellent books have brought them to light (see Appendix D), but some days I think such discussion is "too little, too late." These myths are powerful molders of our attitudes and lifelong orientations to everyday events. And they exact a dreadful toll.

Cultural Myth 1 (For Men): "Only Women Can/Should Nurture"

This is often one of the earliest messages a little boy receives—that women alone are nurturers. When you need food, Mother provides; when you need changing, she hears your cry. When you need comforting because your feelings are hurt, Mom is there; Dad is often absent physically or emotionally. If he is present physically, often he'll shame any emotional expression, using such slogans as "Big boys don't cry," or, "If you don't quit crying, I'll give you something to cry about."

Now don't misunderstand me: the kind of caretaking attributed here to women is critical for healthy childhood development, but as the little boy grows older, it becomes imperative that Father step into his nurturing responsibility as well. It provides a new perspective on life to have Dad feed him, comfort him, bathe him. If Dad is absent or chooses to stay out of this caretaking picture, the little boy begins to formulate unconscious thoughts that all basic needs in life are met by women. That bears fruit later in life, as we shall see.

Female teachers in elementary school and Sunday school continue to send the same message. Unfortunately, many scoutmasters, Indian Guide leaders, and other male leaders also reinforce this misperception. Coaches yell, scream, and curse; women encourage, support, and affirm. It's not hard to see where most men get the idea that comfort lies with women.

The message is reinforced in adolescence when the hormones take over and sexual activity becomes a great source of nurturance. Let's face it: sex itself is comforting and reassuring. When the selection is eventually made for a lifelong comforter—wife—the stage is set for ultimate disappointment. All the women of the world cannot meet all the needs for nurturance in a man—just ask King Solomon.

Part of the deep yearning of the masculine soul is to have an intimate, appropriate relationship with another man—a man-to-man relationship that is vulnerable, genuine, and loyal. Yet that is so rare that it is practically absent in our culture.

So an obvious decision for a man who has bought into this myth would be to seek his comfort solely in a woman. If his wife is not providing this nurturance and he has needs that are not met in same-sex appropriate relationships, he will seek it in another woman. He may reason subconsciously that he must have married the wrong woman since she obviously cannot nurture him fully. And, of course, the initial infatuation in an affair only confirms this thought process.

CULTURAL MYTH 2 (FOR WOMEN): "I NEED A MAN TO BE HAPPY"

This is the other side of the coin. We saw it illustrated in the opening section of this chapter. Owen's wife, rather than address the problems in their marriage, chose to look for happiness in the only logical place to her (i.e., a man).

Little girls often grow up seeing their own mother's unhappiness, hearing their complaints, and seeing them turn to self-nurturance—such as overeating or other kinds of addictions—because their husbands have failed to relate to them adequately. Thus the goal to find the right man, who will ensure happiness for the girl, is set early in life.

The girl's father is a critical figure in this drama. His responses to his daughter can cause her to later mistrust all men, even while she is desperately searching for one. The deficits in the father-daughter relationship can generate an impossible "needs list" for the future husband to try to meet, a bottomless pit of unmet needs created by her father's failure. In that regard, consider the case of Allyson.

All Allyson had ever wanted was to get married and have a family. Now in her early thirties, Allyson was becoming increasingly concerned that time was running out for her to find a mate.

She had been involved in several serious relationships, but she always seemed to come on too strong. She never understood why the men kept breaking it off. She thought she needed to prove to them that she would be a good wife, and in her mind that certainly meant being a good sex partner. But no matter how much she tried to please them both in and out of bed, she just couldn't seem to snag one.

Eventually, however, Allyson succeeded and married. Her new husband drank a little too much at times, but she could tolerate that. It was the first time he struck her in the face that shocked her.

He apologized profusely, and she felt a little better—it was probably just a momentary loss of control, she reasoned. But his drinking worsened, and by the time she was pregnant with their first child, he was consistently violent.

Unknown to Allyson, during the final month of her pregnancy, her husband started having an affair. She knew he didn't seem as interested in her physically, but she chalked that up to normal pregnancy complications. Besides, she would soon have the baby to care for, and preparations took most of her time and attention. She didn't have the energy now to address his lack of interest.

His drinking escalated, and she could sense a giant argument coming just before she delivered. It did. And it was violent. It thoroughly scared her, but, thank God, the baby in her womb was not hurt. She wondered if things would get worse.

As she reflected in the hospital, Allyson vowed to leave him. After another episode or two, and especially one in which he threatened to hurt the baby, she moved out.

While living with her parents, she found herself considering the men in her "Parents Without Partners" group at the community center, trying to decide who would make a good husband and father. She picked one out.

Their friendship grew, and it wasn't long before she moved in with him. He had some of the same habits as her first husband, but she figured she could make it work and thereby make her dream come true.

Needless to say, it didn't. He turned out to be abusive too.

In counseling, Allyson began to look at the list of poor choices she had made. It led all the way back to her dad. Only as she began to realize that she couldn't get from grown men what she had failed to receive from her dad was she able to discard the myth that men are the center of happiness in life.

Eventually, Allyson learned to stop desperately needing a man and get rid of her destructive "any man will do" mentality. Instead she focused on pursuing what was important for her and her child. The good side of the story is that once she didn't need a man so badly, she didn't scare them off anymore. Eventually, with her new attitude, she did meet someone and make a good choice. As far as I know, they're still married today.

In marriages that have suffered an affair, it is critical during the recovery process for both partners to develop close, same-sex relationships to supplement the marriage relationship. Those outside relationships can provide much of the nurturance, empathy, mutual support, and affirmation that both individuals need. And it fleshes out the truth necessary to contradict those cultural myths.

For this reason a sponsoring couple is very helpful for a couple's recovery. In an affair recovery group, a sponsor couple will walk with either the spouse or the infidel (or both, ideally) as he or she works through the affair. If you don't have such a group available to you, you can work through an existing relationship to develop such support.

ENVIRONMENT 2: SPIRITUAL BELIEF PATTERNS

Individuals who have had an affair and also maintain a Christian value system seem to come from one of two major religious backgrounds: either a performance or a dependency orientation. Let's look at these thought systems and how they contribute to affairs.

SPIRITUAL MYTH 1: PERFORMANCE ORIENTATION

This constellation of spiritual practices includes:

1. *A black and white worldview.* This is an attitude that goes beyond maintaining sound doctrine to the point of being doctrinaire and all-encompassing. It is often black and white, with little allowance for gray areas. It's a belief system that has an answer for everything.

2. *Overly rigid worship practices.* Individually, there is often an overly structured devotional time that never varies, is too predictable, and which gradually becomes a forced habit instead of a vital practice with some variety. If the individual doesn't practice a structured personal piety, he may attend a church with a programmed liturgy. Both are rigidly predictable.

3. *An overly measured ministry.* This is a performance orientation in ministry that is out of proportion; it often involves extensive record keeping. This is sometimes true of churches or ministries that are managed like a secular sales force. Don't misunderstand me; there's nothing wrong with moderate or balanced tracking of activity, but when it becomes all-important and people begin to take a backseat to performance, it becomes extreme.

That unbalanced structure is what allows an individual to maintain his or her spirituality in the midst of an affair. In a meeting-the-guidelines-is-paramount orientation, he can compartmentalize the affair and his spirituality, and the two never meet. One example is the highly placed minister who in the morning leads his staff in devotions and then at lunch meets with his mistress. The more tightly structured the religiosity, the more susceptible the individual can be to sexual perversion. He can practice both at the same time and never miss a beat.

SPIRITUAL MYTH 2: DEPENDENCY ORIENTATION

Whereas the first spiritual myth encourages responsibility and measures performance, the second removes individual responsibility altogether. Here responsibility is placed upon another individual, such as the pastor, or a small group of individuals, such as the elders.

Some typical characteristics are:

1. It allows for little variation in behavior, appearance, or even conversation. Church members under this system tend to be clones of each other or of the pastor or of the denomination.
2. It requires an extreme submission to authority, even on matters of personal choice.
3. It exalts the position of leadership over the laity beyond the biblical standard.
4. It reinforces individual inadequacy. The individual is never encouraged to make decisions for himself.
5. Individuals from such a background often resort to a lot of what I call "God talk." This orientation utilizes unmeasurable decision-making procedures, substituting "God led me" or "God spoke to me and said that I should—" for sound thinking. They rarely say things as they are. Everything is couched in a safe and spiritually acceptable fashion. As long as they speak right, look right, and behave right in public, they are right in their minds. They can easily compartmentalize their Christianity while living an entirely different lifestyle outside of church.

When such a dichotomy is practiced by local church leadership, the results can make your hair stand on end! The case below is all too common in pulpits today.

Del was a wonderful pastor—gifted and especially talented. He was comfortable with all ages and had great people skills. In preaching, his approach was fresh, and he said things in such a way that people listened with respect. From the pulpit he spoke with authority, and everything he said sounded logical. You walked away from each service feeling as though you had been in the presence of a master teacher.

Over the course of time, Del became more aware of his ability to sway people's thinking. He went through several phases of processing that thought. At first, it was exhilarating, then it became somewhat frightening as people began to expect more and more of him. He continued to "deliver the goods" Sunday after Sunday, but he found himself growing irritated with those who disagreed with him. They just made his life more complicated; why couldn't they just cooperate with the pastor?

As time went by, Del began to reward those who supported him and distance himself from those who questioned him. He increasingly felt the need for support as the demands of the ministry grew. Loyalty from his staff and lay leaders became all-important to him. Having a loyal team behind him helped him run even faster through his overloaded schedule week after week.

Eventually, though, even his affirming staff was insufficient to rejuvenate him. He needed more than that to pick him up emotionally.

During that time, Del had increasingly applied his talents to issues on the fringe of ministry—scarcely even realizing what he was doing. He had developed opinions on subjects that he knew very little about. He found himself making pronouncements about topics that were, if the truth were known, out of the realm of his expertise.

Worse yet, they were not only pronouncements; they appeared to have the power of edicts with the people in his congregation. Initially their widespread acceptance among the laypeople surprised him, but he rationalized that they needed a strong leader in this day of confusion and chaos. So the cycle was reinforced.

But woe to those who opposed him. Anyone who questioned him found himself cut out of leadership and other influential positions. Persons in the congregation either accepted his official interpretation, or they drifted away. Even their departure was covered over with more "God talk," characterizing those who left as spiritually lukewarm and those who stayed as the truly devoted. They whispered the slogan: "The committed stay; the carnal stray."

Del's growing sense of entitlement to have everyone around him be "yes men" actually set him up for a *series* of affairs. He didn't just have one. He had simultaneous affairs going with three women in the congregation—one of them the wife of a deacon!

Del continued to preach effectively for some time. Each of his illicit partners sat in church and believed her secret relationship with Del was beneficial to him. They all thought their sexual favors were helping him do the work of God. He was under such pressure, they rationalized, as the senior pastor of a prestigious church that he needed release from all the stress.

Even when word of his behavior leaked to the inner circle of the staff, they overlooked and ignored it. After all, they had been conditioned to accept everything he said as right, and he needed their love and support. He appealed to their loyalty never to tell. It was "our secret," he assured them, and for a while that worked.

The dependency orientation fostered at Del's church allowed him to hold accountability at bay. As long as he continued to do what was important to God, he reasoned, he had a right to enjoy God's creation—even if it was another man's wife.

Eventually, Del's affairs were revealed, and his ministry came tumbling down. But his people had become so dependent on him for leadership that they couldn't provide accountability until it was too late.

ENVIRONMENT 3: MARITAL STYLES

In theater, the written script makes each actor's role crystal clear. But in real life, many factors influence what we perceive our role to be. Ideally we follow God's script for our husband/wife roles (Ephesians 5). But the world and our fallen nature sometimes work together to skew that ideal balance of independence and interdependence, introducing dysfunctional roles into the relationship.

In this section we'll look at two role aberrations, where husbands and wives relate to each other in inappropriate ways—ways that can predispose either party for an affair. First we'll examine the case where one spouse sets him- or herself up as the functional equivalent of a parent to the mate; then we'll look at the case where a parent can put one of the children in the place of the spouse.

MIXING SPOUSE/PARENT ROLES: THE SPOUSE AS PARENT

Individuals from dysfunctional family backgrounds with abuse, enmeshment (overly close relationships), or abandonment patterns will often choose, at the time of courtship and marriage, a person to become both their missing surrogate parent and a marital partner. Such a double bind is an impossible role for anyone to fill.

Those who practice this pattern rarely do it on purpose. Unaware of unfinished business with their own parents and their unmet needs from childhood, they choose to enter marriage with gaping emotional deficits that no spouse could ever meet. Often that cavernous need is exactly what attracts the spouse in the first place, because he or she has a complementary need to take care of someone else. The latter is called a "caretaker." When normal, healthy caring is taken to the extreme, it becomes unhealthy.

The marriage seems perfect at first. It's as if the partners have been looking for each other all their lives (and in a sense they have). Eventually, however, such intense need and smothering become exhausting. Resentment and smoldering anger will settle in because both are disappointed when their unrealistic expectations are not met. That anger will corrupt the entire relationship. Adult relationships ideally involve mutual giving and receiving, but this type is totally lopsided.

Plus, it's a one-way street. The adult who is trying to get all his/her lingering childhood needs met in marriage will not be able to reciprocate in caring for the spouse. Unless that individual works through those issues, he will remain at risk to become inappropriately involved with another, as he blindly and desperately seeks to have his love and other needs met by *someone*.

The caretaker spouse with the overblown need to care for someone will often complain about how helpless her marital partner is. Jokingly, she will even count her spouse as one of her children. I know one woman who says sarcastically, "I've three kids to take care of: Billy and Tommy [her actual children], and Herb [her husband]."

The "joke" gets played out in daily living: the caretaker often treats the one-down spouse like a child, a humiliating experience for an adult to endure. Some real-life examples:

- The spouse who buys all her husband's clothes or on a daily basis even lays out what her partner should wear. Now I'm not saying it's dysfunctional for the wife to buy new socks or underwear for her husband to save time while she's out shopping, but if such buying covers his entire wardrobe and is accompanied by belittling comments, it's unhealthy.
- The spouse who doles out an "allowance" to the partner, not on an equal basis but rather on a come-and-beg-because-today-is-payday basis. Each spouse should share equally in the responsibility of financial management, without promoting the idea that "I'm the responsible one, and you're the irresponsible one."
- The spouse who is constantly reminding the other of items you would remind a child: "Don't forget your lunch," "It's cold outside," "Don't forget your jacket," "Watch your step," "How much did it cost?" "Where's the change?"
- The spouse who is always correcting the other's pronunciation, behavior, manners, posture, meal preparation, driving patterns, ad nauseam.
- The spouse who won't allow her mate to grow up, by not

allowing him to drive, always filling his plate at social gatherings, requiring a report of how every penny or every minute is spent.

Although it may seem ridiculous, that degree of caretaking actually goes on between adults. What is ironic is that it often seems reassuring at first. For the adult who was never cared for as a child, it can generate wonderful feelings of significance and love. Unfortunately, the tendency on the part of the caretaker is to keep pouring it on, increasing the behavior instead of moderating it.

Eventually, the behavior becomes suffocating to the one being cared for. Confusion and repressed anger or depression sets in: *Why do I feel so bad when I'm being cared for so well?* he might ask himself. The smothered spouse feels boxed in, trapped, and unable to say what he really feels, for fear of hurting his partner, who is being so nice.

The caretaker's goal (whether conscious or unconscious) is usually to maintain his or her power in the relationship. As long as she can keep the spouse in the one-down position of child, she can be the "parent in charge." Sure, it's hard work always to be in charge, but for the caretaker it beats the alternative of never being able to predict exactly what will happen and thus feeling totally out of control. If you're in charge, you can call the shots—as long as your mate lets you, that is. When the one-down mate rebels against this strange system by sleeping with his spouse's prayer partner, you can guess that things are going to change.

Resentment

The spouse-as-parent relationship style produces a great deal of resentment in both parties. The child spouse is bitter because he has to "take it" just as the caretaking spouse sees fit to provide it. Even if you don't like it, "Father/Mother knows best."

The caregiving spouse also feels resentment, because she receives little nurturing from the one-way relationship. But watch out if the child spouse attempts to change the system by returning some caregiving. The caregiver often panics, feeling uncomfortable receiving kindness. She senses that her power and control may be eroding, so she smothers the "rebellion."

Entitlement

Over the course of time the child spouse becomes demanding. What was initially given freely now is expected, and the child spouse appears to be "spoiled rotten." A pervasive tone of entitlement sets in. The one-down spouse can end up throwing tantrums or pouting if he doesn't get exactly what he wants, just as a child would.

The caretaking spouse also develops a sense of entitlement: "After all I do for you, you owe me _____." Fill in the blank. The payoff may come in the form of sex, tolerance of addictive and compulsive behavior, inappropriate buying, eating, gossip, and so on.

"You owe me" and "I owe you"—it can go on forever unless interrupted by something. Something like infidelity.

Anger

The anger in this parent/spouse mix-up often lurks under the surface in the infidel-to-be until another person shows up who "understands" his or her sense of being smothered or exhausted or being taken advantage of. We'll look in depth at the anger that is a natural result of this aberration in chapter 9.

Exhaustion/Depression

Neither spouse is truly happy with the parent/spouse arrangement, but both are usually afraid to change it. It's exhausting work to continue to cover up unhappiness with pretense. The resulting exhaustion causes depression, which in turn can ironically cause couples to draw even closer. "Misery loves company" goes the expression.

Now we have real helplessness, so the caretaker becomes motivated to increase his or her dysfunctional behavior. Instead of changing gears in the face of the depression, she just turns up the throttle a notch or two. Misery is thus multiplied.

On the other hand, the resultant depression can also encourage a couple to bring some fresh thinking into their marriage in the form of a counselor or pastor. Since it is difficult to adjust to the advice given by the counselor, they may just intellectualize or discount it, preventing the counseling from impacting their lopsided relationship. That allows them to maintain the same pattern.

Couples in this mode will go from therapist to therapist "seeking help," only to move on if attempts are made to change the way the spouses relate to each other. In other words, they say to the counselor in effect, "Please help us, but if you rock our boat too violently, we'll dump you and go find someone who won't upset our pattern." That denial can set up an illicit relationship. Or it may lead one or both of them into an inappropriate relationship with one of their children.

CONFUSING CHILD/SPOUSE ROLES: THE CHILD AS SPOUSE

Role confusion in the marriage is not limited to the spouse-as-parent scenario. Sometimes a parent will become too close to one of the children as he or she attempts to fulfill unmet emotional needs. The attachment can range from too much protection and involvement in the child's life to actual dependency upon the child for the adult's happiness.

In the latter case, the parent has no happiness except what the child manages to produce by his achievements, behavior, dating life, experiences at school, and so on. If left unchecked, this intrusion into the child's life will only intensify with the passage of time. And it has been demonstrated that the pattern is often a prelude to incestuous sexual behavior.

The parent may encourage the imbalance by sharing inappropriate portions of the marital relationship with the child, such as sexual aspects, with the mistaken notion of "improving family communication." Some parents actually will follow their same-sex adolescent children to the bathroom, again with the misguided intention of "closeness." Others may sleep in the same bed with their children beyond appropriate ages (upper elementary). Through such inappropriate actions, the parent forces to the child to take on the role of surrogate spouse.

The parent who is inappropriately close to a child rarely becomes involved in an affair. Why should she risk that? Her own children are now satisfying the emotional needs that she brought into the marriage.

Rather, it's the left-out spouse who is at risk for an affair—he will feel cut off from the one who is extremely close to the children. Initially, he may try a number of compulsive behaviors, such as workaholism, food, alcohol, or pornography, to fill the void left by the now-distant spouse. Eventually, however, the emotional emptiness created by the overattached spouse's behavior soon develops a psychological vulnerability that the "other woman" taps into very quickly.

In such cases, people may ask, Which came first—the chicken or the egg? That is, did the overattached spouse cause the left-out spouse to go searching for affection, or did the distant spouse cause the other to look for affection in the children? It's difficult to answer that, and in any case the answer is unimportant. The pattern is what is important: one spouse withdrew, and the other spouse overattached. The result is often infidelity.

LOOKING AHEAD

In the next chapter we'll look at additional causative factors that lead to adultery. We'll examine family-of-origin patterns (patterns in the family in which you were raised) learned early in each of our lives. We'll observe how learned lifestyle responses—such as poor anger management skills, excessive risk taking, or overabundant control in relationships—can predispose us to infidelity.

5

OTHER FACTORS CONTRIBUTING TO INFIDELITY

D ave and Lynn had been married barely three years, and they were already having violent arguments that included throwing things at each other. Lynn was even hitting Dave, and she was afraid he might start hitting her back. Their eighteen-month-old son had witnessed their last fight, and they both felt terrible about that.

It had got to the point where Dave was threatening to leave, and Lynn was on the verge of asking him to. Instead, thankfully, they came in for counseling.

Both were puzzled by their extreme behavior, being Christians and having grown up in Christian homes. As we explored their situation, I suggested that they do a little homework and find out if their parents had experienced similar discord. As the old saying goes, "Apples don't fall far from the tree," and even though they both held idealized images of their families of origin, I had a hunch that if they did some digging, they might find clues that would explain their behavior.

Dave came back both excited and depressed. He was excited because he was uncovering some family secrets and because he knew he was on the trail to finding healing for their marriage. But he was depressed because he found that his father had deserted his mother for a six-month period when Dave was eighteen months old and his mother was expecting her second child.

Though his father wasn't involved with another woman at the

time, Dave was shocked that he had abandoned his mother at such a crucial time. What terror his mother must have experienced as she saw her man walk out of her life, not knowing if he'd ever return. The true impact of his father's actions was driven home to Dave when, a few weeks later, Lynn discovered that she was pregnant with their second child.

But Dave's father revealed an even more fearful fact when he admitted that his father, Dave's grandfather, had done the very same thing to his wife, Dave's grandmother! Soberly, Dave realized that if he didn't change his relationship with Lynn, he was in grave danger of repeating the cycle in the third successive generation.

Dave asked his dad why he had never known about this family pattern. His father explained that he thought the best way to protect his son from even entertaining thoughts of such behavior was to keep it a secret; he had sworn Dave's mother to secrecy for Dave's sake. Yet keeping it a secret didn't break the cycle; Dave was continuing the pattern all over again.

As I probed to find out more about Dave's parents' relationship, some further clues began to emerge. The desertion had a lasting effect on Dave's mother in that she never fully trusted her husband again. The result was that she emotionally distanced herself from her spouse.

Dave's mother had made a vow to herself after the abandonment: she would raise Dave never to do that to his wife. She would raise him to be a sensitive man. So she became overly involved with him, pouring her energies into him, and neglected her marital relationship (an example of the overattached pattern that we examined in the last chapter).

The fallout of his mother's overinvolvement in Dave and Lynn's marriage was that the mother-in-law was constantly intruding. She wasn't going to let a little thing like her son's marriage stand in her way! She continued her lifelong project of developing her little Dave. Now that Dave was an adult, Mom still wouldn't let go, and she didn't want Lynn obstructing her access to him either. As a result, Lynn was having a difficult time feeling attached to her husband, an absolutely critical element to any healthy marriage.

The mother-in-law's actions naturally caused resentment in Lynn and explained in large part her violent behavior toward Dave. Too, Lynn was finding herself becoming increasingly dependent on her son for her emotional happiness (as opposed to being close to her spouse and finding contentment there), which is exactly what

Dave's mother had done with her son! The pattern, as it began to repeat itself, was frightening.

Dave and Lynn's fighting was a way that both could show that they still cared for each other (you only fight over what's important to you). But as a result of their conflicts, Dave's feelings were rapidly cooling for Lynn, he was entertaining thoughts of leaving, and he was worried.

If their situation had gone unchanged, it's easy to see how Dave would have been vulnerable to another partner who would understand and care for him.

FAMILY OF ORIGIN PATTERNS

Extramarital affairs seem to run in families. Yet that doesn't mean you are absolutely predestined to cheat on your spouse—you can break the cycle. Family history only sets the stage, predisposing you to infidelity if no new thinking patterns are introduced. Even though our parents' (and grandparents') actions influence us, we have to take full responsibility for our own actions. We have to break the cycle, with the Lord's help.

Often, as was the case in Dave's family, the infidelity itself changes the way members of the family relate to each other; they begin to keep secrets from each other, or develop unbalanced relationships, as when his mother withdrew from his father and overattached to Dave.

Overall, with affairs, no one in the family is left untouched—that's how devastating the breaking of the marriage vow is.

A Twisted Heritage: History of
Affairs in the Extended Family

Affairs and even "close calls" (when the attraction does not result in a full-blown affair) rarely occur for the first time in the current generation; they have a history behind them. The existence of affairs in the family tree is usually not discussed. Many times the young couple has to do some homework—some digging—before they can even uncover it in their family history, because those who have cheated are often punished by being cut off from the family tree. Their story is rarely known outside a close circle, almost as if it never happened.

Part of your recovery requires tracking your family system backward, starting with your own parents. Now that you've suffered infidelity and the future of your marriage is in jeopardy, there are no secrets worth protecting anymore. Come clean, and if you find your relatives resisting disclosing information, encourage them to come clean too. Secrets fester and cause problems, so it's best to tell them rather than cover them up.

All of us need to know how our own family works (immediate family, family of origin, and extended family). Men share similar passions and weaknesses, whether they are sons, fathers, or brothers. The same holds true for daughters, mothers, and sisters. If infidelity has happened in your history, you need to know it. The old adage about world history holds true for family history: "He who ignores history is doomed to repeat it." The stakes are too high to allow that to happen.

CLOSEST TO HOME: FACTORS IN THE FAMILY OF ORIGIN

Within each individual family history, certain behaviors seem to surface in individuals who experience affairs. Some of these practices, together with the resultant response in the children affected, are:

Parents Who Practice:	Cause Children to Say:
• Abuse of alcohol and drugs	• "Be there for me—I'm alone"
• Overly rigid discipline	• "Love me, don't hurt me"
• Sexual molestation	• "Don't use me and make me pay"
• Pre-puberty exposure to pornography	• "Don't confuse me or make me doubt myself"
• A history of affairs	• "Don't abandon me; I'll behave better"

It should be noted that the "messages" noted in the right-hand column tend to endure from childhood into adulthood. Such influences can wreak all sorts of havoc in children's development for literally decades.[1]

The two threads that hold the above practices together are:

1. The lack of nurturing delivered to the child.
2. The underlying message that the parent sends to the child is "If there's any happiness available in life, you've got to find it on your own, kid. It's not here." The child grows up and applies that thought to all of life.

Those messages become underground tapes that play over and over in the mind of the adult child. As a result, these grown-up children start a lifelong search for the right person (or sexual partner) to fill their emptiness. Of course, it is a hopeless fantasy.

And that distortion in the child's psyche later predisposes him or her to an affair. Several factors affect how deeply it impacts the child: time frame (how long the environment was endured), chronicity (how many encounters with behaviors such as sexual molestation), intensity (how fearful or painful was the environment), and the child's age at the time of these experiences.

Although all of these experiences are hurtful to the child and destructive to his development, some mitigating factors might lessen the impact: a caring parent who makes up for the parental deficits of the other spouse, a surrogate family (neighbor or relative) with whom the child spends a lot of time, the child's personality makeup (however, all children by their very nature are impressionable and therefore vulnerable), and the onset of early treatment.

Some recurring themes in the individual history of those who experience affairs are feelings of abandonment and lack of affection. Many times these adults were left alone as children. They had too much time on their hands without supervision. No one was available or really seemed to care about them.

Along with feelings of abandonment and aloneness there was a lack of physical and emotional affection. If parents were physically present, they were often emotionally unavailable. They were exhausted and had little to give to the children. Appropriate touching and normal childhood nurturances—warm hugs, even something as common as rocking in Mother's arms—were often unavailable to the small child who later grows up to have an affair. Laughing with the parents, talking with them in quiet moments of closeness, taking peaceful walks together, playful fun times on the child's level—all were missing to some degree.

Part of the recovery process for every reconciling couple is determining which of the infidel's unmet childhood needs *were* met in the illicit relationship. As I work with couples, I am struck by the utter childishness of infidelities. I say that not in a denigratory way but in a literal sense: you get a feeling that those unmet childhood needs are carried forward so that they are fully present in adulthood. The private world of the affair that the infidel and partner create for themselves is much the same world of the narcissistic infant, combined with adolescent sexual attraction. The needy baby has grown up and put the sexual skills learned in the teen years to work.

Seen from that angle, affairs are at their core adult "magical" or make-believe experiences. *The affair is an artificial world spun together by the infidel and partner in an attempt to have their gnawing emotional deficits addressed.*

LEARNED LIFESTYLE RESPONSES

Whether learned in the family of origin or in subsequent adult years, the following seven characteristics tend to typify those who are at high risk for affairs. As you read through them, think about which are true of you or of your spouse. All of us can identify with them to a certain degree, but the more highly they characterize you, the more at risk you are for infidelity.

SUPPRESSION OF EMOTIONS: NUMBNESS AND BLINDSIDING

Both the infidel and the spouse report a feeling of emotional numbness before the affair. The infidel often says he was honestly surprised when he found himself involved with another. The words *sudden, unanticipated,* and *overwhelmed* are common in the infidel's vocabulary when reporting an affair. He commonly reports that he had "no intention of doing this." He was not even aware of what was going on inside him until it was too late. The infidel says to himself, *Focus outside yourself, shut down emotionally, keep it in your head, don't let it touch your heart.*

The suppression of emotions explains in large part the surprise element. Stuffing one's emotions results in the turmoil bubbling up with surprising regularity and in inappropriate moments. One's anger is not destroyed or eliminated when one refuses to acknowledge it—it is simply forced down into the emotional depths and, to use a modern-day word, is "recycled" when it pops back up. For example, when one mate tries to convince herself that she doesn't have any need for love, that doesn't change the fact that she does. And when that need bubbles up, she becomes vulnerable to infidelity. The result is often a blindsided attack on the marriage relationship. The "surprise" isn't really all that surprising when you look at it that way.

People with this pattern use several slogans to keep their emotions below the surface.

- Focus outside yourself. Never look within—introspection is dangerous. Only look at other screens—computer, TV, or movie screens—not your own.
- Shut down emotionally. If you don't feel, it won't hurt. Be numb; that way you'll be safe from pain.

• Keep everything in your head—don't let it touch your heart. Intellectualize, philosophize, and think straight.

Through those or other defense mechanisms, the infidel has gotten out of touch with his or her feelings. This is especially true of Christians perpetrating affairs—their cognitive dissonance (a fancy term for guilty conscience in this case) requires much management, since they know in their heart of hearts that such behavior is contrary to God's law. They often report that just prior to becoming involved with the partner, they had no feelings at all. Infidels are often exhausted, and they feel just plain dead emotionally.

Identifying the pattern of suppression is important for the couple attempting to reconcile. If the person practicing the suppression does not start to change it, long-term recovery will be elusive. Getting in touch with true feelings and being able to communicate them to the spouse is a key to recovery and comprehensive restoration of the relationship.

ANGER MANAGEMENT: DISCHARGE VERSUS RESOLUTION

One of the big surprises for many who have been in affairs is their lack of proper anger management skills. Their slogan seems to be: "Anger is bad; get rid of it as soon as possible, and whatever you do, don't look at the root cause." It's a game of emotional hot potato.

On the surface, they are often the "steady Eddies" who always appear to be in control of themselves (except with their family or a few close friends). They rarely have the communication skills necessary to resolve anger properly. Instead they dodge it with humor, discount it ("It wasn't that important"), deny it ("What, me angry? Never!"), or vent it (watch out for this), but they rarely work through it. When angry, this type of person will either run, rage, or pout; he will feel depressed or explode; he will be stubborn or act out. The tendency is to blame or displace the anger onto another person or experience, rather than dealing with the real source.

That inability to work through anger and conflict is often one of the initial wedges in the marital relationship. It doesn't directly push one of the spouses into an affair, but it does serve as a block to the intimacy both desire and, more to the point, it generates unmet needs that predispose one partner to finding fulfillment in someone else.

BOUNDARY CONSTRUCTION: CONTROL VERSUS COUNSEL

Within the child. Individuals who have had affairs commonly report a pattern of poor choices during adolescence, which are often discounted as a time of "sowing wild oats." Although some form of moderate rebellion is probably necessary and even healthy in adolescents, poor sexual choices certainly are not. In fact, they appear to predispose the adolescent to inappropriate choices in adulthood.

A series of poor choices means the boundaries normally constructed through the slow process of making one good choice after another are never built. I think that is what the Bible means when it speaks of "the mature, who because of practice have their senses trained to discern good and evil" (Hebrews 5:14). They might *want* to chose right instead of wrong as an adult, but the pattern that makes good choices easy has not been assembled in the early identity construction period of adolescence. Thus they are poorly equipped to control their impulses and make wise choices when they become adults.

Between parent and child. There appear to be similar parenting practices in the backgrounds of those who later get involved in affairs. As children they were either over- or under-controlled and therefore grew up to have control issues with their spouse, which can lead to infidelity. For example, an infidel whose spouse over-controls him might rebel and go on the prowl for a more reasonable partner.

Common parenting practices that exhibit control problems are:

- *Parents who control their children too tightly for too long.* The ideal pattern of control is one where direct control gradually tapers off as the kids grow older, especially as they move into mid and late adolescence. When the parents never relinquish their influence, they become intruding parents-in-law to married adult children.
- *Parents who relinquish control too suddenly.* Note above where I outlined a gradual tapering of control. The tapering-off process is just as important as the degree of control.
- *Parents who suddenly increase their control.* Sometimes parents fear that time is running out, that they've been laissez-faire for too long and suddenly impose almost dictatorial standards of conduct. This often happens when the children enter high school. Such a change in gears can be jolting and damaging to kids.
- *Parents who are parenting out of their own adolescent failures.*
- *Parents who feel extremely hurt when children in late adolescence refuse to follow all their counsel.* It's not reasonable that

every single bit of advice should be eagerly accepted by emerging adults. In fact, part of their role at this stage of their lives is to make their own decisions, and that means at times not following every counsel given by parents.

- *Parents who have little tolerance for adolescents' mistakes and grossly overreact to them.* Part of the normal growth process for children is to make mistakes and learn from them in a ridicule-free environment.

RELATIONSHIP STYLE: ABUSE OF POWER VERSUS MUTUAL RESPECT

Persons involved in affairs (I'm speaking mostly of the infidel here) often have a warped sense of power in relationships. They have often suffered an abuse of power in earlier years, so they turn around and use their power to manipulate their spouse, their partner, or both. They figure that if they have power (and we all do to one extent or another), they should use it to their best advantage, often at the expense of others. They have practically no concept of shared power in marriage, or of power used to benefit another person. To share power is to put yourself at risk; to abuse it is to maintain control.

Participants in affairs often have a great need to regain a sense of control over their personal lives. Adultery seems to provide that, at least temporarily; the participants find needs met that previously seemed elusive. Their chaotic search for love is, at least for now, over.

These individuals often report having felt powerless in childhood and growing up in a family where, for example, "children should be seen and not heard." They were not valued as full human beings, they were "always in the way" of the adults, and as a result, they often struggle with feeling unimportant. When such a person finally does find someone—the illicit partner—who respects him as a peer and values him fully as a person, there is almost an overwhelming sense of health and wholeness. It doesn't matter to them that the newfound relationship is an infatuation and immoral—the feeling is so overwhelming and long-sought that the moral matters pale in comparison.

TASK ORIENTATION: COMPULSIVITY VERSUS BALANCE

Individuals who become infidels are often intense, quick, and impulsive. They tend to rise high in the world—they are often successful entrepreneurs, executives, and even pastors. Their slogan is "There's no time like the present—I'll get this done now." Even when they play, it is with great and sometimes overblown intensity. Down times are few and far between. They like to have a lot of things to do, and they love scratching things off the list.

Emotionally, their slogan is "If I can just run a little faster, I won't feel the pain. If I can just stay busy enough, I can stay ahead of it." They could be called "activity-aholics."

Besides being impulsive they tend to be compulsive; that is, they report not being able to stop doing certain things. They frequently do too much of one thing and only become alarmed when the behavior has become nearly uncontrollable. They struggle with different addictions at various times in their lives. Yet at other times and in other settings, they can display great willpower and can seemingly stop certain habits, such as smoking, that other people would have difficulty controlling.

Outwardly they may seem successful, but inwardly there is the gnawing sense that they are out of balance. Again, blame becomes the dominant defense mechanism. They rationalize that they would feel better "if they were just involved with the right person." The illicit relationship fits perfectly with this kind of thinking.

RISK ASSESSMENT: PASSION VERSUS CAUTION

Obviously people who get involved in affairs have thrown caution to the wind. As described in the section above, they have a tendency to be intense and impulsive. They are the consummate risk-takers. They say, "It's always easier to ask forgiveness than to ask permission."

They hate routine, and if they are trapped in a boring or tedious situation (e.g., their marriage), it only increases their vulnerability to an affair. They have a high need to feel alive; they need to feel the adrenaline flowing. They often seek challenges, such as climbing Mt. Everest just because it's there.

In matters of romance, they cherish the fantasy, identifying challenges in relationships in the same way. They find new love interests exhilarating. They enjoy spotting new "targets" and setting out to snag them.

The famous beer slogan "You only go around once in life—so go for the gusto" is their lifelong motto. Thrill seeking becomes their unspoken goal in life. They commonly get speeding tickets; they overload their credit cards, buying "toys" and taking vacations they can't afford; and so on. However, secretly maintaining a mistress on the side may be thrilling, but walking that knife's edge can have disastrous consequences when you fall.

ENTITLEMENT: "I DESERVE A BREAK TODAY"

Speaking of advertising jingles, there's an even more famous slogan that illustrates this characteristic thinking pattern of those involved in infidelity: "You deserve a break today." Entitlement thinking is epidemic in the general population today, and it usually finds expression in binge eating, binge spending, and so on.

Applied to infidelity, it finds a home in the thinking of the infidel who feels stressed out in his marriage or life situation. The various stressors begin to pile up in his mind, and pretty soon he has a list as long as his arm to justify why he deserves an additional love interest in his life. He is quick to justify his actions and to minimize the wrongness of his actions.

And it can apply to the partner's view as well. She may reason that since the infidel is so stressed out, it's OK for him to fool around. It's similar to the story of the pastor we examined in the last chapter who had multiple mistresses simultaneously in the congregation; they pitied the poor senior pastor who was so overburdened. He deserved a break today, and they were more than happy to help supply it.

COPING WITH TRANSITION IN THE LIFE CYCLE

Change is on every corner in the North American lifestyle today. As a result, confusion and turmoil are almost normal. People are so mobile and the pace of life is so frantic that instability is practically a way of life. But destabilization does exact its toll.

Such events as a change in job, a drop in income, a cross-country move, a pregnancy, a health crisis, or a death make an individual vulnerable to infidelity, especially if entitlement is part of his or her coping style. It is during periods of destabilization and transition that a relationship with another partner looks most appealing.

When life circumstances upset or destabilize a person's life, an affair is often his attempt to restructure and stabilize his life, especially from an emotional or nurturance point of view. But the price of such "stabilization" is high—too high. And it rarely provides a permanent stability; it's a false solution to real problems.

ARE YOU AT RISK FOR AN AFFAIR?

I originally created an evaluation like the one below to identify, prior to adultery, individuals in the ministry who were at risk for infidelity. Yet it applies to anyone—not just to pastors, although those with Christian backgrounds will identify most closely with it.

First, though, a caveat: This is not a scientific instrument, and it should not be used as such. It does not have absolute predictive power. Rather, it is meant to be used as a tool to identify personal growth areas for you and your spouse to discuss and develop. It is designed to help you evaluate your personal history and lifestyle for parallels with those who have been involved in adultery.

PERSONAL PATTERNS PREDICTING INFIDELITY

PERSONAL AND FAMILY HISTORY

1. Did you grow up in a family that used a substantial amount of alcohol?

    _____ Yes _____ No

2. Were your parents strict disciplinarians, possibly even abusive at times?

    _____ Yes _____ No

3. Were you sexually molested as a child?

    _____ Yes _____ No

4. Did you experience early adolescent heterosexual activity with an older partner (baby-sitter, older sister's friend)?

    _____ Yes _____ No

5. Were you involved in pornography prior to puberty (magazines, video)?

    _____ Yes _____ No

6. While you were living at home, was either of your parents involved in an extramarital affair?

    _____ Yes _____ No

7. Were you sexually active with a variety of partners in adolecence?

    _____ Yes _____ No

LIFESTYLE PATTERNS

Please use the following criterion to answer questions 8–25: The higher the score, the truer the statement.

8. As an adolescent I did not get along with authority figures, and I continue to have conflict with the law or my supervisor.

    1   2   3   4   5

9. I feel driven, unable to relax or have fun.

    1   2   3   4   5

10. My self-control and anger management skills are strengths in my life.

    1   2   3   4   5

11. I like testing the limits that surround me, such as the speed limit, tax and banking laws, church policies, and so on.

    1   2   3   4   5

12. I enjoy getting through a project so that I can get on with the next one. It is important to me to have a number of projects waiting for my attention.

    1   2   3   4   5

13. I feel alone even in my marriage and am unable to share my fears, deepest feelings, and the longings of my heart with my spouse.

    1   2   3   4   5

14. I recognize in myself the tendency toward compulsive behavior, such as with food, exercise, work, spending or saving money, fast driving, and so on.

    1   2   3   4   5

15. I have lots of acquaintances and appear to be close to my family members, but I don't have one intimate friend.

    1   2   3   4   5

16. I like to win and am a fierce competitor in whatever I do.

    1   2   3   4   5

17. My dating life was marked by a series of broken relationships that I ended.

        1   2   3   4   5

18. I feel stressed out, almost numb, from all the demands of my responsibilities in life.

        1   2   3   4   5

19. I like to be around important people and find myself playing up to them.

        1   2   3   4   5

20. My financial history contains a series of bounced checks, a large debt-to-income ratio, poor credit, regular use of credit cards to support my lifestyle, or possibly even bankruptcy.

        1   2   3   4   5

21. I have trouble expressing my anger in ways that provide relief without wounding others emotionally.

        1   2   3   4   5

22. I don't mind conflict and find that it actually helps me feel better and more in control.

        1   2   3   4   5

23. I like to see what I can get away with by living "close the edge."

        1   2   3   4   5

24. An area that the Lord has to help me with is a tendency to harbor grudges and a desire for revenge.

        1   2   3   4   5

25. Most of those who know me would say that I am intense, easily irritated, and have high standards of excellence.

        1   2   3   4   5

CIRCUMSTANTIAL FACTORS

Give yourself 5 points for each of the items you have experienced within the past year.

26. Lost a close loved one (child, parent, spouse). _____
27. Suffered a major stressor (job loss or promotion, divorce, medical diagnosis or hospitalization, cross-country move). _____
28. Approached a major life transition (pregnancy, midlife, retirement). _____

TEST SCORING

Questions 1–7
    "Yes" answers count 10 points each. If all seven questions are answered yes, give yourself an additional 40 points.
    Total score for questions 1–7: _____

Questions 8–25
    Total the numbers that you circled.
    Total score for questions 8–25: _____

Questions 26–28
    Five points for each category experienced.
    Total score for questions 26–28: _____

                                        TOTAL SCORE: _____

EVALUATION OF SCORE
    Questions 1–7. A score over 50 for this section places you in the high risk group.
    Questions 8–25. A score over 70 for this section places you in the high risk group.
    Questions 26–28. These are the trigger mechanisms that often send a person at risk into an affair.
    Total score. A score over 100 places you in the high risk group.

    One word of warning—high risk individuals are more vulnerable than they realize. Whatever you do, do not discount your initial score—talk it over with your spouse, and start working on some of the issues discussed in this book.

LOOKING AHEAD

    This concludes the section that examines exactly what affairs are and why they happen. Starting with the next chapter, we begin to delve into the healing process that needs to take place following infidelity.

In looking at some causes of affairs, it is clear that external structures will not protect an individual from the temptation of adultery. Real protection comes from the inside.

We'll be looking at that "real protection" in the next section. Lasting recovery is built on self-awareness—knowing who you are and where you come from. It is built on knowing what you need to work through and how you act in relationships with significant others in your life, and, finally, on your own personal spiritual beliefs.

NOTE

1. See Dave Carder, Earl Henslin, John Townsend, Henry Cloud, and Alice Brawand, *Secrets of Your Family Tree: Healing for Adult Children of Dysfunctional Families* (Chicago: Moody, 1991) for a full discussion of adult children issues.

SECTION 2:
HEALING FROM AFFAIRS

6

UNDERSTANDING THE RECOVERY:
THE INFIDEL'S PROCESS

I used to do some white-water canoeing. It's a somewhat dangerous sport, but if you do it right, danger is minimized and enjoy-
ment maximized. The process is what's important in staying
safe, and we followed our checklist very carefully as we approached
the water.

First, we'd get a map. We didn't want any surprises.

Next, we'd study the obstacles. As we approached each set of
rapids, we would beach our canoe and study the water patterns
from above the swirling eddies and plunges. Then we'd plot our
course, get back into the canoe, and paddle furiously to build up
speed. Canoes can be difficult to control unless they are going
faster than the current.

Once in the rapids, it's nearly impossible to choose a different
course. So you do what you planned, knowing that you will probably come out OK at the bottom if you follow the correct procedure
and refuse to panic.

In many ways, white-water canoeing is similar to picking up
the pieces of a shattered marriage. If you do it right, you can exit
the roaring rapids successfully. But if you don't, jagged rocks and
swirling whirlpools are just waiting to do you in.

Stay on course in the turbulent times, and you will make it.
This material has been tested and refined through many years of
work with couples who have made it, and it will work for you, too,
if you'll hang in there and do the tough work.

Come back and review this chapter when you think you are straying from the course. With God's help and your joint commitment to each other, it is possible to survive the perilous plunges of the roaring water ahead.

MAPPING AFFAIRS AND RECOVERY FROM THEM

The diagram on the opposite page displays the recovery process in graphic form. Study it carefully. It is permissible in the recovery process to take a breather (a roadside rest stop, if you will) from all the hard work. Set the processing aside for an agreed-upon period, and allow yourself to enjoy the reprieve. We'll discuss each segment briefly and then look at the infidel's curve in detail in this chapter and at the spouse's curve in the next chapter. The better you grasp this pair of curves in your mind's eye, the better you'll understand this tumultuous process.

At this point it's appropriate to make some general observations about both curves. The infidel's curve occurs first and is divided into four phases:

Phase 1—Growing Mutual Attraction
Phase 2—Emotional and Sexual Entanglement
Phase 3—Destabilization of the Affair
Phase 4—Disclosure and Resolution

The spouse's curve is also divided into four phases:

Phase A—Awareness
Phase B—Anger
Phase C—Anguish
Phase D—Reattachment and Recovery

Notice that both curves occupy about the same amount of time, in a relative sense. Even though the infidel's curve begins first, the two curves are more or less comparable in a chronological sense. This indicates an important rule of thumb for recovery from affairs: *In most cases it will take the spouse as long to recover as it took the infidel to get into and out of the affair.* For example, if it is an eighteen-month affair, the spouse will need eighteen full months to recover. In sporadic, longer-lasting affairs, the spouse will need about two years to recover. The two-year rule is a common time frame used in Divorce Recovery and Grief Workshops for the person who needs to rebuild his identity.

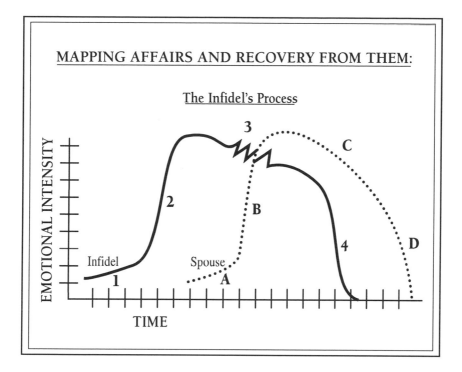

MAPPING AFFAIRS AND RECOVERY FROM THEM:

The Infidel's Process

That statement may be startling to some of you (it seems too large a time frame), but I urge you to keep reading. Almost all of the couples who reviewed the rough draft of this book—folks who've been through the agony of this recovery process—firmly agree that that rule of thumb is accurate in most cases.

So give yourself (or your spouse) adequate time to process the shattering break in your marital relationship. You may feel as if you should be over it by now, but cut yourself some slack—Rome wasn't built in a day, and the affair (and more important, the cracks in the marriage that contributed to it) didn't develop overnight either. The recovery process will take time.

Second, as you look over the chart, note that the emotional intensity (shown by the height of both curves) is the same for the spouse as it is for the infidel. Thus the second rule of thumb is: *The spouse needs to have emotional reactions that are just as intense as the infidel's.* That is, the spouse needs to feel anger that is as intense as the infidel's infatuation, anguish as intense as the infidel's joy, retaliation as intense as the infidel's deceit, announcements as intense as the infidel's secrecy, and so on.

Please don't misunderstand me—I'm not saying that the spouse should lose all control and obliterate the infidel through physical and verbal violence. I'm simply saying that the spouse needs to be brutally honest with herself and her mate and discontinue the pattern of denial that may have led to the affair. To respond otherwise is unhealthy—it's in essence a suppression of emotions and won't contribute to true and lasting recovery. Only when the spouse is truly in touch with her feelings of rage at the betrayal can lasting progress be made. Utter emotional truthfulness is also a key to discovering the reason for the affair.

Now let's look at the infidel's curve. As we examine the material below, keep in mind that this is an entangled, or Class II, affair.

PHASE 1: GROWING MUTUAL ATTRACTION

IN SECRET AND UNAWARE

The affair often starts innocently enough between two parties —a smile with no sexual overtones, a fleeting thought, a sincere appreciation of the other, an occasional meeting at a business function, even regular daily contact on the job, none of which is sexual. Generally a growing appreciation of the other's skills, abilities, and achievements can gradually lead to feelings of romantic or sexual attraction. That is the beginning of the secret.

Christians especially hate to acknowledge this attraction. Yet we're all sexual creatures, created by God with that dimension of our personality. Some sexual feelings toward others (even those we're not married to) is normal. But many believers cannot believe such feelings are OK and so they deny that they experience them. Guilt and shame follow. Denial is the defense mechanism of choice.

Yet denial doesn't solve anything. In fact, it usually exacerbates the problem because in the stages of denial, the desire to be around the other person "goes underground," and the infidel-to-be actually initiates contact with the partner unconsciously. Given the right set of circumstances and hormones, the affair literally becomes an accident waiting to happen, since the individual is unaware of the growing attraction.

A CONSCIOUS FANTASY

The growing sense of appreciation and attraction allows a whole new fantasy world to develop within the future infidel. Yet doing the "safe thing" (i.e., by daydreaming about him/her instead of making contact) actually feeds the attraction. The infidel keeps the attraction uppermost in his mind and begins to relish the feelings that the fantasy produces. He begins to concoct imaginary experiences (often nonsexual, to keep it "safe") with this person. He wonders "What it would be like if—?"

Actually, a person with that degree of emotional involvement still has a good chance of bypassing the affair if he can talk with someone else about his feelings and perceptions. It's normal for attraction to occur between males and females who are in constant association with each other. It's also natural to be able to appreciate beauty and develop admiration for another member of the opposite sex, even when happily married. The safety is in being able to talk about it with a close Christian friend who can hold you accountable and prayerfully walk through the attraction with you to keep you from stumbling.

SHARED FEELINGS

The starting point of the affair occurs when the individuals involved share their mutual feelings for each other. The actual verbalization of what had previously been unspoken thoughts and fantasies releases all those pent-up feelings. It is at this point that the affair takes on a life of its own. It will not go away of its own accord. Individuals report that this mutual acknowledgment "touches" something deep inside their souls that they cannot forget. Few couples can refrain from expressions of affection once this acknowledgment is made. This is the point of transgression within the marriage, and this is the starting date used for recovery purposes (see chapter 13, "Emotional Affairs").

PHASE 2: EMOTIONAL AND SEXUAL ENTANGLEMENT

The relationship develops new intensity when the two entangled people mutually acknowledge their feelings for each other. Once that happens, it is extremely difficult for the relationship ever to return to what it was initially. Now the cycle becomes self-perpetuating, since talking about one's feelings with the partner is exactly the wrong thing to do (i.e., it inflames the passions you're trying to control). Again, sharing the feelings with a trusted third party, who will hold you accountable, is far and away the better course to take.

A CRY FOR HELP

Many times, one party will attempt to talk to other people about her struggle, but her language style, the content of the conversation, and her description of emotional involvement is so superficial that the listener is not fully aware of how close the relationship is to becoming a full-fledged affair. In other words, the person struggling doesn't fully come clean in sharing the level of attraction. This is especially true of Christians—they tend to portray a false image of everything being under control.

For example, one woman I know was volunteering in a ministry at her church, working very closely with one of the pastors. She began to feel strongly attracted to him, and he to her. In her concern, she shared a limited version of her struggle with her husband, but she didn't tell him everything. The husband made an appointment with the pastor to take him to lunch. Did the husband lay down the law with the minister? Did he keep tabs on the situation by later asking his wife how the struggle was going? No! He simply had a nice lunch with the pastor and casually mentioned that he hoped he would manage his friendship with his wife carefully. The roaring flames of their passionate affair started up soon afterward. Their two families nearly fell apart, and the church was severely damaged. When your mate sends you an SOS, take it seriously. It may be muted, so be sure to tune in. It takes great courage to bring this subject up to one's spouse—don't discount it. If she is talking to you about it, she needs more support.

Such minimizing behavior is counterproductive to say the least; I could extend my canoeing analogy to describe a canoe that is approaching a waterfall, but one person doesn't want to alarm the other. Even though he knows the waterfall is close, instead of saying, "Hey, we've got to get to shore soon or it's all over!" he says, "Do you hear that pretty sound in the distance? I wonder what it could be?" Being vague about impending danger is foolish and dangerous. That applies just as much in matters of romantic and sexual attraction as in the navigation of rivers.

When the cry for help does come, it is commonly just prior to giving in to the partner, as with the woman and the minister above. In fact, it is often the failure of the listener to hear how intense and deep the struggles are that literally provokes the onset of the affair. Many times the person chosen to hear the struggles doesn't know what to do. She herself may have often struggled with similar attractions and made it through, so she assumes her friend or spouse will too. Or, if the future infidel does let on to his true level of feeling for the other woman, often the fright of such a revelation provokes such denial in the wife that she is incapable of acknowledging the intensity of his feelings.

When there is no response to the cry for help, the person

sending the cry says to himself, *See? She doesn't understand me. I'm going to spend time with someone who does.* That's why utter transparency is so critical to a healthy marriage.

That is the last barrier to be broken before the affair begins. This is not a time to ask the person if he wants help; he is often so confused that he is uncertain if he does or not. He doesn't want to give up the dream that is emerging. He likes the vitality that comes from living on the edge. He still has enough respect for himself to think that he can make it on his own.

Neither is it time for the spouse to accuse her mate who is considering adultery of his many sins and failures. Rather, it is a time for action. Now the spouse must initiate a different kind of relationship with her mate. It is time to listen and communicate acceptance—to build intimacy as the chief protection against getting involved with someone else.

DID SEX OCCUR?

Once the infidel and partner reveal their mutual attraction, I've found that the development of the sexual aspect to the relationship is just a matter of time. Usually sexual involvement follows such a discussion immediately and is quite intense. Thus, following a "help me" conversation as outlined above, you need to take action quickly—before the flames erupt.

But sometimes the process of sexual involvement is more drawn out. Simple gestures and other normally docile expressions of affection may be all the entangled couple allow themselves. The gestures, however, are supercharged with emotion, far beyond their normal and usual expression. They provoke an emotional involvement that is extremely intense and bonding.

Even though intercourse might not occur in the affair, every touch and glance can be highly charged with emotion. Highly erotic feelings can be exchanged in mere eye contact and nonsexual touch—even in a handshake. It is exactly those feelings that make affairs so special.

Most spouses, upon disclosure of the affair, desperately want to know, "Did sex occur?" The issue of intercourse is almost irrelevant, however, when it comes to gauging the level of emotional involvement. It's the emotional involvement that the infidel must recover from in a Class II affair. Sex usually does become a part of this emotional involvement simply because it becomes too difficult for couples to not consummate their intense feelings of attachment. In fact, when the illicit relationship does reach the level of experiencing sexual intercourse, the intense emotions are released through the very act itself. And, though in a strict sense there is never any "positive side" to sexual involvement outside the God-given bonds of marriage, the stage is now set for the couple to experience remorse and guilt.

PERVASIVE DECEIT

Through that very intense phase of the relationship, maintaining the affair requires widespread deceit. Both parties begin lying to their respective families, friends, and coworkers.

It becomes "their little secret." They don't tell anyone else. Thus they enter an artificial world about which only they know. That usually means planning get-away weekends, spending money that belongs to their respective spouses and families, buying special gifts for each other, and generally pulling the wool over the eyes of everybody who knows them.

But it doesn't last long. It usually endures for only a relatively brief time because those extra bills catch up to them, they miss many business and familial appointments, concentration begins to suffer at work and at home, productivity falls, and slips are made in the secret arrangements.

Those cracks in the plan—and the fear of disclosure and exposure—often provoke one or both partners to initiate a separation, for a time anyway. Their little secret becomes their little millstone around their necks. But unless at least one of the partners seeks help from outside their dual party of deceit, they are bound to get back together.

PHASE 3: DESTABILIZATION—ON AGAIN, OFF AGAIN

During the destablization stage, fear of being caught, fired, divorced, or shamed fuels the urgency to get out of the relationship. Yet looks are deceiving. Though on the outside the affair looks like it may be falling apart, in reality it is being stabilized.

Let me explain: to endure through this stage requires a tacit agreement of mutual maintenance. Often, one partner will break up, and after some time the other calls with a pretense for getting together. The individual who broke off the relationship agrees, out of a sense of responsibility or whatever, and immediately the affair starts up again. It's like a forest fire that never goes out: it just dies down, to restart later under the right conditions.

This apparent destabilization of the affair is actually its most powerful maintenance. In behavior modification terms, such behavior is called "intermittent reinforcement." The most powerful behavior-shaping pattern known, its on again/off again pattern makes the affair almost impossible to end. It's like a spider spinning a web around its prey; many turns with a weak thread make for an iron-like bondage. The separation/togetherness cycle actually intensifies the feelings and guarantees that the affair will not end. The longer that process goes on, the more powerful the attachment and attraction become.

In some affairs, this phase can go on literally for years, with many months separating the periods of togetherness. Times together are so good, yet so far between, that the relationship is never actually threatened. It is the old pattern of the binge drinker who thinks he will never become an alcoholic because he only drinks heavily two or three times a year.

This dance, this mutual maintenance pattern, wears down the desire to break off the relationship. Often it is only after one of the binges that an intervention can take place to begin the actual separation process and return to normalcy.

Often during this stage, the spouse begins to suspect the possibility of her mate's involvement with the partner. Symptoms include unexplained bills, unusual or inexplicable time away, abrupt changes in schedule, emotional detachment in the infidel, changes in mood and dress, and unusual loss of sexual interest. The spouse might even confront the partner with some of these changes, and the denial and the contortions that are necessary to protect the affair begin to undo the conscience of the infidel.

Also during this period of time, growing exhaustion and depression begin to creep into both partners' lives. Part of the destabilization process is that they begin to need each other to "medicate" the fear, emptiness, and new irrational "reality" they now both live in. When they are with each other everything seems OK, when in reality everything is falling apart.

By denying and covering up, the infidel makes things worse. The longer the affair is maintained in secrecy and the more denial and deceit that occur, the longer recovery will take when the affair is over. The longer the affair goes undiscovered, the more destruction it wreaks on the conscience of the individuals involved—spouse, infidel, and partner, who often has a spouse too, so he or she has guilt as well.

A recovery process must begin with a clean break from the partner. All shared artifacts—pictures, mementos, and other physical representations of their history together—need to be expunged from the infidel's life.

This means the partners separate physically—move to different locations, change jobs, and so on. It certainly requires them to go to different churches. If such a decisive break is not made, the recovering infidel will struggle with the knowledge of the partner's whereabouts and will be tempted to renew contact during the bouts of doubt and rejection by the spouse that occur in subsequent phases of recovery.

PHASE 4: DISCLOSURE AND RESOLUTION— OUT OF THE CLOSET

It is often after one of the binge experiences during the "on again" phase that the infidel decides to reveal the affair to his spouse. The disclosure is both an acknowledgment that he needs help to get out of his bondage and also a symptom of his emotional exhaustion and depression.

Disclosure can also be an expression of the infidel's ambivalence about getting out of the affair: he says he wants out, yet he really doesn't want to end it either, so he leaves a trail of clues that will allow him to be discovered without having to be responsible for betraying his partner who created such a wonderful world for him.

The infidel is really in a double (or triple) bind. He is trying to please many masters—his partner, his guilty conscience, his spouse—and it's agonizing to be caught in the middle. That's why Jesus was so emphatic about it being impossible to serve two masters—you can't do that and maintain your sanity at the same time (Matthew 6).

Trying to please all these parties (including God, if the infidel has a shred of religiosity left) causes a split in the infidel's personality, with lots of accompanying anguish. He feels torn because he truly is torn. Parts of his psyche belong to different people! On any given day, the different parts will have varying degrees of influence on his behavior and speech. Hence the infidel will often vacillate back and forth between the partner and the spouse. He is the kind of man the Bible talks about: "a double-minded man, unstable in all his ways" (James 1:8). He is "like the surf of the sea driven and tossed by the wind" (v. 6). Those who have been there can relate to that description. It's roller coaster city.

This behavior drives all of the parties involved crazy. The roles change back and forth, causing further confusion. In some cases, it can actually get to the point where the mistress becomes the wife, and the wife takes on the role of the mistress.

The initial period of disclosure can be both traumatic and relieving for the infidel. It's traumatic because he finally has to face the truth that he has violated the most precious promise he ever made in his life. But it can have its comforting side as well. After sharing the ominous secret he has been carrying around for months (or years), it's not uncommon for the infidel to have the best night's sleep he's had in a long time, while the spouse remains sleepless from anguish and rage. The spouse may go into shock and lose weight, take up smoking again or return to other bad habits, or suffer other physical maladies as a result of the explosive revelation. Suddenly the roles have switched in this marriage: now the infidel is the strong one, staying rational "for the sake of the family" as the spouse falls apart.

The key step has occurred—disclosure—and now many results are propelled into action. Whether the infidel voluntarily disclosed the affair or was discovered doesn't really matter. As the expression goes, "the die is cast," and the players in the drama leap into action.

Needless to say, it's a lot easier to trash the marriage and for both parties to flee the difficulty of reconstructing the relationship. Yet to divorce now means that you only take all of this unfinished business with you. It will require you to work on this by yourself. Should you refuse and try to bury it, it will contaminate all future relationships you might develop. Once buried, it often leaks out into your children's attitude toward their future marital commitments, and it shows in their hesitancy first to get married and second in their doubts about whether their marriage will last. But for those who have hung in there and done the difficult work, it's all been worth it. Besides the personal benefits of picking up the pieces, God commands us to hold marriage in utmost sanctity: "Let marriage be held in honor among all, and let the marriage bed be undefiled; for fornicators and adulterers God will judge" (Hebrews 13:4). He will help you both as you seek to put things back together.

LOOKING AHEAD

In the next chapter we'll look at the spouse's reaction to disclosure. It's an absolutely critical juncture in the marriage. The sparks are going to fly, the tears will flow; it's really "make it or break it" time for the couple. The spouse's reaction to the now public fact of the infidelity is the critical factor determining which way the marriage will go—back together with proper processing, or into the trash can.

7

UNDERSTANDING THE RECOVERY: THE SPOUSE'S PROCESS

When the spouse finds out about her mate's infidelity, a dramatic moment is forming up in the history of the couple. How she finds out—whether through the infidel's confession or her suspicion and confrontation or the proverbial "grape vine"—is irrelevant.

How she reacts—whether by throwing the bum out or ignoring the betrayal or something in between—will determine many things. It will help determine whether he'll continue with the partner, whether the spouse herself will prolong her own agony or address it, and whether they'll stay married. In a phrase, it's the moment of truth. Although she may try, there's really no sitting on the fence from this moment hence. It's either make progress by doing the work of recovery or prolong the cycle of dysfunction.

In this chapter we'll again look at the affair chart, with the curves for both the infidel and spouse. If you are a spouse or a friend seeking to support a loved one going through the agony of an affair, you'll benefit a lot from this discussion.

And if you're an infidel, this chapter will help you understand what your spouse is going through. Even though you were in the driver's seat in initiating the affair, at this stage you're in the passenger's seat.

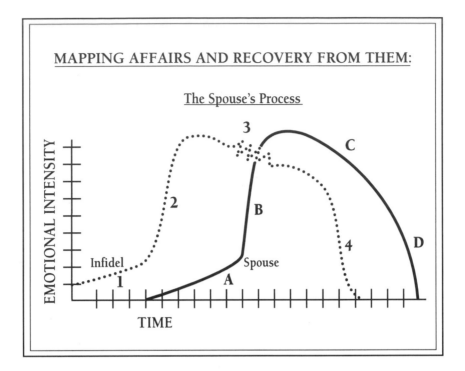

MAPPING AFFAIRS AND RECOVERY FROM THEM:

The Spouse's Process

PHASE A: AWARENESS—IS HE OR ISN'T HE?

Hindsight is 20/20, and so it goes with affairs from the spouse's point of view. Just prior to actual disclosure, the spouse will often come upon subtle or even obvious clues with increasing frequency, bits and pieces of information that spell out "a-f-f-a-i-r," but only when the spouse looks back.

Those pieces of information contribute to the spouse's feeling foolish in the wake of the discovery: "Why didn't I see it coming? How could I have been so stupid?" The self-incrimination goes on endlessly as the spouse berates herself for not picking up on the signals that now seem clear.

The spouse eventually begins to mistrust herself, just as the infidel mistrusts himself. If her vision was so obstructed, what senses *can* she trust? Obviously, the subconscious desire to deny what was happening fueled the lack of recognition, along with the fact that she fully trusted her husband prior to disclosure. It's reasonable that she didn't detect the affair up to a point, but the feelings are tumultuous now, and reason often gets thrown to the wind.

There is a growing sense of shame from perceived inadequacy. Often the spouse selects a course of action to counter her shame during the awareness phase, such as:

- trying to make herself more presentable through external changes—changing her hair, starting a diet, buying a new wardrobe, and so on.
- initiating sexual activity or some other behavior that she thinks will please the infidel, who has usually moved away emotionally. This is extremely dangerous in this day of AIDS—*all sexual contact should cease until the infidel is tested for STDs* (sexually transmitted diseases). You may think that is too harsh, but in actual fact it's a matter of life and death. We no longer have the luxury of giving a loved one the benefit of the doubt—the stakes are too high (i.e., AIDS is fatal). For more information on this topic, see *Back from Betrayal*, by Jennifer P. Schneider, M.D.[1]
- cutting off the doubts and suspicions she may be having about her mate's extracurricular activities (if prior to actual disclosure) and focusing time and attention on the children or others who will not provoke anxieties about the infidel. This is basically a strategy motivated by denial and fear that her suspicions could be true.

Sadly, even though such changes may actually be what the infidel needed from her, they are often "too little, too late." I have found that Christian women who come for counseling during the suspicion phase prior to actual disclosure will commonly deny that infidelity could be a problem in their marriage. They still believe it would be a bad reflection on them if it were true.

However, when the affair is finally disclosed, many of the same wives will know who the partner is, how he got involved with her, and other such details—without being told. The awareness was lurking just below the surface.

A special word to the spouse at this point: this is not the time to compete with the supposed enemy, the partner, or to try to win the straying infidel back by being extremely nice, attractive, compliant, cooperative, and so on. Those strategies, if they might ever have been successful, will exhaust you now. Pursuing that line of attack, you would have to perform at ever-increasing levels for the rest of your life to reassure yourself that all is well in the marriage.

Rather, the key to recovery is that both of you join forces to look at the situation that truly exists and work together to make this marriage *different*. Now is the time to confront the betrayal head-on. Only by going right into the eye of the storm will steady and lasting progress be made.

PHASE B: ANGER

YOU'VE BETRAYED ME

At discovery, the spouse's emotions are usually intense. The anger, hurt, bewilderment, betrayal, and numbing shock are almost overwhelming. The betrayed spouse will be angry, and she needs the freedom to ventilate her rage. The language of anger is never pleasant; however, it is not only OK to say it with intensity and force, but *it is absolutely necessary for true recovery to occur.* People do not get better until they get mad.

If denied, that anger "goes underground" and eats away at the innermost spirit of the person. It is very important for the violated spouse to be free to express the rage that he or she feels.

After the first surge of anger comes the need for information— what happened? when did it happen? how often? and so on. This is the time for the violated spouse to ask the offender those all-important questions. Men seem to want to know the details of the sexual activity; women commonly report wanting to know if their husband loves the other person. Whatever the need, the information is important and shouldn't be squelched.

There is no good reason to hide information from the injured spouse at this point. The precious marriage vow lies shattered on the floor—there is nothing left of the marriage to protect. Therefore, the infidel who has been discovered should share each and every bit of information that his partner wants to know.

Often the infidel thinks that as the questions come, he should tell only what he thinks is appropriate, so he withholds details, covering up certain aspects of the trail. Nothing will anger the wounded spouse more than being subtly deceived at this point by double talk or half-truths. Eventually, all truth will be known anyway.

This is the time to tell it all, or at least tell it at the level that the spouse wants to hear it. There's a difference between the two. Many of my counselees who have gone through recovery from affairs say that getting into too much detail can create tortuous mental images for the injured spouse that can haunt her for years. But you need to walk this fine line of disclosure and honesty carefully, and be sure to err on the side of too much disclosure rather than too little. The ideal, of course, would be to satisfy the spouse's need to know without ignoring any major revelations. The main point is to own up to what you have done and to admit humbly the full range of injury and transgression. Don't try to alter the facts subtly to protect yourself. Just as deceit is no way to build a relationship, it's no way to rebuild a broken one.

Withheld information becomes "unfinished business" that will have to be dragged along through the balance of the marriage. The more time that passes without the unfinished business being revealed, the more difficult it will be to bring it up. Should the marriage stay together, this secret will become an albatross around the neck of the infidel, who will have wished that he or she had completely "come clean" at the anger stage, when it was most appropriate and helpful.

THE SPOUSE NOW HOLDS THE REINS

The power to continue the marriage has now passed into the hands of the wounded spouse. Her reaction—whether to process the affair properly or to run from all the pain and seek a divorce—will dictate in large measure the outcome of the marriage.

One of the great fears on the part of the spouse who has just discovered the affair is that if she expresses as much rage as she feels, she will drive her spouse into the arms of his partner. That could happen; but, remember, he has already been in his partner's arms. You couldn't keep him out of her arms before you knew about it; now simply being angry is not going to drive him to her—more is involved here than that!

Besides, there is nothing of the marriage left to protect by "walking on eggshells" at this point. If you are going to live together in harmony in the future, you need to live together *differently*. It's time to start over. The most sacred aspects of this marriage have already been violated. Now you both have to begin to rebuild.

PHASE C: ANGUISH

GRIEVING THE LOSS

During the anguish phase, some recovery can begin. But it won't be steady progress—rather, it will probably be two steps forward and one step back. It's a rocky time emotionally, but that's part of the normal process of grieving the losses: loss of trust, of the once-pure marital relationship, and so on.

Just about the time that the violated spouse thinks she is getting over the pain, it will suddenly resurface. But be encouraged; gradually the pain will become less intense and less frequent, and the good times between the down times will lengthen.

This grief process is similar to grieving the death of a spouse.

Violated spouses do indeed report many responses that parallel those of widows:

- They feel abandoned by their mate.
- They feel alone in their grief.
- They feel as if they could have done something to prevent this.
- They feel like a marked person. They don't fit in with normal couples anymore.
- They have a lot of unfinished business with their spouse that is now off-limits or has been overshadowed by what has occurred.
- They feel terrified of the future.
- They feel they should be doing better than they are for the time that they have been in it.
- They will even pretend nothing has happened (such as the widow who sets a plate for the lost partner at the dinner table).

Grieving is important, but it is even more important to know what you are grieving for. Some find it helpful to list the losses on paper. I recommend that you try that, being as transparent and honest as you can.

Crying in front of other people as you process your grief is perfectly permissible. Grief is not always predictable, not always controllable. It is certainly all right to cry in front of the infidel. In fact, he needs to see—and feel—the damage his actions have wrought. Be totally honest about your sadness.

RELEASE

During the anguish phase, the spouse needs to hear that she has release, that she does not need the infidel to survive. She lived twenty years or so without this individual prior to marriage, and she can learn to live without him again. Put another way, personal survival is not dependent upon the maintenance of the marriage. Often her self-image is so inextricably bound up with being married to her mate that this is a new and frightening thought to her.

Often the spouse's dependency needs are overwhelming at this juncture; she isn't really sure whether she could survive without him. It is a critical crossroads because the spouse needs to see that, with God in her life and her feet on the ground, she can survive without the infidel. That means she has options, and options promote a feeling of power, something often new for the spouse.

Once she can see other options, she begins to think more clearly; she feels less smothered, and her decision-making faculties can kick into gear.

But don't get me wrong—I'm not urging the spouse to "choose" divorce at this point. God hates divorce (Malachi 2:16) and wants couples to do everything possible to reconcile. But that's ahead of where the spouse is at this point. She doesn't need to hear that God is forcing her to reconcile with that lousy, no-good, two-timing man. Her feelings at this point are often that she needs to get free from the bum! So, based on God's provision that divorce is allowed in cases of adultery, the spouse may consider her option of release from the mate (Matthew 19:9).

If she does not accept and believe that release, she will not fully express her anger, for fear of losing this very important person. If she believes that she must stay with the infidel for spiritual or financial reasons, she will not recover. You can't be brutally honest with someone whom you need in order to survive.

The ideal is that she'll use this newfound power to restore the relationship and not just crush it and throw it away like a soda can. The chief benefit of this power is that it equalizes the equation; now they can deal with each other as equals (often unlike before the affair).

GUARANTEES

One of the first things an angry and grieving spouse wants is the guarantee that this will never happen again. Often Christian spouses think that if they can just get their infidel partner to walk the aisle to the altar, confess his sin in front of the congregation, read his Bible daily, or be convicted by the Holy Spirit or disciplined by the church, all will be well. But nothing could be further from the truth.

Any or all of those practices might be appropriate, but none of them will provide the guarantee that the wounded spouse is looking for. The closest thing to a guarantee that the infidel won't stray again is for him to feel fully the pain that he has caused the wounded spouse. Let me underline this point: promises to "behave" won't endure; neither will artificial boundaries such as a curfew each night after work. *The only lasting remedy is for the infidel to feel the agony he has caused the spouse.* If he truly loves his mate (and he usually does down deep; that's why they got married and why he came back), that will hurt him so much that he won't want to inflict more on his loved one.

But getting the infidel to experience the hurt of the spouse won't happen immediately—it could take many months. Remember, it will take as long to recover from the affair as it did for the infidel partner to get involved in it. So allow some time for him to feel her pain.

FORCING THE CHOICE

I am not in favor of waiting for an affair to run its course. There's nothing helpful about prolonging the agony or the deceit. You need to start the work of restoring the marriage, and confrontation is often the first step. Doing so will help the spouse regain some self-respect and get over her feelings of helplessness. If the spouse becomes aware of the affair, then I recommend an intervention, which is a programmed confrontation to help the infidel feel the spouse's pain and force him to take action.

The spouse, by her actions and communication at this juncture, puts an end to the status quo of the affair from the infidel's viewpoint. In other words, up until now, the infidel has been able to have the mistress *and* the wife. Now it's time for him to choose to either leave the partner and restore the marriage, or lose the marriage relationship completely. From this point forward, he cannot "have his cake and eat it too"—he *must* choose between the spouse and the partner.

Bringing the infidel to the point of choice can be done orally or in written form, as demonstrated here. The essence of what the spouse must communicate to the infidel is that it's *his* move now. The spouse fully releases him to his choices (and their consequences), but there is no more time to "sit on the fence." Either the infidel chooses to come back to the spouse—while forsaking the partner—or the marriage is over.

It is important to prepare appropriately for such a process with another party, preferably a trained counselor, pastor, or trusted friend who can help guide the intervention. I also strongly recommend reading *Love Must Be Tough,* by James Dobson.[2]

Some points to keep in mind as you consider this option:

1. You will only have one opportunity to do this. Do you feel good about the timing?
2. This is the ultimate statement of release. Do you mean it, or are you only attempting to manipulate him with guilt and/or fear?

3. Are you really willing to go through life without the infidel, should he choose the other partner over you? The intervention will "call the question" and force the infidel to take action. One course of action is, of course, going off with the partner, but that may happen even without the intervention.

Those are tough questions, and your decision whether to force the infidel to choose will usually take shape as you work through your particular feelings about the situation. There is no one perfect answer that fits all situations. Read the sample letter below, and consider how you could adapt it to your own situation.

Dear Richard:

This letter is the hardest I've ever written. You are the love of my life, and I thought I was the love of yours. But I'm beginning to wonder if I was wrong.

Now with the revelation of your involvement with Julie, I just don't know what's true anymore.

Were our eighteen years together just a lie?

Am I having a nightmare just now in trying to believe that you've been with her on the sly for almost a year? In my heart it seems like a bad dream, but in my head I know it's true.

I've had my faults as a wife, I know. And I'm willing to work on them. But at this most difficult juncture in our marriage relationship, I want to let you know clearly that I'm releasing you to your choices.

I love you very much, and I made a commitment before God and a promise to you to love you, and you only, forever. However, true love really sets people free.

I hope you will choose to stay with me as my husband, but I would not want you to do so out of compassion over how your departure would affect me. Should you ultimately choose to leave, it would be extremely difficult for me, but I am an adult and know that God will help me recover. I would eventually go on with my life.

If you choose to come back, I want you to know that I am fully willing to accept my responsibility for putting this marriage back together in a more mutually satisfying way. I know that I need to make personal changes for any future relationship to be successful. I also know that if you choose with me to save our marriage, our mutual recovery will very probably be slow, difficult, and painful.

We both will surely feel like quitting along the way, and working

*through our issues will stretch both of us to the breaking point. But
you have my commitment to this process, and I hope and pray that you
will join me in it.*

*But you, too, are an adult and are free to walk away if that's
what you truly desire. I only ask that, should you choose to leave, you
carry out your decision appropriately and without deceit.*

*I think this letter states clearly my true feelings, and I thank you
for listening. I ask you to search your heart and make a decision within the near future as to whether you want to restore our marriage or
not.*

Richard, regardless of your final decision, I wish you the very best.

*Love,
Ashley*

Be careful about your motives. You must mean what you say
and say what you mean—for example, you must be willing to set
your spouse free, if that's what you say in your letter. *Do not force
the choice with the sole motivation of obtaining a reconciliation.* It is
OK to desire reconciliation, but if that is your sole motive, you are
being manipulative. You have to be authentic in releasing your mate
to make his own choices.

What if he can't/won't make up his mind? What are you the
faithful spouse to do in that situation? You really only have two
options prior to filing for divorce. (1) You can choose to accept the
spouse and let the affair run its course. You would not be the first
Christian woman whose husband has a mistress. In fact, in many
cultures it's tolerated. I'm not necessarily endorsing this as the best
option, but in some cases it is, given the circumstances—such as
small children, financial need, and so on. (2) On the other hand,
many women report that they cannot knowingly accept a mistress.
It is too painful for their own self-respect. For them, I would suggest a separation. This option must require financial protection for
the spouse. It usually requires legal assistance. It will require the
keeping of numerous records (to protect yourself in the future, if
the outcome is divorce).

PHASE D: REATTACHMENT AND RECOVERY

The reattachment phase is essentially explained in the balance
of the book, so I won't go into too much detail here.

It is difficult to say exactly when reattachment and recovery begin and end for the spouse. Certainly the onset of reattachment can be seen when the previous stage (anguish) begins to subside. But exactly when it is over varies widely. For now, a couple of points deserve attention: proper time frame and reaching out to others.

TIME FRAME

Hurt always takes time to heal. Reattaching often takes about as long for the spouse as it did initially for the infidel to detach from her and become involved in the affair. During this time, you'll experience the common symptoms of crying spells, bouts with depression, and angry flare-ups, but they are much more manageable than before.

Many will be the long conversations you have until 2:00 A.M. There will still be hurt and withdrawal and isolation, even though you two are slowly growing closer. Chapters 10 and 11 will focus on a series of intimacy and trust-building exercises that are helpful in this regard.

SHARING THE SECRET

It can be helpful near the middle or late sections of the recovery process—whenever you both are ready—for you to share your secret with another couple. It won't be easy, but it is so therapeutic that I highly recommend it. It might be done as a testimonial or as an encouragement to another couple who are in the midst of their own struggle.

Whatever the case, once you have shared this great devastation you have come through the worst part. You are achieving recovery if you feel safe enough with your spouse to talk about it with others. Such action is a fulfillment of 2 Corinthians 1:3-4: "Praise be to the God and Father of our Lord Jesus Christ, the Father of compassion and the God of all comfort, who comforts us in all our troubles, so that we can comfort those in any trouble with the comfort we ourselves have received from God" (NIV).

LOOKING AHEAD

Now that we have seen the main steps that both the infidel and spouse must take in the recovery journey, it's time to launch into the most intensive detective work of the process. In the next chapter we'll look at how to decipher "the message of the affair."

The message will be useful to you both as you seek to reconstruct a healthy marriage. It explains in a very specific way why the affair happened and shows you how to overhaul and reprogram your relationship in the future.

NOTES

1. Jennifer P. Schneider, M.D., *Back from Betrayal: Surviving His Affairs* (New York: Harper & Row, 1988; also under the title *Back from Betrayal: Recovering from His Affairs* (Center City, Minn.: Hazelden Foundation, 1989; New York: Ballantine, 1990).

2. James Dobson, *Love Must Be Tough* (Waco, Tex.: Word, 1983).

8

WHY? DECIPHERING THE MESSAGE OF THE AFFAIR

Perhaps the most excruciating question the spouse has to deal with, night after night, day after day, following disclosure of the affair is, "Why?"

"Why me, Lord?"

"Why now?"

"Why did he do this to me?"

"Why with her?"

And so it goes ad infinitum. Such endless torture can haunt the person who was betrayed and to some degree the betrayer. It's not crystal clear to him either.

The question, "Why?" looms large and seems virtually unanswerable sometimes. Yet identifying "the message of the affair" is key to making lasting and certain progress toward recovery. Both parties must work together in ferreting out the message. Usually the situation is so convoluted that it requires true determination to dig it out.

The message of the affair is simply what the infidel wants the spouse to know about himself and the marriage. The goal for both to figure out is: what emotional and physical nurturance did the infidel receive from the affair that was unavailable in the marriage?

For whatever reason, prior to straying, the infidel felt unable to express the message adequately with words. So he "told" the spouse via his actions. The infidel might have attempted to talk about it before the affair, but (1) he didn't have the emotional or communicative resources to identify what he really wanted to say, or (2) he wasn't even aware of what he was feeling inside.

Of course, the message for each couple is unique to their particular relationship. But most messages contain a combination of the following components. I've expressed them in the form of "I" statements—you might try them on for size, especially in filling in the blanks with your particular need or issue:

- I'm feeling alone and afraid that you are going to leave me. Nobody in my life has ever stayed around for me to lean on, and I'm sure you won't either.
- I feel like a little child inside, but I'm afraid it wouldn't be appropriate to act that way in your presence.
- I have this secret _____ that I want to share with you, but I'm afraid you will make fun of me or try to change me.
- I have had a number of experiences lately which, if I shared with you, I fear would cause you to respect me less.
- I know I am increasingly unhappy, but I don't know how to change, and I'm afraid of how it will turn out.
- Something _____ is happening to me, and I need to talk about it, but I can't, so I think our marriage needs to change—we both need help in communicating the hard things to each other.
- Something _____ is very important to me, but I don't want to act like a child, demanding my own way. I don't want to appear to be a beggar, either—that's humiliating.
- I think I'm figuring more out about each of us. The more you do _____ , the more I respond like _____ . That's been interesting to watch, and although I know you don't like me analyzing things, I think it's part of the answer. I wish I could share it with you.
- I miss all the _____ I used to receive in my family of origin, but I know you think that they are crazy, so I'll just keep this particular need to myself. I know you were not used to _____ in your family, and I guess I should be satisfied with that fact, but I'm not. I need to talk with you about this, but I'm scared.

There are many other components of the message that the two of you will need to explore together. The important thing is not to finish exploring the message too quickly. Your understanding of the message will develop over the course of your recovery; time will help the two of you to sort it out.

Often the spouse has no clue about the message while the infidel is in the midst of the affair or even shortly thereafter—she is so confused by her conflicting emotions that she cannot see clearly. But to the infidel, the message of the marriage has become increasingly focused—he often knows in his heart of hearts why he is seeking fulfillment of his needs elsewhere, and that is the essence of the "message."

A complicator from the spouse's point of view is that she is often afraid that deciphering the message will change the role of who is guilty about the infidelity, and that doesn't seem fair to her. In other words, immediately after disclosure, the spouse sees in abundantly clear terms the word *guilty* written all over the infidel's face. *He's the one who strayed, and I'm the innocent one,* goes the line of thinking at this point. But as she begins to sort out the real reason behind his straying, the spouse must shoulder her share of the responsibility for it. Many times this "responsibility" is a passive acquiescence, an adjustment on the part of the spouse to the infidel's patterns, demands, expectations. This "adjustment" becomes dissatisfying to both of them, but usually the entangled affair is not just the infidel's fault.

Understanding the message of the affair not only gives the spouse a sense of power—she finally understands what her mate was getting from the affair that was not present in the marriage—but it also provides the infidel with a sense of hope. For the infidel, the sense of being understood by someone other than the illicit partner is critical to keeping him in the process of recovery; otherwise, he'll be tempted to bail out and leave for good. He will only stay if he feels truly understood. The need to be understood in the midst of this pain and turmoil is critical to his staying out of the partner's arms.

Showing empathy and understanding for the infidel's pain is not justification of his behavior. It is not being "soft" on the person who has acted inappropriately, and it is not overlooking the sin of adultery—it is simply a way to keep the infidel in the process of recovery. There will be a time in the future to confront the sin and deal with the guilt. Now is the time for understanding, not condemnation.

THE TWO CENTRAL GOALS FOR THE INFIDEL AND SPOUSE

In uncovering the message of the affair, two goals—one for the infidel and one for the spouse—need to be kept firmly in mind. The infidel needs to feel deeply the hurt his infidelity has caused in his spouse, and he also needs to know that the spouse is attempting to understand that his needs were not met in the marriage. On the flip side of the coin, the spouse needs to be willing to feel the unmet needs of the infidel and also realize that at this point she has the power to make or break the marriage.

The spouse does indeed have permission to dissolve the marriage because of infidelity, but if she can connect in a deep way with her mate's pain, she may (and hopefully will) choose to work on healing and restoring the relationship. She has often felt like the powerless one in the marriage, yet now she has the upper hand. Often this realization alone empowers and gives hope to the spouse, after she has gotten over the shock and humiliation of the initial disclosure stage.

Likewise, if the infidel can deeply connect with the spouse and the searing pain his betrayal has caused, he will be highly motivated never to cause such pain in his loved one again. Yet the connection between infidel and spouse is usually stale, to say the least. That's part of why the affair happened.

A common problem is that the infidel doesn't want the spouse to change. It's as if he is saying, in resisting the tough work of reconciliation, "I gave you months—even years—to change, and you wouldn't. Now that I've found someone else who will meet my needs, I don't want you to change just so that we can reunite. Besides, how do I know you will change permanently? I suspect you're just doing this to manipulate me into letting go of someone who is very special to me." Regardless of such feelings on the conflicted infidel's side, however, spouses need to feel free to implement changes they think are appropriate.

One of the keys to processing the affair at this stage is identifying intimacy deficits in one or both of the marriage partners. *All Class II affairs are caused primarily by intimacy deficits.* Even when the infidel's focus seems to be on the erotic, that is always encased by a need for emotional closeness; that's what defines the entangled (Class II) affair. As a couple you need to identify what intimacy deficits there are between you and what you can do about them.

The more apparent the deficits in the marriage, the more apparent the message of the affair will be. Many times the spouse knows the message months, and even years, in advance but either refuses to, or is unable to, change the situation. She may hope that the other positive patterns in the marriage will offset the acknowledged deficit. But that will not occur. An example is a husband who knows deep down that he is a workaholic and withdrawn from his spouse but thinks the fabulous luxury home he has provided offsets the pain he has caused his wife. He is unable to change his pattern of behavior or refuses to ask for help. His motto is "Just run faster and the problem will probably go away." The sad truth is that it won't.

The deficits need to be viewed as separate entities that exist until directly addressed or improved. They never just disappear with the passage of time or hopeful wishings. Sometimes one or both of the mates will try to make that happen—for example, the spouse may set aside her needs or deny them in order to focus on the positive aspects of the relationship, but the actual deficits are still present and render her at risk for unfaithfulness.

This sense of unmet needs is a part of all the relationships that we are in. None of us is perfect or able to meet all the needs of another. Even before the Fall, when Adam was still a perfect creature, he still had unmet needs. Jehovah pronounced the first negative in the Scripture about the human condition when He said, "It is not good for the man to be alone" (Genesis 2:18). So there is a void in each of us that only a spouse can fill. Even a perfect walk with God did not satisfy all of Adam's need; he needed a key human relationship as well.[1]

The purpose of this chapter is not to make you or your mate feel guilty. To have accusation heaped upon shame and failure is more than most individuals can bear. There is usually already enough shame and guilt around to last a generation or two. Rather, the purpose is simply to uncover the reasons the infidel strayed.

The rationale behind this goal is that the infidel will finally feel heard and understood—even somewhat vindicated. And the injured spouse will finally have a sense of power and influence in her mate's life. The message of the affair forms the foundation for true reconciliation. However, if the message is not heard, the marriage has no hope of surviving.

Hopefully, you will get some help in this process. Often a close friend can assist in helping the hurting spouse understand the message. Take advantage of any close friendships you have for this support. If you don't get any offers to help, don't let that hinder you— go to your same-sex friend and ask for help. Many times the anguish of the affair is deepened because of an internal sense of failure on the part of the spouse. She knows that if she had done things differently, she might not be in this position now. Yet it's so hard at this stage to sort things out that some help is desperately needed.

Another caution to the wounded spouse: don't dismiss certain needs of the infidel too quickly. Sometimes you may think that the infidel is fabricating reasons for his behavior and dreaming up deficits in the marriage, but please understand that his feelings of guilt and failure are often forcing him to highlight each and every possible flaw in the marriage. Instead of broadly dismissing such a list, try to find a major theme or two emerging from the scattershot of items. Beware of being overly defensive on your part—you could miss a key message.

For example, an infidel may say that he simply wanted a change. He may deny that there's anything deeper or more intimate in his motivation to stray. But that's rarely the case in my experience, especially among Christians. People don't just switch mates the way they change outfits for social events. There is usually a deeper and more emotionally charged reason behind one's decision to betray the marriage vow, and your joint goal is to dig it out. Stay transparent yourself, and be persistent in wanting to decipher the message. Eventually it will surface.

One helpful method for figuring it out is to write out a list of the statements the infidel makes. Often there may be many statements that don't reflect on the infidel's needs, such as "You're too fat," but don't let that discourage you from searching for the theme of the infidel's unmet needs; if you look long and hard enough, doing that tough communicative work, you'll find them.

LOVE LANGUAGES: GRANT, MICHELLE, AND YOU

Most of us know some things that we would like from our spouse but which we rarely receive. (The length of that list may correlate to the relative health of our marriages.) Ironically, unmet needs in our own life cause us to extend love to our spouse in ways that we would enjoy but in ways that may be foreign to him/her.

An example would be a husband who values financial security and bends over backward to supply abundant finances to his mate. But she is hardly concerned with money and would rather be close to him and poor than distant and wealthy. Failure to meet your spouse's needs or attempts to meet his or her needs by loving him/her in a manner that only you enjoy produces the exact opposite of what you intend: frustration and anger.

Several writers and researchers have helped to identify the various love languages we all understand.[2] Love languages are simply avenues of communicating—the ways we feel cared for, infatuated with, cherished by, or just plain understood by another. Since most of us know what we enjoy and what makes us feel special, we have a tendency to express love for another person in the same way. However, that usually doesn't work. In essence, when you try to minister to your mate in your own way, you haven't learned his or her love language. In fact, part of the message of any affair is that someone else has figured out your spouse's love language!

Take the case of up-and-coming attorney, Grant, and his wife, Michelle. They discovered this truth in a painful way that almost sounds (in a black humor sort of way) like an episode of "I Love Lucy."

Grant was a young lawyer who had just passed the bar exam. Michelle was a busy full-time mom with three young kids. She knew they had a bright future, but the present seemed dismal and grinding.

Michelle shared little quality time with Grant. When he was available, she was consumed with the kids; when she was available—during the kids' nap time, for example—he was either working or traveling to meet with clients. Michelle knew her other friends had the same frustration, but that was of little comfort—she still needed more of her husband.

One day she began to cook up a getaway for the two of them. *This will be a perfect way for us to get reconnected*, she thought happily. She made a deal with some friends who agreed to watch the children on a swap basis and traded her car for another family's van for the weekend so they could take along their bicycles. Michelle remembered riding her bicycle as a child at the beach. The warm fuzzies of that memory, combined with the romance of a mid-California beach village, were irresistible to her.

Just thinking about the weekend lifted Michelle's now chronic feelings of depression. Planning it consumed her—she decided to make it a secret surprise for Grant. Even he began to notice her cheery spirit and was relieved that she was feeling better. He didn't ask what caused it (note the lack of communication); he just noted the improvement to himself as he busily dashed from one responsibility to another. *Michelle's really improving on her attitude—that's one less hassle to slow me down.*

Because the weekend date was several weeks away, Michelle's

happy anticipation built. As she watched Grant get busier and busier in the intervening period, she often thought how glad she was that she had planned the interlude. Grant would need time away, and he didn't even know it was going to happen. Every time she thought about what she was about to pull off, she almost giggled out loud.

For his part, Grant interpreted the change in his wife's demeanor as permission to work a little longer and a little harder. He started spending extra hours at the office, which his bosses noticed. They reinforced his dedication, and Grant felt free to commit himself even more intensely to his work. After all, his wife seemed to be happy and understanding about it all.

On the other hand, Michelle began to worry that Grant might plan to work on the weekend they were to be away; so being the bright, young, energetic mother that she was, she called his office and talked with his secretary. They worked out a scheme where Grant's Friday would be free of appointments. The plan called for Michelle to swing by the office in the van with the suitcases packed and the bikes loaded, pick Grant up, and whisk him away. She and his secretary laughed on the phone as they planned it—they both got a big kick out of it.

Meanwhile Grant was beginning to see that one case was becoming particularly thorny. The case was consuming him day and night, and he was yearning for a big block of time so that he could devote himself completely to the trial preparation. *I'm always being interrupted—I wish I could get some sustained effort together to get this case in shape for the trial next week,* he worried. He tried working a little harder and a little smarter, but the clock was going too fast and it became increasingly apparent that he was going to have to cancel appointments in order to get the case done by the trial date.

One day early in the week of the big surprise, Grant decided to check his appointment book. *What would be the easiest appointments to postpone to create more working time?* he wondered.

Grant was delighted when he saw all day Friday blocked out. *What an awesome secretary I've got,* he thought with satisfaction. He had a sudden surge of gratitude for her wonderful capabilities of planning ahead. *This is working out great.*

He was so busy the next morning and so tired from the night before, that he failed to thank her for her thoughtfulness. He thought again about it that evening after she left and jotted himself a note to be sure and thank her tomorrow. When he mumbled a few words of appreciation in passing, he thought that she seemed to smile awfully big. That made him feel even better, because he knew attorneys had a way of being rather abrupt, and he didn't want to get into that routine. *Glad she appreciated the compliment.*

Throughout Thursday, Grant found himself putting off little decisions on the case, thinking he would give them special attention on Friday. They were too important to be too hasty with, and he grew increasingly excited about having a whole day to work on the case. *I'm sure I can put this one away in about twelve more hours,* he strategized.

When he got home late on Thursday, Michelle seemed cheerier than ever. Grant seemed so exhausted that Michelle was tempted to tell him right then and there, but she decided to wait and show up on Friday morning, as she and his secretary had planned. That would heighten his pleasure, she reasoned.

About mid-morning, after the morning rush hour, Michelle drove to the office. She had taken plenty of time for specially primping herself and had taken the kids over to her friend's house early in the morning. She and the girlfriend who was keeping the kids were giddy with excitement. Her girlfriend even shared her secret envy of Michelle. She was sure that her husband would never enjoy such a surprise and remarked how fortunate Michelle was to have such a wonderful husband as Grant.

As soon as Michelle walked into the office, she knew things were not right. The secretary looked worried and explained that Grant had instructed her that he was to have no interruptions whatsoever. Absolutely nothing was to distract him. He was even ordering lunch in.

Michelle's initial reaction was to feel some distant twinges of anger, but she wasn't about to let anything disappoint her at that point. Surely Grant would love her plan. So into his office she marched and revealed her special surprise.

Before she and Grant walked out of the office together, both were wounded and hurt.

Grant's body went to the seaside resort, but his heart and mind stayed in the law office all weekend. He hated riding bikes, and he especially hated riding bikes along the beach. Even sex wasn't all that good, and he felt bad that he was hurting Michelle so deeply. But he was also angry that she hadn't checked with him and that she had wasted such a valuable time slot without consulting him.

As a kid, Grant had never liked surprises. There had always

been plenty of them when he was growing up in his dysfunctional family; now he hated any unpredictability. His favorite times were quiet times alone, doing what he wanted to do. He loved Michelle, but it seemed to him that everybody was always wanting something from him, and the weekend was just a repetition of that weary theme. He pretended to enjoy it, and, frankly, there were a couple of moments that he did forget about the job. The sunset was gorgeous as he sat on the veranda of their rented condo.

Michelle had decided to take a nap just prior to supper. As she drifted off, she thought about how strange it was that Grant always enjoyed being by himself so much.

They both went home disappointed—he, still bogged down in the court case; and she, severely disillusioned at the end of her great expectations for their connectedness. Michelle had tried to love Grant the way she liked to be loved. Mothering was a daily grind at times and didn't change much from day to day, so she needed a change of pace and wrongly assumed Grant wanted the same. Grant, on the other hand, was working toward a trial that would soon be over. She loved surprises; he loved stability. She wanted attention; he wanted solitude. She wanted to play; he wanted to work. They were on different wavelengths. Instead of the weekend drawing them closer, it simply alienated them further.

Although Grant and Michelle didn't wind up being the victims of infidelity as far as I know, examples like theirs show how bricks build the walls that separate couples. Even if they didn't get divorced, such abortive attempts at loving each other put couples at risk for affairs.

If you want to show true love to your mate, you need to do it in a fashion that will register with him—in his love language—and make him feel understood, cherished, and cared for. You need to understand what her language of love is, and the material in the balance of this chapter provides a way to sort it out. But first, to heighten the effectiveness of the material, stop and take the following inventory.

YOUR LOVE LANGUAGE

Write out twenty things your spouse does to or for you that makes you feel special, cared for, cherished, and understood. Yes, I said twenty. Each of you—the husband and the wife—should write these out on a separate sheet of paper and keep it for an exercise later in this chapter. They could be things that are already occurring in the relationship, things that were done way back in dating days, or things that have never been practiced in the marriage at all. This is a kind of wish list. The infidel needs to be sure to include the items that made the affair special for him/her.

In my experience, the first six to ten items are usually fairly easy for people to come up with, but the last ten to fourteen are more difficult. If you don't know what you enjoy, how in the world is your spouse supposed to figure it out? She can't read minds; it's up to you to tell her.

Make the list before you read the balance of this material; you'll get more out of it that way. Don't feel bad if you can't come up with all twenty right out of the gate; this is a starting point only and the basis for an important exercise in determining the message of the affair.

So mark your place in the book, and go get pen and paper.

Love languages can be grouped into five common themes, which are discussed below. If you've tried to come up with twenty things your spouse could do for you and failed, perhaps this information will spark more ideas. If they apply to your particular situation, go ahead and add them to your list.

1. VERBAL

The first theme refers to any spoken or written communication items on your list. It can include receiving cards, notes, poetry, and other forms of written expression that might appear on your list. Often couples love special phrases that carry emotional significance, or "pet names" for each other; all those and more can appear on your list.

2. GIFTS/TASKS

The second love language says "I've been thinking of you" through gifts. It's the basis for the famous advertising slogan "When you care enough to send the very best."

If that's your feeling, say so. Most of us feel special when there are little gifts along the way to remind us of the other person and of what we mean to him or her. The gifts can range in simplicity from candy and gum, to cards, perfume, diamonds, and dinner out. It's not the cost that makes the gift meaningful; it's the thoughtfulness behind it.

Gifts and tasks are put together because they require the giving partner to be thinking of the other person. Most of us feel cared for if our mate does one of our regularly required chores unexpectedly. In an affair, the partners often do little tasks for each other that cement the relationship and help form their own private special world. Many times the infidel even does household repairs for the partner.

The wounded spouse has a hard time understanding that; but often she herself has contributed to her spouse's lack of doing little jobs for her. It only takes one or two criticisms for the way the mate completes a task, or the way something has turned out, for him to cease doing it. Most of us will not persist in doing extra jobs that we don't feel comfortable doing, especially if we are fearful of criticism after they are completed.

A caution here: many of us who come from environments where the Protestant work ethic was highly emphasized are really overgrown taskmasters. When we let that ethic become overblown and out of control, we end up treating our spouses as servants or hired hands. If that describes your situation and it's part of the message of the affair you are trying to recover from, then you need to listen to it; you also need to draw an appropriate boundary. Such well-meaning but overblown behavior can be destructive. If your spouse wants you to do, do, do, and not be emotionally close, then tell him gently that he can hire those kinds of things done. You married him to be in relationship, not to be a slave!

3. NONSEXUAL TOUCH

Many times in a marriage the couple has gone from loads of physical affection in their dating days (ranging from holding hands to more extensive expressions of affection) to having only sexual intercourse once they are married. This is especially true of Christian couples who (rightly) eschewed sex before marriage. After it becomes "legal" when they tied the knot, they may use it exclusively as their sole means of expressing love. All those lingering touches and safe expressions of caring have disappeared. That is a loss, especially from a woman's point of view.

Many times, an affair rekindles feelings of infatuation simply on the basis, at least initially, of nonsexual touch. Hand holding, hugging, cuddling, walking arm in arm, and other playful touches commonly build the attraction to the partner. Thus one message for the recovering couple might be "We've lost the playful touching we had at the outset of our romance."

If that's your case, set a time limit for not having sex at all, and concentrate on nonsexual touching in expressing your affection. Then, later, you can add the sexual aspect again. I know of one couple who decided to refrain from sex for one whole month, concentrating instead on other forms of expression. It worked wonders in their marriage.

4. Erotic/Sexual Activity

Dress, language, behavior, indeed, anything that is provocative to the partner and sexual in nature, is a part of the erotic language. Males in general report more intense sexual thoughts and activity than do females in adolescence and their twenties. Sexual dissatisfaction can be a seedbed for many other disappointments in the marriage.

Often the couple puts too much demand on the area of sexual activity. They expect it to solve conflict, bring them closer together, and keep them infatuated with each other. But that's asking too much of it. Good sex is an expression of all three of those areas (conflict resolution, closeness, and infatuation) but certainly will not meet all needs in all those areas.

In fact, sex for the infidel in the affair often was not what the wounded partner thinks it was. Infidels commonly report that sex wasn't all that great, especially in a Class II affair. That makes sense in that the entangled affair has a high emotional component to it—sex doesn't have to be that good, since both individuals are in it for much more than that.

What is not being recognized is the key to all successful marital relationships: sex doesn't make relationships good; it only makes the good ones better. Building a quality relationship involves a lot more than abundant sexual or erotic activity. Frequently when I talk with couples who are struggling through recovery, I hear the violated spouse say she knew this was an important arena in the marriage and that it had become a source of conflict, anger, and withdrawal.

Often sex has become the only means for one partner to feel close to the other. If that is the only avenue of closeness, the arena of sex will eventually deteriorate under the demands that are being placed on it, and then one of the partners will move into a high-risk category for inappropriate behavior. Most men and women desire to have more of their person explored than their sexual anatomy; they want emotional closeness and soul-to-soul understanding.

When infidels talk about the affair, they typically say things such as, "I could tell her anything," or, "He would listen to everything I said," or, "There weren't any secrets between us." And the partner says about the infidel, "I knew everything about him—he talked and talked and I listened." Married couples often substitute sex for this kind of intimacy, much to their detriment.

5. FOCUSED TIME

What do you do together with your disposable time? Both the quantity of time you spend and the type of activity that you do together are important. Many times affairs center on simple activities that are available to any couple: a weekend away, a stroll on the beach, lunch at a cheap little restaurant, a game of tennis, a workout at the club, taking in a movie together, or just a ten-minute chat at the end of the day.

Focused time is time spent with just the two of you. The key is that there are no other distractions—no other couples, no children, no office responsibilities lurking in the back of your mind, nothing except what the two of you are doing.

This particular love language is probably the first barometer to indicate that you as a couple are reconciling adequately—you are beginning to spend more time together, even if at first it's always working on your "stuff," talking about issues related to the affair, or expressing emotion and hurt about the experience. At least it's focused time. Maybe it is the first time you two have spent intense time together in months or years. Later you can start spending focused time on non-recovery issues, but take it one step at a time.

LOVE LANGUAGE ASSIGNMENT

Step 1: Be sure you've made the list of twenty things that bless you "in your language"—those things that your spouse could do to you that make you feel special, cared for, cherished, or understood. (You should have done this already, but if you kept reading, stop now and make the list!)

Step 2: Take your list of twenty items and review each one in light of the five love language themes. Transfer each of them onto the chart below, labeling each one with a "V" (verbal), "G/T" (gifts/tasks), "NT" (nonsexual touch), "E/S" (erotic/sexual), or "FT" (focused time). Some of them might seem to require more than one descriptor, but be decisive and try to restrict each to one language. For now, don't show each other your charts; later, you'll compare them. After you have labeled each of your twenty items with a descriptor, tally up the occurrences of each of the categories.

Most individuals find that they have one primary love language—the category with the highest score. It is often followed by one, or sometimes even two, languages that would be in second place. Usually two or three of the categories don't mean anything at all to a person. When and if a mate tried to express love in those languages, the spouse would say, "It's all Greek to me."

This exercise of determining what is important to you and to your spouse is important for rebuilding intimacy. Some other ways to utilize this exercise will be given in chapter 11, but for now suffice to say that it is important to understand what your spouse's love language is.

Step 3: Before you look at your spouse's chart, do the following in the space provided below the charts.

1. List, in order of importance, what you think your spouse's love languages are.
2. Give yourself a 1–10 rating (10 being high) of how well you think you have met your spouse's love language.
3. Rate on the same 1–10 scale how well your spouse will think you have met his/her needs in the five categories.

One final caution: don't sabotage the benefits of this experience by saying in your mind, "He's only doing this because I told him he had to," or, "It's not spontaneous, so it's not real." If your spouse agrees to do this, it's because he's motivated to one degree or another. Assume he's being sincere, and you be sincere too.

This is not meant to be an exam or test but rather an opportunity for both of you to process important issues in your relationship.

LOVE LANGUAGE CHART
FOR HUSBANDS

Special Behavior	Theme (e.g., Verbal)

How many occurrences?

_____ Verbal

_____ Gifts/Tasks

_____ Nonsexual Touch

_____ Erotic/Sexual

_____ Focused Time

_____ Total Score

Number in order of importance what you think your spouse's love languages are:

_____ Verbal

_____ Gifts/Tasks

_____ Nonsexual Touch

_____ Erotic/Sexual

_____ Focused Time

Score yourself, on a scale of 1 to 10 (where 1 is "bombing out" and 10 is "got it down") regarding the five love language themes. Be honest—your process with your spouse will be better off by not pretending.

How Well Do You Think You Are Doing?	Themes	How Well Will Your Spouse Say You're Doing?
	Verbal	
	Gifts/Tasks	
	Nonsexual Touch	
	Erotic/Sexual	
	Focused Time	

LOVE LANGUAGE CHART
FOR WIVES

Special Behavior	Theme (e.g., Verbal)

How many occurrences?

_____ Verbal

_____ Gifts/Tasks

_____ Nonsexual Touch

_____ Erotic/Sexual

_____ Focused Time

_____ Total Score

Number in order of importance what you think your spouse's love languages are:

_____ Verbal

_____ Gifts/Tasks

_____ Nonsexual Touch

_____ Erotic/Sexual

_____ Focused Time

Score yourself, on a scale of 1 to 10 (where 1 is "bombing out" and 10 is "got it down") regarding the five love language themes. Be honest—your process with your spouse will be better off by not pretending.

How Well Do You Think You Are Doing?	Themes	How Well Will Your Spouse Say You're Doing?
	Verbal	
	Gifts/Tasks	
	Nonsexual Touch	
	Erotic/Sexual	
	Focused Time	

Plan some time to talk about the results of this inventory with your mate. It might not be easy, but it will be some of the best time and effort you've ever spent, especially at this critical juncture in your relationship.

LOOKING AHEAD

Do you like fireworks?

If so, you may enjoy the next chapter—in fact, if you let yourself feel authentic and valid anger at appropriate times, you will likely process the affair in a healthy manner. But if you're like most people involved in affairs, processing anger is difficult for you.

In the next chapter we'll look first at how to feel your anger and hurt, and second, how to process it correctly.

NOTES

1. For further discussion on the need for connectedness, see John Townsend, *Hiding from Love* (Colorado Springs: Navpress, 1991); Henry Cloud, *Changes That Heal* (Grand Rapids: Zondervan, 1992); and Dave Carder et al., *Secrets of Your Family Tree: Healing for Adult Children of Dysfunctional Families* (Chicago: Moody, 1991).

2. I recommend books such as Willard Harley, *His Needs, Her Needs* (Old Tappan, N.J.: Revell, 1986); Gary Smalley and John Trent, *The Language of Love* (Pomona, Calif.: Focus, 1988); Gary Chapman, *The Five Love Languages* (Chicago: Northfield, 1995).

9

Anger in Affairs: Getting Good Out of Getting Mad

Jim couldn't sleep. He hadn't had a decent night's sleep in a week since he lost control that night with his wife, Karen. When he had confronted her about her "late nights at the office," she admitted her six-month affair with her surgeon boss.

Jim had flown off the handle, alternating between angrily cursing her and tearfully begging her to break it off. For some reason he kept rushing in and out of the house, trying to regain control of himself. He didn't know whether he should strangle her, shoot her boss, or shoot himself.

That creep, he thought as the fever rose within. *Cheating on his own wife and trying to ruin my marriage—if I just knew his home address, he'd be sorry he ever touched her.* Then his fury would turn on Karen.

But he'd catch himself and try to rein in his anger—he suspected that her boss already had a lot more appeal to Karen than he did. She had come to their marriage from a wealthy family, and Jim had never really gotten on track with his career. He knew he shouldn't bad-mouth the guy—not now. He might drive her back into his arms.

Look at her, she's so beautiful, sitting on our broken-down couch. He stood over her threateningly, asking question after question. After another dash outside into the blackness of their front yard to keep from strangling her, he ran back in and fell on his knees, beg-

149

ging her forgiveness in tears for being so lazy and not providing for her.

When Karen seemed to hesitate in extending her forgiveness, Jim flew into a rage and threw her favorite bone china figurine across the room, exploding it into a million tiny pieces against the wall. Seeing a tangible example of his fury, he burst into tears again, covered his face with his hands, and slowly sank to the floor.

How long he lay there crumpled on the floor he didn't know, but Karen never reached out to him. She just sat there, frozen. Eventually Jim's rage returned. Calling her filthy names, he ran out the door and drove away into the night.

He didn't know where to go except to the now dark medical complex where Karen worked. He imagined that Karen was calling her boss now from their home. *Let them talk—I don't care anymore,* he thought bitterly.

As he walked angrily around the darkened building like a prowling tiger, trying to find some order in his swirling emotions, he noticed a loose brick in the landscaping near the entryway and toyed with the idea of heaving it through the second floor windows of the offices. Or heaving *all* the bricks through *all* the windows in the building. Luckily, he discarded that plan. *Boy, I'm starting to really lose it now. Better drive home and try to recover my sanity.*

When he got home, he wondered if Karen was even there anymore. Perhaps her lover had come to pick her up, upon hearing of his ravings. When he got inside, however, there she was, asleep. *How can she sleep on a night like tonight?* He woke her up and made her promise not to see her boss anymore and to quit her position as soon as he could get a better paying job. Then they even made love, but that didn't help.

Now shortly before dawn, Jim's mind was still racing with bitter questions that seemed unanswerable. He was afraid of losing Karen. She was the best thing that had ever happened to him. His actions had almost got completely out of control again last night, and he promised himself he would control his passions—if not, she just might leave him, and then where would he be?

As Karen got ready for work, Jim found himself hating her and wishing she wasn't going into the office to see that rich jerk again. He wanted to hurt Karen and make her cry. He knew he should send her out the door reassured that they would make it, but his rage kept him from caring. He managed not to hurt her physically, but when she finally did leave, she was in tears.

As soon as her car was out of sight, Jim panicked. He jumped into his car and sped after her. Finally catching up to her at a traffic light, he jumped out and ran to her car window with tears running down his cheeks. She was crying too. He kept her at the intersection through the next light, apologizing and bawling like a baby. The other drivers just drove around them, and the whole scene was like one out of a class B movie, but to Jim it was a real-life nightmare.

Karen was late as she walked into the office, having tried to repair her tear-streaked makeup in the car before entering the building. The phone was ringing. Pulling herself together, she answered it in the most businesslike voice she could muster.

It was Jim, angry at himself and confused for humbling himself so thoroughly in the intersection. He begged her again to break off the affair. Confused and tired of Jim's tirades and tears, Karen hung up on him just as her boss walked in.

Jim's back-and-forth behavior—alternating between towering rage and humble apologies—is common to the spouse who is suddenly confronted by the infidel's unfaithfulness. The betrayed one is carried along in violently swirling eddies of emotion, and it seems the rip current will suck him out to sea at any minute.

In Jim and Karen's case, Jim's anger eventually subsided to the point that he and Karen were able to start communicating and make progress toward reconciliation. They came for counseling, and Karen decided to quit her job and call off the affair. Jim allowed the jolt to his marriage to motivate him to begin to work on his issues. Today both are doing well in recovery.

ANGER, THE NATURAL RESPONSE

The initial revelation of the affair produces a crisis experience. The natural response—indeed the healthy response—is anger. There are both positive and negative aspects of this anger, which we will examine herein; later in the chapter, we'll look at what happens when spouses do not get angry at the revelation of an affair. For now, though, let's look at common responses.

Many times a spouse has suspected for some time that something is wrong with the marriage. She might have even confronted her mate about the possible illicit involvement on more than one occasion, only to be met with numerous denials. Often when the infidel finally reveals the secret of the affair, the spouse knows who the partner is without being told.

In my experience, male spouses often react with rage at their mate's affair, whereas female spouses express more hurt mixed with anger. Male spouses often want to kill the infidel's partner—and even choose to believe at times that their spouse was just a victim, that she was seduced, that she didn't willingly participate in the affair. The male spouse often wants to see the infidel as the passive, rather than the active, partner. In this reaction, the male spouse tips his hand as to the amount of personal ego involved—he's such an awesome spouse that she probably was stolen away; she would never want to stray from him.

The true picture, however, is often different. The spouse is rarely totally whisked off her feet by the "evil partner." She almost always plays an active role. The male spouse usually doesn't express much interest as to whether or not his wife loves her partner; instead, he wants to know the details of their sexual activity.

The female spouse usually will cry, yell, and scream but is less physically violent or threatening toward her infidel husband and his partner. She often wants to know what feelings the infidel has for his partner. Does he love her, and did he bring her into their home or bedroom?

After the initial eruption, the betrayed spouse usually begins to obsess about the affair. Obsessing simply means to stew on something; to run it over and over in your mind, to be unable to remove it from your thinking processes, to feel overwhelmed and unable to get it out of your day-to-day thoughts.

A person who is obsessing asks questions that cannot be answered and may not even wait for the questions to be answered. His or her thoughts are chaotic and unconstructive.

GETTING IN TOUCH WITH THE HURT

THE SPOUSE'S HURT

As mentioned in chapter 7, the spouse often feels like a widow after disclosure. Her recovery process parallels that of a spouse who has lost a mate to death.

Initially, however, an affair produces a very different set of emotions: the feelings of being a fool; of being taken advantage of by someone she trusted; of overshadowing shame and persistent guilt. We all have imperfections in our relationships. Immediately those come to mind, and suddenly we feel guilty.

It is not uncommon for spouses to report a fleeting sense of total responsibility and blame at the revelation of the affair. In addition, they often report feeling exposed: "Now everybody in the world will know what I am really like." Plus, there is the pain of betrayal—the sense that someone you completely trusted has just pulled the rug out from under your feet.

All feelings of safety and security can be lost. Only as the spouse reaffirms her trust in God and herself (e.g., "I can survive without the infidel if I have to" and "God will still be my strength") can her sense of security be restored.

A reminder here for spouses who struggle with identifying and ventilating your anger: that's often part of what contributed to the affair in the first place. It is often inappropriate caretaking, such as protecting your spouse from your anger, that encouraged the infidel to have the affair initially. Such a pattern develops as one spouse denies his or her own feelings in order to focus on the mate's feelings, which are counted as more important.

During the anger phase following disclosure, don't hold back your hurt and anger. You may think, *I can't kick a man when he's down*, but consider this: your expressing legitimate anger in a non-retaliatory way does not constitute "kicking" him; you're just processing the affair correctly. Remember, you are trying to do it differently from how you have ever done it before.

There will be tears. True, crying can be a form of manipulation if it is insincere. But it can also be a normal, healthy expression of feelings in a time of crisis. You will have to decide what is an honest expression of your pain.

The biblical character Joseph is a great example of being "all mixed up" in the initial phase of a personal crisis (Genesis 42–50). Joseph was the darling of his father's heart, and his brothers were jealous to the point of hatred. One day their anger overcame them, and they spitefully sold him as a slave to some traveling Ishmaelites. Many years later, Joseph had become acting ruler over all of Egypt. The surrounding lands were suffering a severe famine, and Joseph's brothers came to Egypt to buy food.

When they appeared, Joseph wept and raged against his brothers all at the same time (Genesis 42). He expressed anger and grief in the same setting. His confusion, incoherence, and mixed-up emotions are typical of initial confrontations that involve betrayal. Actually, it was a sign of health.

Joseph was so overwhelmed by their unannounced appearance that he knew he wasn't making any sense, so he sent them to prison for three days. Joseph's behavior exhibits definite anger. His actions are more understandable when we realize that it had been many years since he had faced his brothers. His feelings had lain dormant for a long time, and the reunion reawakened them.

Joseph handled it in a healthy way. He didn't try to take care of his brothers when they became bewildered by the accusations he was making against them. If he was trying not to upset them and worrying about their reactions, he would have said, "Oh, brothers, I'm sorry that you're so scared now. I didn't mean for it to be so intense for your poor little minds. Here, let me wipe away those tears and make you feel better. I'm sure you must be in a terrible mood after having ridden your donkeys all the way down from Israel."

Joseph said nothing of the sort. Yet that's what some spouses do when they see their partner grieving. They try to "make it all better," as a mother would do for a toddler.

If your partner has had an affair and betrayed you and his wedding vows, you need to be angry. And you don't need to hold his hand when you express your true feelings.

THE INFIDEL'S HURT

The revelation of the affair is often so painful for the spouse that the infidel feels he cannot grieve. He may think, *We both can't fall apart at the same time.* So he tries to "be strong and take his medicine." In his mind, he deserves this because he caused it.

Thus the infidel will often show no tears of hurt. He may fear that tears will be interpreted as a desire to return to his former partner. But when the infidel insists on "being strong" and showing no emotion, his behavior only convinces the spouse that he has no remorse. On the other hand, if the infidel does grieve, the spouse can believe he cares for her and that his heart is still tied to the marriage.

That trap of not being able to grieve is really the exact opposite of what the spouse wants. The spouse needs to see and feel the infidel's hurt. Grieving helps heal the wounds and gives the spouse permission to look at his or her contribution to the affair's development.

Think of it like this: if the infidel is strong, trying to behave "correctly" and keeping himself from grieving, then the spouse has to do all the grieving, falling apart, and irrational behavior for the both of them. However, the more overwhelmed by pain the infidel is, the sooner the spouse will be able to begin (and end) her grieving, and the sooner they can both make progress toward healing.

OBSESSING

Part of what fuels the tendency to obsess about the affair is the bewilderment that comes from betrayal. There is a tendency to ask more and more details, as if sufficient information will take the pain away. The spouse often asks unanswerable questions, such as, Why? How could you do this to me? Why did you do it with him (her)? It can go on relentlessly, causing sleeplessness, physical symptoms, untold mental anguish, and in the extreme case, suicide.

Some amount of obsessing is natural, but when it persists and the spouse is unable to get it under control, it becomes dysfunctional. In that sense, it causes the spouse to "get stuck" and unable to move on to processing the other issues that will yield healthy recovery.

Obsession is a cyclical rage that is self-perpetuating. It emerges in the following pattern:

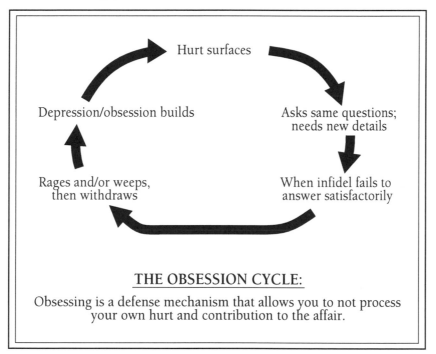

Hurt surfaces

Asks same questions;
needs new details

When infidel fails to
answer satisfactorily

Rages and/or weeps,
then withdraws

Depression/obsession builds

THE OBSESSION CYCLE:

Obsessing is a defense mechanism that allows you to not process your own hurt and contribution to the affair.

There will be no recovery without both parties accepting their appropriate share of their contribution to what happened. Otherwise, the one who refuses to accept responsibility (e.g., the spouse who denies her role in the breakup) is powerless to influence the outcome. *The greater contribution each party assumes for the affair, the more control he/she has over the final outcome.*

The tendency to ruminate on the affair should be a signal to the spouse that it is time to do more processing. As the unanswerable questions and uncontrollable emotions surface, they should be expressed constructively. Crying long and hard over the hurt alone, especially at the outset, is helpful. Talking it through with your mate is a must.

It is common for couples to report that the tendency to obsess ebbs and flows through the recovery process. The spouse often reports intense obsession shortly after the revelation period. As time passes, however, your obsessing periods should become less intense, have a shorter duration, and be farther apart from each other. You may get over obsessing if you practice this self-talk routine: "I don't need to think about it again, because it only gets me depressed. I feel a little better now than when I went through it the last time. I'm making slow but steady progress, and I don't need to put myself through the agony of those questions again."

Another option for the spouse who can't seem to get through the obsession is to get a picture of the partner, buy a plastic whiffle ball bat, lay the picture on the bed, close the windows, send the kids outside, and beat the picture until you cry and feel some relief. Many spouses report definite relief from the obsession after doing this exercise. It also protects the relationship and helps keep the spouse from ventilating her anger on her husband.

If you are seeing a counselor during this time, it is important that obsessing be controlled in the sessions. At its base, obsession is often a defense against processing your own hurt and contribution to the affair. If left uncontrolled, it will eventually thwart the marriage from getting back on track. It keeps the spouse from adequately grieving through her pain. If it is not kept to a minimum, it will force the infidel to begin to focus on his own survival, driving him away from the reconciliation process.

POSITIVE ASPECTS OF ANGER FOR THE SPOUSE

There are several benefits to being "good and angry" at the infidel who has betrayed your joint commitment to each other.

IT SHOWS YOU CARE

You only get mad about things that really matter to you. Thus anger shows that the spouse cares about the relationship and values it.

Anger not only shows that you value the relationship, but it also tells you something about the nature of it. The level of anger upon disclosure of the affair demonstrates the level of relational intensity, and to a great degree, the identity of the relationship. For example, cruel anger often demonstrates that it is a cruel relationship; quiet anger may show that there is little emotional intensity between two mates. As discussed in the previous chapter, anger demonstrates what the message of the affair is all about. It is important to the couple's recovery that the anger be appropriately expressed.

IT HELPS WARD OFF DEPRESSION

Anger, strangely enough, helps keep the spouse out of the downward spiral of depression. Usually depression is the result of repressing or denying appropriate feelings of anger. In contrast, expressing anger helps keep the overwhelming, black feelings of depression away. As such, it helps protect the spouse from the emotional self-flagellation that can prolong one's misery—and even lead to suicide in extreme cases. It makes the processing of this broken relationship, and the restoration of it, more manageable.

Initially, the anger dumps all the responsibility upon the infidel, and that's to be expected. But that will change as the spouse begins to see beyond the infidelity to look at the overall relationship. We will look at that process shortly.

IT PROVIDES ENERGY

When you are angry, you have lots of energy. Anger provides energy to do the necessary work of recovery. Normally we think of anger-related energy as negative and destructive—and it can be, if not expressed appropriately. But when we are honest with ourselves and our mate about the hurt that we feel, that energy can be channeled toward a constructive recovery. Then we are able to find good in something that is often seen as only bad.

IT HELPS CLEAR YOUR MIND

Anger helps people think more clearly than, say, depression. Depressed people report confusion, mixed feelings, and withdrawal into silence. Expressed anger allows a person to verbalize what is going on in his cognitive processes and therefore allows him to strategize and reason more effectively.

In the anger phase following disclosure, the spouse needs a clear head. She is about to begin the confusing process of sorting out the tangled webs that she, the infidel, and the partner have woven.

It Helps You Survive

Anger is a natural consequence of being injured or hurt. Justifiable anger is part of the survival mechanism that God has built within us. It is the same kind of anger—righteous indignation—that Jesus expressed in the Temple to the money-changers who had contaminated and discounted their righteous vows (Matthew 21:12-13).

It's no accident that God often calls corrupt religious practices prostitution or adultery (Hosea; Jeremiah 23:9-14). If God got angry at those who went a-whoring after other gods, a spouse has every right to be angry at the infidel who has gone a-whoring after another partner.

NEGATIVE ASPECTS OF ANGER FOR THE SPOUSE

Retaliation/Bitterness

Recognize that your initial desire to make the infidel hurt as you are hurting is highly counterproductive. That aspect of anger almost always involves bitter feelings of retaliation—the desire to get back at someone, to exert "justice," to make him pay for what he has done.

Clearly, the desire for revenge crosses the line of appropriate expression of God-given anger. Such feelings are destructive in light of the eventual goal of restoring the relationship—but initially the spouse doesn't care. After that first flush of rage, however, she needs to realize that such retaliatory motives are damaging. Rather than seeking her "pound of flesh," she needs to channel that energy into confrontation and address issues that have been long neglected.

One-Sided Blaming

It is important to acknowledge your initial sense of failure and the countering desire to blame the affair completely on the infidel. Part of the shock that you will begin to feel after the initial revelation is the possibility that you, too, might have contributed to the conditions that led up to the affair. One of the immediate defenses against this emerging perception is to blame the infidel completely and not share in the responsibility.

Difficult as it will be, resist that urge, and look at your relationship from the big picture. Before God and your mate, honestly be open to what lacks you may have contributed to the marital relationship. The more you can understand the causes of the infidelity and the *mutual* flaws in your relationship, the better chances you have for lasting recovery as a couple.

"LINING UP THE OPPOSITION" MAY BACKFIRE

Your initial need to tell everybody—indeed anybody who will listen—what the infidel has done to you may not produce the results you want; in fact, it may backfire. Telling everyone you know is not only counterproductive to long-term marital happiness, but it also may mask a motivation in your heart similar to the one discussed above: the refusal to share the responsibility for the breakup. Such behavior keeps the eyes and ears of your friends safely focused on the infidel, not on you.

True, you will want (and desperately need) emotional support during this crisis, but when the telling goes beyond one or two close friends, the specter of gossip, character assassination, and backbiting comes into view. You may be extremely mad at him now, but telling a long list of your (and his) friends and acquaintances about his long list of sins will only hurt you in the long run.

If you poison his entire social circle against him by telling them what a bum he is, he will be reticent to come back into relationship with you. That will drive him back into the partner's arms, since he's loved and accepted there. Indeed, through the partner he may be in the process of making new contacts in her social circles, and they may very well think he's a great guy.

Remember, he and the partner have created their own little world that is safe and full of "warm fuzzies" for him. If you increase the discomfort of his world with you, your misguided attempts at "support" will result in further alienation of the infidel.

IF THE SPOUSE DOES NOT RESPOND WITH ANGER

Some spouses, even upon disclosure of the affair, continue their codependent, dial-tone relationship, instead of getting angry. They deny their emotions in the name of "not rocking the boat" or "being a good Christian" and end up freezing the recovery process, dooming it to failure.

Again, it takes two to tango: (1) both the spouse *and* the infidel create a marital environment where an affair takes place, and (2) it takes both parties to put the relationship back together following disclosure. If one party refuses to participate (in this case by not getting angry), the process of recovery is stymied.

If you have trouble expressing your angry emotions toward your cheating mate, give serious consideration to the following characteristics of the "angerless" spouse.

STOICISM

The stoic spouse feels compelled to maintain a stone face and a "stiff upper lip" so that things won't fall apart, no matter how upsetting her world is. Such people project the attitude that they can take anything—emotionally they're a combination of Superman and John Wayne. Yet such "strong" behavior can actually be counterproductive to the healing process.

Granted, stoic behavior may sometimes be necessary for the protection of the children (anger shouldn't be directed at them) or to hold the family together during this crisis. However, it is never healthy if that is the only response of the spouse. Stuffing emotions can generate a series of physical illnesses and feeds addictive behavior.

FORGIVING TOO QUICKLY

The spouse who refuses to get angry wants to "get over this" and stop feeling the incredible hurt soon. And she means soon— like yesterday.

In so doing, she is usually denying how intensely personal the betrayal is. Her spouse has just broken the most important promise he ever made in his life, yet she refuses to admit it. For a multitude of reasons, it's too scary for her.

Often she wants to look good to others, even in the midst of all the destruction. This is especially true if she wants to look like a super-spiritual Christian who is full of "grace" for the offender. (Grace is good, denial is bad. Forgiveness will come later.) She doesn't view hurting or anger as socially acceptable, so she feels a tremendous hurry to "get this over and done with."

She often feels as if it is her responsibility to pretend forgiveness and that to respond in any other way would be childish, irresponsible, juvenile, or unspiritual. Many Christians, including pastors, reinforce this behavior. They tend to reward good outward appearances and shame emotional honesty. (In chapter 11 we'll talk again about the spouse who forgives too quickly.)

EXCUSING THE AFFAIR

The spouse who excuses the affair often has a great need to be in charge of the outcome. Being in control is usually typical of his or her approach to life and relationships. The tendency to excuse the affair (especially on the part of wives) is often expressed in a somewhat sarcastic and resigned-to-one's-fate tone. "What else would you expect from a man? My dad did this, and my mother survived—I suppose I will too."

The attitude that "nothing terrible that you do can surprise or upset me" renders the infidel powerless—the spouse is refusing to play by the rules (i.e., when someone betrays you, you will get angry), so the process is truncated. That kind of response shows that the spouse still has not heard what the infidel was saying through the affair—"I am unhappy, and things between us need to change."

The spouse's decision to discount the pain and power of the affair usually reflects an abusive childhood experience. The defensive reaction of dismissing pain rather than feeling it is a learned response. Its effectiveness was only temporary in childhood, and it will be only temporary in adulthood.

Such a pattern really becomes dysfunctional if the infidel has more than one affair. When that happens, the spouse's repeated dismissal of her anger telegraphs the message to the infidel that "Your behavior is normal; you don't have to change a thing; all is fine on this end."

That is exactly what happens in an alcoholic family when the nonalcoholic spouse doesn't insist that help be sought. By that response, she dubs abnormal behavior as normal, and the cycle is self-perpetuated. She begins to assume that her pain-filled, abnormal experience is everybody else's pattern. That's why adult children from dysfunctional families have extreme difficulty getting a handle on what "normal" behavior is. The infidel-spouse interaction, when unfaithfulness is merely dismissed, is very much the same.

As the spouse begins to get in touch with her own contribution to the affair, the infidel receives permission to get mad. But that can only happen as the spouse owns up to her contribution—otherwise, the infidel is too busy parrying the blame being launched his way. He is too occupied with self-protection to begin self-examination. If the spouse avoids blaming, however, and assumes her contribution to the affair, the infidel can relax his defenses and will start to feel his own frustration—and more important, the hurt behind the anger.

THE INFIDEL'S RAGE

Initially, the infidel's anger is often smothered by guilt and shame, and he doesn't feel angry. Many infidels report waiting for the storm to blow over before they can blow up.

What anger could the infidel possibly need to get in touch with? the spouse may ask. Actually anger (or frustration, which is a mild form of anger) pushed the infidel toward the affair in the first place. Sure, that started a long time ago, and the infidel may not even be aware of it anymore, but it's still there and usually unaddressed (if it *had* been addressed, very possibly the affair would not have happened). If the spouse refuses to feel her anger, this latent frustration in the infidel may reignite, and he may reexpress his exasperation with the relationship pattern he and his mate have been practicing.

Keep in mind when you're in the maelstrom of anger that the affair in and of itself did not produce the anger. The frustration and resultant anger were usually already present in the relationship prior to the actual illicit involvement. Disclosing the affair simply highlighted the friction already at work in the relationship.

In summary, we can see why defensiveness and blaming are so counterproductive to healing the marital bond: the more the spouse blames, the less the infidel feels his own hurt and anger, but the more the spouse focuses on her contributions, the more free the infidel is to review his own hurt and anger. Although it may seem ironic, this highly charged, emotional seesaw is healthy in the long run.

PRACTICAL WAYS TO PROCESS ANGER

Remember the message of the affair as you seek to process your feelings of rage. Whatever you do, do not do more of the same. For example, if workaholism was part of the problem, cut back or reevaluate your business commitments. If the infidel started sleeping with his partner in the bowling league, find another leisure activity (or at least another league!). *Do things differently.* Though returning to the familiar routine provides a temporary escape in this time of crisis, simply doing more of the same is only a setup for another affair.

The following is a list of responses to working out and working through anger. Some of them may seem insignificant, but you might be surprised by how helpful they will be to you. Many of the couples I've counseled have reported great success in employing them to help process the powerful feelings that are part of the recovery process.

Discuss Your Feelings, But Separate Them

Tell your mate how you are feeling during this difficult time. A healthy response from the spouse (or infidel) is to empathize and understand the other's feelings. But even that healthy pattern can get out of hand if taken to the extreme. For example, you don't need to feel responsible for your mate's feelings. Those feelings belong to him or her, not you. Even though you're "one flesh" in spiritual terms, you're still two distinct people, and whatever feelings the other is having are OK. He or she owns those feelings; you cannot control them.

Nothing is off-limits for discussion. The worst has already happened. That realization can be helpful in giving either party permission to bring up whatever issues are important.

Keep a Journal

Express your feelings in a private journal. Write to God, write to your mate, write to yourself—do anything to get those thoughts out on paper. That discipline provides a wonderful release of emotions—a catharsis—and serves as a road map to indicate where you've been, where you are now, and where you're going. You might even read from it with your mate in one of those heart-to-heart discussions, to communicate exactly what you're going through.

Chart the Ebb and Flow of Your Recovery

Charting is helpful after a certain period of time has gone by. Use some of the charts in this book, or even your own calendar at home to mark the days that pass as "good," "bad," or "surviving." After the month is over, chart the month. Or you may chart your improvement on a daily or weekly basis. Whereas journaling primarily captures the present, charting is a backward look. Using them together can help you know that you are on course, versus drifting in a sea of emotional upheaval.

Implement Personal Changes

Make personal changes that both of you know are long overdue. Don't put them off any longer. Now is the time for a little self-nurturance—don't feel guilty! Go ahead and make those changes you have been considering, such as getting a new hairstyle, changing your dress, starting an exercise program, beginning new, personal, fun relaxation times, and so on. For example, if your spouse's grumpiness kept you from playing golf, go play a round when your schedule allows it. You'll need to make improvements in your lifestyle to help you cope during this crisis, when nurturing from your mate is probably at an all-time low.

Of course I do not mean that you ought to max out your credit cards in an attempt to salve your feelings of depression! Neither am I suggesting that you should go buy a $80,000 Porsche and ruin your budget. I'm talking about healthy, normal changes to your routine or lifestyle. Eventually, as your recovery progresses with your mate, the natural spouse-to-spouse nurturing will return.

If one mate chooses to implement personal changes and the other does not, the non-changing mate must be careful not to interpret the other's changes as attempts to manipulate him or her. The changes are simply a way for each individual to say, "I am going to do for myself what I've known that I needed to do for a long time."

Cultivate a Same-Sex Relationship for Support

Often individuals report so much shame and guilt during this time that they withdraw from their friends. Yet exactly the opposite needs to happen. During this difficult stage, resist the temptation to distance yourself from others around you.

Take time for others, especially those one or two friends whom you can talk to during these difficult days. Each partner needs to take time to develop a same-sex friendship with someone who will serve as a listener and provide feedback without being overly corrective or free with advice. (The caution that it not be an opposite-sex friendship should be clear enough—the danger of another affair sparking in such a setting is enormous.) Now more than ever, you need someone who can help you see things from a different angle, someone to affirm your recovery and help you sort through your thoughts, behaviors, and feelings.

There should be a tapering to this "lean on me" process, however. At the outset of working through the affair with your mate, you'll need to lean heavily on the same-sex friend. But as you progress as a couple, you'll lean less on your outside friend and more on your mate. When that begins to happen, you'll know that some reattachment is occurring.

Talk About It

There's something highly therapeutic about simply verbalizing your feelings with another person. Talk about them with Jesus in prayer (get someplace private and speak your prayers out loud—it helps a lot), with your recovery friend as outlined above, with a Christian man or woman who has recovered from an affair, with your spouse in heart-to-heart talks, or with significant others in your life, such as close siblings or cousins.

You will probably experience the urge to tell everything to your mother, but that could prove to be more problematic than helpful. Usually mothers of adult children are biased and lack the objectivity required of a friend. Unless you have an exemplary relationship with your mother, where she fully allows you the proper amount of individuality and freedom as an autonomous adult (instead of treating you as "her little girl/boy"), talking it over would probably be best done with someone else. (Sorry, Mom.)

MAKE AN ANGER LIST

Making a list of things that make you angry will help when you feel as if the swirling emotions will never stop and that each day you are more and more confused. Write down what you're upset about, and leave no stone unturned. Get it out of your head and onto paper. Then you can rank the list, discuss the items with your mate and with Jesus, and so on.

If you enjoy checking things off lists, it will feel great when, after discussing a point and processing it sufficiently, you can make a glorious check mark next to that item. But beware of too easily marking off the items—some of your frustrations will be deep-seated, and you need to be honest with yourself about when and how you process them.

FEEL IT

Feeling your feelings instead of denying them is a major theme throughout this chapter, but it doesn't hurt to make the point again, with some examples. Perhaps you can think of more. The overarching principle here is to express the anger in an unregrettable fashion, that is, in a manner that is appropriate and won't hurt others or yourself.

These ideas would fit within the "unregrettable" parameter:

- Crying, yelling, or screaming in private
- Grabbing your son's baseball bat or a broomstick and beating your pillow

- Going for a long run, vigorous walk, bike ride, or fast swim
- Participating in a sport that involves hitting a ball: tennis, raquetball, softball

UNDERSTANDING THE DEPRESSION CYCLE

It is common for both of you to feel "down" at times during the recovery process. Part of the ebb and flow of recovery is to feel sorry for yourself and even for your mate at various times. The following chart helps explain this process, which can be rather puzzling.

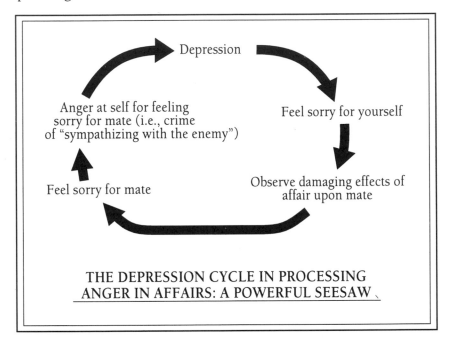

Depression

Feel sorry for yourself

Observe damaging effects of affair upon mate

Feel sorry for mate

Anger at self for feeling sorry for mate (i.e., crime of "sympathizing with the enemy")

THE DEPRESSION CYCLE IN PROCESSING ANGER IN AFFAIRS: A POWERFUL SEESAW

As we saw in the story of Jim at the beginning of this chapter, one moment you can feel sorry for your mate, and the next minute you want to kill him or her! As you look at the above chart, keep in mind that the infidel may have these feelings toward the spouse or vice versa.

Though difficult, periods of depression are actually opportunities for growth, insight, and a commitment to do things differently in the future. They are the points at which the counselor will make interventions. If you're not in counseling, you can recognize that the dips in your emotions may be the time to propose a new development in your relationship.

Following are some common depressive themes that recur in individuals who are involved in the recovery process. You'll probably recognize several or all of the feelings involved.

THE SPOUSE'S FEELINGS

"I'm exhausted. I can't do any more processing right now. I need a break." Short, mutually agreed-upon breaks are OK. Just beware of the danger of skipping out on the recovery process. Sometimes requests for breaks can really be glossed-over statements of fear of addressing tough issues. In that case, it would be better to hang in there and face the pain or anger than quit now.

"I'm confused. I thought I was doing exactly what you wanted before, and look where that got us!" That statement simply indicates that one mate is not clear on the message of the affair. Keep talking, following the guidelines set forth in chapter 8.

"Why should I try to take care of you differently? That might not work, and then where would I be?" That statement usually cloaks fear of the failure to resolve the problems in the marriage, or fear that it will be impossible to recover and do things differently. In addition, the reference to "taking care of you" probably indicates an unhealthy role in the marriage relationship. Remember, the infidel is an adult and doesn't need to be cared for as a child.

In these and other statements of frustration and depression, the trick is to identify what attitudes they represent, then address that root belief. That way, progress can be made, and time won't be wasted going down a rabbit trail.

THE INFIDEL'S FEELINGS

Before disclosure

"Our marriage will never change; there's no sense even telling my wife about my affair. Anyway, I don't deserve a better marriage, now that I've messed up." This infidel is already depressed before disclosure. These feelings reveal that the infidel is prejudging the ability (or disability) of his spouse to change their relationship. But that's foolish—the spouse could surprise the infidel in her willingness to look at tough issues and be willing to change. The true question is, Is the infidel willing to live in a healthy way by disclosing the affair, or is he insisting on maintaining the charade?

"It would kill her to find out. At least now everything looks OK from her point of view, and I'm reasonably happy to have my mistress and my wife. It's better to leave things the way they are." Again the

infidel is making assumptions for the spouse. She probably doesn't really think that everything is OK. The infidel is in maximum denial—denying both reality and his own pain as he tries to live in two diametrically opposed worlds. The anguish of maintaining such a lie over the long term will eventually catch up with him.

"The whole church will know." That may be true, but it's no excuse for not coming out into the open and letting truth fall on the situation.

If the affair is ongoing (i.e., it has not been disclosed, or even after disclosure the infidel will not dump the partner), depression is often expressed as anxiety or mounting tension. The infidel may withdraw increasingly via TV, music with headphones in isolation, drinking, or even tranquilizers, sleeping aids, or other drugs. Physical symptoms often become apparent as expressions of tension: chronic fatigue, unexplained headaches, gastrointestinal disruptions, heart palpitations, and extreme irritability.

All of that turmoil demands relief, so the tension builds for yet another visit to the illicit partner, who appears to understand the infidel's pain. Thus the cycle is self-perpetuated, as the partner provides relief for the infidel in a world set apart from reality.

After disclosure

If the spouse knows and the affair is over, the depressive messages have a different tone.

"See, I never should have told her. She was better off before she knew. Look how badly it hurt her." That statement indicates that the infidel believes the lie that "what you don't know can't hurt you." But truth and honesty are the basic currency of any relationship, especially the marriage relationship.

"The marriage is over. Now I've lost everybody. The kids hate me, my wife hates me, the in-laws hate me. No one understands. Everyone in our family has turned against me." That reaction will become self-fulfilling if the infidel refuses to process and recover from the affair correctly. If, on the other hand, he sincerely tries to pick up the broken pieces, the marital, and even the child-parent, relationship may very well end up stronger than before. Modeling a reconciliation process to your children is also a powerful example.

The cure to depression is change. Pain promotes taking risks to do things differently. Denial not only drives the other mate away, it also drives the pain underground, from whence it will resurface later. Stay with the pain, and wrestle it through.

Jesus illustrated that process in the Garden of Gethsemane, just prior to His crucifixion. At that time He was agonizing over the cross. Jesus understands what it means to work through unasked for assignments, such as putting a marriage together after an affair.

Jesus' great temptation in the garden was the desire for relief from His assignment to die for humanity. You will have crazy thoughts about running away, getting a quick and dirty divorce, murdering the partner, letting attorneys "kill" the infidel in court. Jesus too asked His Father for escape, but at the end of His request, He said, "Yet not My will, but Thine be done" (Luke 22:42). His example can give us hope.

LOOKING AHEAD

The anger stage is a very painful time of wrestling with feelings of pain, grief, and abandonment, but it will eventually produce good in your life and in the life of the marriage.

After you process the anger, you and your mate will need to reestablish trust, that commodity that was blasted to bits in the moment the spouse learned of the betrayal. It can be done, but it must be done right. In the next chapter we'll look at how to do that.

10

CAN I TRUST YOU AGAIN?
REBUILDING TRUST

Herb had been married to Carol, his high school sweetheart, for thirty years. For nine of those years, however, he had been involved with Crystal, his on-and-off mistress. Herb's affair with Crystal had been disclosed several times, and Carol had responded to each revelation in a different fashion. At the first disclosure, she had responded with tears, but not many—she almost immediately formulated a quick forgiveness. She hoped that by doing so, their marriage would survive and the problem would fix itself.

Yet nine years later, Carol was still dealing with her husband's ongoing infidelity. Her "quick fix" had turned out to be no fix at all.

Three years after the first revelation Carol began to suspect that Herb was reinvolved with Crystal, so she used an intervention (see chapter 7) to try to grab Herb's attention. On that occasion, as at the initial discovery, Herb had stopped seeing Crystal for a while. But they never sought more than two or three counseling appointments with their pastor to resolve the problem permanently.

When their last daughter married and left home, Herb got involved with Crystal yet again. Carol sensed it almost immediately, and Herb tearfully acknowledged it. Together, they entered marital counseling with their pastor, where the focus was on relational and communication skills. A year and a half later, Herb started seeing Crystal again. Apparently they needed more than work on their communication skills! They needed to get at the root of the problem—simple confrontation and repentance were not fixing it.

AN UNSPOKEN CONTRACT

At first glance, Herb and Carol's case looked like sexual addiction, with the chaining of relationships that so often occurs there. But as we further explored the triad of relationships among Herb, Carol, and Crystal, I found that there was very little sex going on between Herb and Crystal, the partner. *The real issue appeared to be that Carol had never gotten truly angry at Herb's betrayal, and Herb had never fully grieved following the first exposure of the ongoing affair.* That, as we saw in the last chapter, is the first critical step: the spouse must get mad about the betrayal. Only then will the infidel understand the damage his actions have caused.

As I got to know Herb and Carol, I saw that there was no honesty in their relationship, and hence no foundation on which to build trust. Trust cannot flourish where there is any hint of doubt that the other is not being 100 percent truthful. Herb knew that Carol should be angry at his actions, yet she continued to forgive him too easily, so he doubted her.

I began to see that Herb and Carol both needed to be with each other for all the wrong reasons. In other words, they had developed an unspoken "contract" that they couldn't break. According to the terms of the agreement, Carol had actually trained Herb to think that parts of the affair were OK. After all, she would never leave him, as long as he would just agree to quit seeing Crystal for a while each time she found out. Herb, on the other hand, could reassure Carol of her importance to him by temporarily suspending his illicit relationship, with much weeping and gnashing of teeth. The arrangement even extended to the illicit partner: Carol had "trained" Crystal to temporarily release Herb, knowing that in a short while he would sneak back.

The dance was maintained by dishonesty and deceit, highly toxic factors in a marital relationship. Yet each individual understood the distorted rules of the game. In fact, often in such "dances," if you ask any of the parties what will happen next, they can predict it with an uncanny accuracy, since they all know the steps.

When I first met with Carol, we explored her anger. She had none. She was numb, simply frustrated that she couldn't "raise her last little boy," Herb. She was looking at her mate through the eyes of a parent instead of spouse. The issue of terrible betrayal of an adult-to-adult agreement (the wedding vow) had never occurred to her because she was so busy parenting him.

I decided to tell Carol what I thought was the root cause

behind their dance together. I suggested maybe Herb didn't respect her because she had never gotten angry enough to earn his respect or to motivate them both to do things differently. The floodgates burst with wails and tears, and Carol was unable to consider the possibility rationally.

I like to think that she did consider the idea later, but I can't be sure, because they discontinued marital therapy at that point. Apparently the threat to their familiar steps was too great. Part of the tragedy of Herb and Carol's case was that they tried to rebuild the trust without first dealing with the anger and pain. They had the process backward. The result was a chain of events that repeated itself over nine years: revelation, repentance, and backsliding into adultery again. And it caused untold agony.

By her inability to get angry, Carol was preventing Herb from processing his grief and their mutual loss, which would be the key to his never cheating on her again. Unwittingly, Carol was prolonging the misery for both of them.

THE ONLY EFFECTIVE "GUARANTEE"

Upon disclosure of the most traumatic of marital fears, the unfaithfulness of their previously trusted mate, many spouses look desperately for guarantees that it will never happen again. Examples might include her insistence that he come home from work by a certain time, that he report each and every expense to her immediately, and other such structures, rules, and curfews. Although that is natural and understandable, such guarantees usually are artificial at best. They fail to address the root causes of the infidelity.

The spouse needs to face this difficult truth: ultimately, there are no guarantees. No matter how desperately she wants to be able to bank on the fact that the infidel will never stray again, no external scheme can provide absolute surety. What can be done, however, is something we'll examine in this chapter: that of having the infidel fully realize the hurt and loss his actions have caused. That internal motivation will provide more surety than any external restrictions ever could.

THE SPOUSE HOLDS THE KEY

In the highly charged emotional atmosphere following the affair's disclosure, the wounded spouse often becomes somewhat incapacitated, too confused to carry out even the most mundane tasks, such as caring for the house, normal grooming, appointments, and so on. In her grief, she often goes without eating, sleeping, or even caring for the children appropriately.

Note the relationship between the spouse's actions and the abilities of the infidel to enter the healing process, as noted in the chart below.

HOW THE SPOUSE "CONTROLS" THE RECOVERY PROCESS

As the Spouse . . .	The Infidel Can . . .
1. stops attacking and obsesses less	begin to relax; won't have to be the strong one
2. begins to grieve less	begin to feel his own pain and start to grieve
3. begins to forgive the infidel	begin to forgive himself

Notice that even though a major break in the relationship has occurred, the recovery process is still intimately linked with how the spouse responds. That seems to contradict what I said earlier: that both partners share responsibility for the affair's development in the first place. That still holds true—both partners need to identify their responsibility in establishing the environment that allowed the affair to occur. But now in the recovery and rebuilding scenario, the spouse definitely holds more power than the infidel. Not only does the spouse control "if" they will stay together, but she also controls the "when" of the recovery process at this point.

GRIEVING THE INFIDEL'S LOSSES

The initial rebuilding of trust in the marriage must start with identifying and grieving the losses that have occurred in the relationship. It is important for the spouse to see the infidel grieve. That is the best guarantee for faithfulness that the spouse can hope for—that is what will keep the infidel from building another emotional attachment like the one that led to the affair.

Second, grieving provides a sense of finality to the affair. It allows both mates to feel as if it is over and done with. When the infidel weeps in remorse and shows his sorrow in other ways, both mates can relax without worrying that the experience might suddenly repeat itself without warning. Put another way, one doesn't truly grieve over something that's not irretrievably lost. If the infidel is harboring a plan to pick up the illicit relationship later, he isn't too upset about giving it up now. Ironically, some spouses unconsciously send signals to their mates that they don't want them to grieve. That might sound surprising, but it happens for some of the following reasons.

1. Grief often signals a fundamental change in the marital relationship. Especially if the infidel is the kind of husband who has not been able to show much emotion in the past, his weeping will be upsetting for both parties. Such behavior may frighten the wife, and it probably isn't easy for him, either.

2. Intuitively, the spouse knows that the grieving infidel now needs her, yet she feels uncertain about providing comfort to the betrayer. To comfort this individual by whom she has been so deeply hurt might appear to let him off the hook prematurely. It might signal that things are OK, and she knows that they aren't! She is conflicted—she can't provide comfort for him and grieve for herself at the same time. At the same time, she may be haunted by the fear that if she does not comfort him, she may only drive the infidel back to his partner. The spouse thus walks that fine line of tension between keeping the infidel in the pain and out of the partner's bed.

3. The spouse may interpret the infidel's sorrow as a longing for the missing partner. She knows intuitively that the current miserable state of the marriage stands in sharp contrast to the idyllic private world created by the infidel and his partner. She knows that the infidel has just moved from heaven to hell, but she can't feel sorry for him quite yet.

4. Many times the family experiences (e.g., the demands of the children, schedules, dual careers, and so on) do not allow the couple to process their pain at the same time. When one grieves, the other thinks he has to stop his own grieving process and "be strong for the family's sake." That's unfortunate in one sense, because sometimes during the recovery phase, the mates should grieve together. Weekends apart from the children can be helpful in this process.

Though the spouse's pain is more easily understood (especially by outsiders), the infidel's pain is just as deep. That is especially true if the revelation of the affair is accompanied by a career or job loss, as is often the case with ministers and others we hold in high esteem, such as political office holders or candidates.

The apostle Paul talks about sexual sin as a sin against the self (1 Corinthians 6:18-19), and, seen in this light, infidelity certainly damages the perpetrator (the infidel) just as much as the victim (the spouse). The infidel needs to identify his injuries and feel the pain he has inflicted on himself.

It's helpful to develop an actual list of the infidel's losses. The following section addresses the possible losses. You might think of more or of particular adaptations to your situation.

THE LOSS LIST

The loss of self-respect. The infidel has to look in the mirror each morning, and the loss of self-respect can lead to serious depression.

The loss of the God-given boundary that was a natural defense against extramarital involvement. Once one has ventured into the waters of infidelity, it's easier to reenter them later. This is a perfect example of what God's Word exhorts us to be and do: "Be wise in what is good, and innocent in what is evil" (Romans 16:19).

The loss of a clear conscience in the sexual arena. Black marks on the infidel's conscience can occur before and after disclosure, and they represent a weight of guilt on his mind. That is compounded if there are adolescent children in the family who are struggling with their own emerging sexuality. Teens can wind up with a lot of anger in the face of such behavior by the infidel.

The loss of free and unhindered sexual expression with the spouse. Sexual play that had previously been innocent and something only they shared may be discolored by comparisons, shame, and disappointment. In place of sexual freedom, there is now a certain tentativeness and suspicion threatening to rear its ugly head. It reminds me of a country song (that genre seems to deal with infidelity quite regularly) titled "Don't Close Your Eyes." In it, the spouse asks the infidel not to fantasize about being with the partner—the mere closing of her eyes causes worry and suspicion in the spouse's heart. This worry can be worked out and minimized through therapy and many of the guidelines contained herein, but it's not easy.

The loss of trust with the spouse. Following disclosure and prior to reestablishing the trust, there is often no tolerance for tardiness or any of the other normal vicissitudes of life without provoking doubt and anxiety on the part of the spouse. Once betrayed, an individual is always suspicious, looking out for himself or herself, and refusing to assume the best. The infidel is, in effect, "guilty until proven innocent." That is a dark cloud to live under day after day.

The loss of natural openness between friends and acquaintances. Now the infidel is concerned about who knows what and how much. If they don't know, should they? If you decide to tell them, what do you say? How do you say it? There is tension in always being on the defense. It can pollute one's previously pleasant social circle.

A job change or loss. This always compounds the marital and family losses. It often brings about a new standard of living and even a different neighborhood, home, and school. Those changes alone are tough adjustments for most families, but to be forced to go through them under such circumstances makes the process all the more difficult.

The loss of being human and being able to have normal shortcomings. In a normal marital relationship each mate allows the other to have idiosyncrasies. They "cut each other some slack," provide unconditional love, grace, and so on. But once infidelity has occurred, there is no place for failure, at least initially.

The loss of the artificial world that the infidel had created with the partner. As stated previously, the marital relationship should have developed its "own little world" to make it special, but in its stead the infidel and partner created one. It was illicit, but nevertheless its loss generates a deep sense of sadness for the infidel.

Other unique losses. Any affair produces individualized losses, whether they be financial or emotional, or loss of reputation and career. Fill in the blank with your own unique costs.

SOME DOS AND DON'TS FOR BOTH MATES

In the grief process, there are some dos and don'ts. Talk them over with each other, and review them periodically.

1. *Don't* try to make it better. It will get better if both mates stay in the process, but if you try to fix everything prematurely, the process will be interrupted.
2. *Don't* provide too much reassurance that everything will be OK. A little is good, but too much can make the other circumvent the pain and just wait for the situation to magically fix itself.
3. *Don't* feel bad for not getting better more quickly. Give yourself all the time you need.
4. *Don't* feel responsible for making the other person weep. You aren't responsible for her feelings—her feelings belong to her, not to you.

5. *Don't* try to talk him/her out of weeping. Weeping is healthy at this point.

6. *Don't* distract him/her by an inappropriate touch or comment. Too much affection will distract both of you from the hard work at hand. And it may be only a ploy on your part to "fix it" and get out of the pain.

7. *Don't* speak to another person about the spouse's grief when it surfaces in a public place. Let the spouse speak for herself if she wants to speak at all.

8. *Do* reach out and touch your spouse appropriately when he or she is grieving. The timing and location of the touch should be appropriate, such as a pat on the back, a holding of the hand, or some other light touch. Ask for instructions from your spouse—what would she like? What would be comforting? Sometimes it is important for her to grieve alone with you sitting quietly by her side. Most of us want someone sitting nearby silently—Jesus did in Gethsemane; He asked His disciples to watch and pray.

9. *Do* provide tokens of appreciation—verbal and written notes of appreciation "for being there for me while I'm grieving." A thank you is helpful. If you need something else while you are grieving, tell your spouse. Don't expect him/her to read your mind regarding your needs.

10. *Do* be willing to talk about the grief. Plan specific times to discuss the pain that you share. Don't take the "phone tag" approach to grief discussions: "You want to talk, but I don't want to now. I wanted to yesterday, but you weren't available then." A good grief discussion can include topics such as, What was this particular episode about? What thoughts triggered it? What do I (or you) want to say, now that the grieving is over? What do you need from me as this wound heals?

11. *Do* be honest with friends and associates, should a grief episode arise at an inappropriate time. It does not have to be humiliating or embarrassing if it springs up unexpectedly. It is your spouse's emotional response to some thought that you probably have no control over. Allow your mate the space to react authentically to the crisis in his or her own way.

GRIEVING THE PAIN INFLICTED ON THE SPOUSE
WHEN THE INFIDEL WON'T ADDRESS THE TOUGH ISSUES

By now you may be saying, "Dave, all this sounds good, but

my infidel husband absolutely refuses to talk about our difficult issues. He says he just wants to forget that it happened and go on."

Such a scenario is unfortunately all too common. The infidel is stubbornly refusing to delve down into his heart and deal with the real issues. On one level, you can't force another adult to do anything he positively doesn't want to do. But on another level, you can do some things to break through the denial and get him to address the difficult emotions involved. You need to shake him out of his complacency and reluctance to do the hard work.

This technique is for the infidel who:

- refuses to work through the pain
- says the affair is over and wants to go on as though nothing has happened
- wants to do the hard work but can't seem to get started
- says it really wasn't his/her fault and won't accept his/her share of responsibility
- appears to be completely unrepentant and has only terminated the affair because it was uncovered or because it was necessary to save a career
- broke down initially but thinks that that was a sufficient fulfillment of his/her Christian obligations and doesn't want to process it further

If any of the above cases describes your situation, the following process, which I call "telling the story," could prove to be helpful. It is a special review of the affair from the spousal perspective and is intended to turn the stubborn infidel around to embrace the repair process that both parties need.

Warning: what I'm about to describe might get you riled! Some readers will not like it, because they will think it is inappropriate. It might appear to be vengeful (or at best, unnecessary). Many spouses reading this section will think they cannot do it. (Most, after reading about Nathan below, may wish that there was a prophet they could call on the phone to come over to carry out this task!) Remember, this assignment isn't for everyone; it is only for those spouses whose marriage partner refuses to do the hard work of recovery, and whose situation lines up with the criteria presented here. The experience of many people shows that this is a powerful way to evoke emotion from the infidel. And it's a biblically based maneuver, as we'll see below. But it does shock those who believe that the phrase "Don't rock the boat" is sacrosanct.

The purpose of this intervention is to provoke a necessary and desired emotional response rather than wait and see what happens naturally. It was developed in alcohol treatment circles to use when an alcoholic refused to acknowledge his/her need for treatment. Rather than allow that individual to fall to the bottom on his own, those doing the intervention "bring the bottom up" to the individual by giving him an ultimatum: either go to treatment or leave the family. The goal is that the infidel either acknowledges the need to work on repairing the relationship or acknowledges that it is over.

An intervention is always a powerful experience and is probably done best with help from a third party, such as your pastor, counselor, or a mutual friend. But if none is available and you believe the relationship is stuck, don't back down—the stakes are high enough here for courage to rise to the occasion; the future of your marriage is literally at stake. Individuals confronted each other for centuries prior to counselors and pastors, and God will help you do it now in your hour of need.

The purpose of telling the story is to help the infidel feel the pain he has inflicted on his spouse, and to lovingly motivate him into recovery, thus shattering the myth that simply running from the messy situation will "fix it." First we'll look at two modern-day examples. Then we'll look at two biblical ones.

In the modern-day examples, there are two routes you can choose:

1. By posing a "what if" scenario where the infidel imagines what he would feel like if the spouse had an affair with the infidel's golfing buddy, for example, or
2. By using a word picture that involves something dear to the infidel.

You may flinch at option 1, but believe me, it works. I need to stress how firm are the defenses in some infidels' minds against feeling the full effect of their infidelity upon their mate—and therefore you need a high-powered tool to penetrate those defenses. This method will do it in most cases.

When the spouse describes in graphic detail her being intimate with his best pal, the hair will stand up on his neck—she'll have his full attention! He may accuse her of "playing dirty pool" in posing such a scenario, but that's her opportunity to turn the tables by pointing out how dishonest (and therefore equally "dirty") his cheating was. And besides, hers is only a "what if" illustration; his actions really happened!

The principal goal of the intervention is for the spouse to communicate her hurt and to knock down the infidel's defenses, and it won't be easy to penetrate them. But it is possible. The point is to start the process of repentance, remorse, and reattachment lovingly. He must fully feel the weight of his actions before he can start the process of separation from his illicit relationship and reattachment to his mate.

The following letter illustrates the second kind of intervention, the word picture that involves something dear to the infidel. Letters work well in this setting because the infidel can't interrupt you and you can revise and fine-tune the message before the actual confrontation. A woman wrote the following letter to her husband, who did not want to process the affair. Fortunately it broke through his refusal to talk, and they were able to process some vital issues; but unfortunately, he chose not to return to the marriage. Again, none of these suggestions can be guarantees.

As you read this, think about what you would say in your unique letter, should you choose this method of intervention.

Dear Hank:

Back in the mid-'60s there was a boy who was just starting to notice things around him. At the top of his list of favorite things was cars—especially the Ford Mustang. His interest grew to the point where he spent a lot of time looking at Mustangs at every dealer who sold them.

Then one day, it happened: he saw the perfect one. It had been custom made and had every option the young man could dream of. He visited the lot every chance he had until finally in 1969 he was able to buy his dream car.

He was so proud! He spent countless hours caring for it—he washed and waxed it even more than was necessary. He vacuumed the inside and even kept the inside of the trunk spotless. He put much love into his car! Only the best chamois would touch his paint—an automatic car wash would never be acceptable. He applied the soapy water to the car carefully; it was like petting a favorite pet. He rinsed it with a cool, gentle mist. The drying and polishing were the most tender of rituals.

As he ran his chamois cloth over the shiny surface, he admired every inch of the body, every curve, and every piece of chrome. The car was so special in his heart that he pampered it until it shone like no other car in town.

The same rules applied for the engine's maintenance. Only the most expensive name-brand parts were purchased for this, his most valued friend. It never seemed to be work to care for his car, because dreams of its becoming a classic someday occupied his mind and made all the toil seem worthwhile.

The man became one with his Mustang. No one could know him without knowing his car. He talked about it constantly and took every opportunity to show it off. It truly was the joy of his life.

If his car could talk, she would say that all his attentions were wonderful. She would tell how special the strokes of the man's hands made her feel and how secure she felt because she knew that if he cared enough to treat her this way then he would protect her forever.

But one day, things changed. The devoted owner noticed a Mercedes driving down the block. He began eyeing it and, although he never intended to change loyalties, something about the other car attracted him. It wasn't completely new—it had had two other owners before him—but something about that Mercedes appealed to him.

He began neglecting the care of the Mustang. He didn't wash it quite as often, and trash even collected inside. Fortunately, only about six months passed before he realized what was happening. He was shocked by his own fickleness, so he took the time to clean things up on the Mustang. He stopped thinking about the Mercedes and again put his time and interest into his first love.

But as time passed, he found himself interested in other things. Friends, career, parties, and fun took up a lot of his time, and his Mustang became less and less important to him. The car started to get dirty and didn't even run all that well anymore.

If she could have, the car would have cried out for "the good ol' days." Periodically the man would sort of clean it up in a hurry or do a little tune-up, but his passion just wasn't there anymore.

The Mustang was still useful to him, so he kept it around to satisfy his needs. Occasionally someone would tell him what a great car he had and how fortunate he was to own it. He even got an offer or two to take it off his hands, and he gave some thought to it, but he never followed through with the sale.

Even though the Mustang was about to become a classic—it would be priceless if restored properly—all the owner could see was an aging automobile. For a short time he considered fixing it up to show it *in car shows, but it looked like too much work, and he was looking forward to a change when he would buy the Mercedes.*

By now he was so tired of looking at the beat-up Mustang that he just gave it away to a friend who saw its potential. Needless to say, the friend was thrilled.

Now he eagerly acquired the Mercedes and drove it every chance he got. He felt proud of himself that he had "moved up" to the German luxury car, and he tooled around town often.

It felt good for a while, but gradually the thrill went away, and he strangely found himself wishing for the old days of being with his Mustang. There were definitely good things about both cars, but the Mustang had been with him through so much in his life that she held a special place in his heart.

He considered briefly buying her back from the man he had deeded her to, but when he proposed this plan, his pal firmly declined. The new owner was in the process of restoring the Mustang and had even entered her in several upcoming car shows. There was no way he'd give her up as easily as the first owner had.

The man now sank into a deep and terrible depression, since he had given away his first love and was stuck with a third-time-around Mercedes. It was a good car to be sure, but it just wasn't the same as his old friend.

Hank, if you haven't guessed it by now, you are the car owner, I am the Mustang, and your mistress is the Mercedes. I want you to understand my feelings as our marriage has grown distant over these many years.

If you, like the car owner, feel like restoring your first love (and I sense you do, down deep), let's work at it together. Let's get some marriage counseling. It won't be easy, but together we can restore the brilliant shine our relationship once had.

Will you join me in doing the tough work to restore our marriage?

Love,
Mary

Such a letter, especially when it uses an interest significant to the infidel (i.e., substituting the Mercedes for the Mustang) can have powerful results.

Now we will look briefly at two biblical examples of intervention.

NATHAN'S STYLE

Nathan used a "what if" story that would touch David's feelings, one that would provoke pain and cause him to react. Nathan didn't just want David to say it was wrong; Nathan was looking to break David's secret wide open. He wanted David to see it from the other side, from the victim's point of view. Nathan's motivations were that justice be done and that, in love for David, he be restored to God and man. Those motivations certainly apply when approaching an infidel too.

David would have been on guard when Nathan requested an audience with him. Knowing Nathan's relationship with God, David might have suspected that Nathan even knew about his affair.

However, when Nathan approached the king with a story about a little lamb, David's guard was immediately dropped. That is part of the strategy of an intervention. If you lead with "How could you have—?" and other hystrionics, the defenses immediately go up.

Nathan asked David what he thought should be done to the man who stole the sheep, and David took the bait—hook, line, and sinker. David exclaimed, "The man who did this deserves to die!" (2 Samuel 12:5 NIV).

JOSEPH'S PATTERN

After their father, Jacob, died, Joseph's brothers feared for their lives and sent a message to Joseph begging for mercy. They had wrongly assumed that it was Jacob who had been protecting them and did not realize that Joseph had already worked through his anger at them and his desire for retaliation. His response to them is classic: "You intended to harm me, but God intended it for good" (Genesis 50:20 NIV).

In that beloved verse, we see all the characteristics of genuine forgiveness, and we can take that to heart as we approach the infidel. Let's look at his statement, applying it to the situation of the infidel and spouse.

"You intended to harm me, but God intended it for good."

TOWARD THE INFIDEL:

- It doesn't let the infidel off the hook.
- It doesn't excuse his behavior.
- It describes his evil intentions.
- It doesn't sugar-coat the pain he inflicted on the spouse.

FROM THE VICTIM:

- It requires a new attitude toward the infidel.
- It sees a new purpose in the original pain.
- It reaps a new benefit from experiences that were never viewed as beneficial.

GROUNDED IN TRUTH:

- It acknowledges God at work in the process.
- It supports the sovereignty of God in the midst of pain.
- It provides new hope that trauma can be turned in the exactly opposite direction of what the infidel had originally intended.

The attitude expressed by Joseph is the kind of attitude we are working toward in an intervention: true forgiveness of the infidel by the spouse. This kind of forgiveness protects the victim (the spouse) from generating new victims in her own generation; retaliation is out of the question. This kind of forgiveness provides internal guarantees that those who are close to us will never hurt as we have hurt—ever.

The brothers thought their father's *presence* was keeping them safe, when in reality it was Joseph's healthy *process* that kept them from reaping the retaliation they deserved. Joseph knew the high cost of forgiveness and wasn't even tempted to make them pay for what they had done.

Having said all that, however, we need to understand the process Joseph went through in order to be free from the spirit of retaliation. We may not choose to follow his example in every aspect, but it does provide a pattern for twentieth-century Christians who are hesitant to confront those who have injured them.

His story is worth reviewing in the context of marital affairs because it is a story of betrayal and abandonment—the essence of marital infidelity. Remember, this is simply offered as an option for the spouse who believes the infidel is "stonewalling" the recovery process.

When Joseph's brothers appeared on the scene in Egypt, they were not exactly welcomed with open arms. The list below spells out Joseph's responses to his brothers in those first couple of visits.

1. He accused them of being spies.
2. He threw them into jail for three days and three nights.

3. He brought them out of jail for further accusation.
4. He sent them home with their money returned to their luggage, thus terrorizing them even more and causing intense anguish throughout the course of the journey and the months that followed. They knew in their hearts that they would have to return to Egypt again and return the money.
5. He put his silver cup in their luggage, again confounding and confusing them.
6. Upon their return, he accused them again of being spies and of not paying for the grain, even though he knew their money was put back in their sacks deliberately.
7. He required them to bring their younger brother back to him—Benjamin, the apple of their father's eye—claiming that it would prove they were honest men and not spies. Furthermore, he required that they leave one of their number, Simeon, with him in case they didn't return.

Note that until that point Joseph had not revealed his identity to his brothers, nor did he direct any kind of statement of forgiveness toward them. It was only when the brothers begin to talk fearfully among themselves in Hebrew (Genesis 42:21-24) that Joseph broke down and wept twice privately, and finally he weepingly revealed who he was (45:1-3). The drama and anguish in this story make it one of the most dramatic narratives in Scripture.

At that last, critical juncture Joseph revealed his identity because he believed his brothers had finally experienced all the terror, anguish, abandonment, and betrayal that he himself had felt in the pit, on the camel train, in a strange country, in jail, and before Pharaoh. By then Joseph literally had put his brothers through everything he had experienced at their hands. They had to experience the same pain that he had experienced before he could release them. He had to know that they had somehow associated their present trials with what they had put their brother through as a boy.

Once Joseph believed that the brothers had felt firsthand the pain their actions had caused him, he no longer needed to "torment" them. The job was complete, the past was over, and he could release them from their guilt. I trust you're seeing the parallel to the infidel/spouse situation by now.

That is the purpose of telling the story to the stubborn spouse who refuses to process the pain caused by his infidelity. Telling the intervention story is not appropriate when the infidel *definitely* wants to leave the marriage. Its use must be restricted to an infidel who wants to stay in the marriage but refuses to work on the pain and is pretending that nothing has happened.

Once the spouse chooses to tell the story, the content, the timing, the preparation, and the style of delivery are all very important.

CONTENT OF YOUR STORY

As you begin to put your story together, remember that the purpose is to help the infidel feel both parties' pain. There is no perfect story: Nathan chose the story of a poor Israelite with only one sheep in contrast to a rich man who had many. Joseph chose to provoke fear and guilt and dread in his brothers' lives by making them relive parallels to his experience.

One of the most direct ways to get the story across is for the spouse to put together a verbal presentation of what it would be like for him/her to have an affair with the infidel's best friend. This would be an inappropriate approach prior to an affair. But now that the affair has occurred, all the protection that the marriage originally had is gone.

Telling the story, regardless of the method, is a brutal, straightforward attempt to break down the infidel's resistance. It's employed not to torture the infidel but rather to bring about restoration when prospects look especially dim. In some ways it's a no-holds-barred method but is necessary in many cases when the infidel's mind seems to be made up, and he is emotionally frozen.

The more graphically and intensely the spouse can tell the story, the more powerful its impact will be upon the infidel. Do not shy away from being direct. Anything you may describe has probably already been done by the infidel, and your marriage is at stake.

TIMING FOR THE STORY

Even as you put the story together, it is crucial that you consider your expectations.

- What do you hope to have happen as result of the story?
- What would be the most disappointing response?
- How would you handle that most disappointing case? What would you say?
- Why are you not willing to wait? Identify reasons for doing it now versus later.

The content is important, but timing is everything. Nathan chose a time when David was tender. God will give you that opportunity. Watch for a time when your infidel spouse is in a transition, such as David was at the birth of his child. Maybe he is feeling pensive, somewhat depressed, or detached. God will help you in this process; He hates divorce and is committed to restoring marriages.

PREPARATION FOR TELLING THE STORY

You might want to write the story in letter form to read to the infidel. That way his interjections cannot interrupt your train of thought.

If you decide to describe your having an affair with your spouse's best friend, do the following:

- Choose a friend who is meaningful to the infidel.
- Choose a friend whom you know something about so that you can personalize the story and make it realistic.
- Choose a setting and experience that have real possibilities; make it believable.

Next, choose the setting carefully in which you are going to deliver the story. Make it private so that you are both free to express yourselves without interruption.

Prepare in prayer. This is going to take courage and require the kind of timing that only God can provide.

Rehearse the story with a friend who will be critical yet supportive of what you are doing. Say it exactly as though you are saying it to the infidel. Put yourself into it completely. If you do not have access to a friend, put an empty chair in front of you and tell the story out loud to the empty chair. You need to hear yourself tell this story in all of its detail at least once.

STYLE OF DELIVERY

When you are ready to tell the story, ask your mate if you could have some of his or her time. Say that you would like to talk about the affair one last time. In return for some undivided attention, you can promise not to bring it up anymore. In other words, if he will listen to you just once more, he will be free of it, which in most cases is exactly what the infidel is looking for at this point. You should receive eager agreement for the session.

Ask in advance that he give you his full attention. That means no TV, newspaper, or time constraints facing you at the end of the story. In other words, this cannot be a "quickie" conversation—you'd rather wait than slip it in between his other commitments.

Tell him that you, too, want to put this behind you, but you haven't been able to do it yet and that you think that this session will help you as well.

If you have chosen to write it in letter form (and I would encourage you to), you will need to tell him that you have chosen to write your thoughts and you would like to read them, to get it just right.

Here's some critical advice before the sparks start flying and the smoke starts swirling: *Whatever you do, do not quit until the breakdown occurs.* As the story gets more intense, the infidel might try to thwart what he sees coming by interjecting objections, countercharges, and the like. At that point you might need to:

- remind him of his promise that he was going to hear you until you finish, or
- stop until he gives you his full attention once again (but don't be thwarted—insist on restarting where you left off), or
- slow down in your delivery for the full impact to be experienced—don't rush it, or
- wait before finishing if he begins to grieve so intensely that he cannot concentrate. This is part of the result you're looking for. Even though he may begin grieving, be sure to finish your presentation before you consider the session over. The complete story must be told for the long-term health of all parties.

Remember, this is your last chance. Drive the point home. *This is your one and only shot.* In many ways it's like cancer surgery: you need to cut out the cancer mercilessly for the sake of the patient, and in this case, there are two patients who are married to each other.

Don't settle for anything less than what you have been looking for from your mate. There is no purpose in holding anything back. Take this promise from God to heart and hang in there: "Be strong and courageous! . . . The Lord God is with you" (Joshua 1:9).

LOOKING AHEAD

With the rebuilding of trust comes a deeper level of relating, that of intimacy. Even though the spouse may feel that she will never be able to sleep with the betrayer again, or allow herself to be

held by him, it is possible to regain that lost aspect of your relationship.

It's not easy, but it is achievable. We'll look at this high goal in
the chapter that follows.

11

"And They Shall Be As One": Restructuring Intimacy

Angela was depressed—really depressed. In fact, she was borderline suicidal. She didn't know why, and her husband, Stuart, was equally puzzled. Their communication and sex lives were practically nil, and Stuart was worried. So he brought Angela in for counseling. *He* was doing fine, he said—it was *she* who needed the help.

I insisted that Stuart stay around for the first few sessions—I wanted to get an idea of their history together. After much discussion about various factors in their relationship, I began to find the clues I was looking for.

Stuart had indulged in a short Class II affair with his secretary five years earlier. Both Stuart and his wife vigorously assured me that they had gotten over it long ago.

Yet here was Angela about to end it all, with no apparent cause. I hypothesized to myself that their resolution of the affair left something to be desired and that there were still major factors left unresolved between them.

Angela claimed that she had forgiven her wayward husband, but I had a hunch that hers had been a surface-only forgiveness and that her depression was the result of buried hostility toward him. We went to work to try to find the answer.

Angela had grown up in a Christian home where anger was not allowed—in fact, it practically didn't exist. No one ever got mad; they all just got quiet. It was an unspoken rule that if you were angry you stayed away from everybody else in the family, lest you say something you would regret later. There was the accompanying attitude that feeling angry was sinful.

Stuart, on the other hand, grew up in an alcoholic family where everybody was angry all the time and said so—in no uncertain terms. At times, it was like World War III in his home.

When the two met at a small Christian liberal arts college, Stuart immediately fell in love with Angela's serene family. He had always wished for the even keeled emotional tone he saw there.

Angela, on the other hand, loved Stuart's emotional honesty and intensity—everybody always knew where Stuart stood. If he didn't like something, he told you so; likewise, if he was pleased, you knew that too. She soon became most proficient at pleasing him and enjoyed his approval almost constantly.

ANGER REGULATIONS

When Stuart fell for his secretary at work, Angela felt tortuously conflicted. She thought she should be angry at Stuart (or at the other woman, or at someone), but she couldn't figure out what she really felt. In hindsight, we can see that all the old rules about anger in both their families of origin came into play at that juncture.

From Angela's family of origin:

- If you're angry, keep it to yourself (internalization).
- Don't express your angry feelings in any way; such feelings are sinful (religious shame).
- Withdraw from everybody while you're angry—it's too dangerous to relate to anyone during that period (isolation).
- "Stay away from Angela—she's mad" (the flip side of the previous rule—others withdraw too).
- When you get tired of isolation, come back to the group, but pretend that everything's OK (denial and deception).

From Stuart's family of origin:

- Don't act angry; that's something only alcoholics do, not Christians (religious shame).
- Don't remind me of Dad's temper; I still hate what he did to me (rejection).

• Don't provoke my anger by yelling at me; no one will ever hurt me again, so I can't allow you to express any anger (fear and denial).

All of those "anger tapes" started playing in Angela's heart upon hearing about Stuart's affair, and they affected the marriage relationship. Her immediate reaction was to forgive quickly, because of her fear that Stuart might leave her and the children. She determined to go on as though nothing happened and be a "hero of God's grace." She kept a stiff upper lip in their church circle and was viewed as a paragon of virtue. People spoke with reverent tones about her amazing ability to "let bygones be bygones" in extending her forgiveness. (In hindsight we can see why they were so amazed—the forgiveness wasn't real. No wonder they thought it superhuman—it was!)

In her heart, however, Angela was dying a slow death. Stuart seemed appreciative of her quick forgiveness—after all, that was his style too: his slogans of "Move on," "Get over it," and "Don't look back" helped him to soon forget it too. He dropped his illicit relationship and arranged for his secretary to be transferred to a distant office, and she resigned rather than move. So all looked well from Stuart's point of view.

Little did he know that a growing depression was engulfing his wife and beginning to affect her health. When he finally brought Angela in for help, she had very little of herself left to consider her anger at Stuart. In fact, she had almost forgotten the affair. It took some digging to link her feelings of "frustration" with the incredibly swift processing of the betrayal. As I explained the process outlined in this chapter with her, however, the light began to dawn.

When Angela finally got angry and both she and Stuart began to grieve, it was like a huge festering sore that had finally been lanced. Their relationship worsened at first as the anger surfaced (*This is what I get for taking my wife in for help?* mused Stuart a little angrily). But when Angela finally expressed her rage and began to struggle toward forgiveness on the basis of her true feelings, instead of denial, she was able to approach forgiveness. In effect, she was moving toward forgiveness right through her anger, not by going around it. As a result, Stuart developed an entirely new respect for her.

When Angela chose to forgive her husband, Stuart knew it was for real this time, and he could therefore begin to grieve his losses. Angela discovered a whole new person—her real self—to share with her husband. At the end of that long and arduous process, they were able to stand before the congregation and share their testimony of healing without shame.

Stuart, who had begun to feel like a second-class citizen in the church, could finally begin to feel better about himself, because his sin had been fully recognized by the one he had hurt—his wife. The two have a newfound respect for each other, and the children are doing a lot better too.

But the best part is that they know for certain that they have forgiven one another. As a result, they know that their relationship is growing closer as time goes by, not more distant.

BURYING THE PAIN ALIVE

The central barrier to restructuring intimacy in the marriage is the issue of true forgiveness. Mutual forgiveness is the ultimate goal in affair recovery and the only foundation upon which healthy intimacy can be rebuilt. Yet you can't just forgive out of the blue. As we have seen, you must feel your anger and your losses. You must also fully understand the plight of your mate and of the marriage, and the "message" of the affair. Then and only then can you extend a lasting forgiveness to your mate.

FORGIVING TOO QUICKLY

One of the most frequently encountered barriers to such complete and lasting forgiveness is when some spouses want to forgive too early. We examined this in an earlier chapter in detail, but it bears repeating here because authentic forgiveness depends upon properly processing the offense.

Either because of her own family of origin background, her Christian beliefs, or the advice of some significant other in her life, the spouse often attempts to forgive immediately. The spouse who attempts to forgive too quickly actually buries the pain alive. She doesn't process it correctly, and she suffers the following losses:

- She never has a chance to forgive the infidel and thus experience the reconciliation that is key both to affair recovery and to long-term marital health.
- She will never be able to say, with Joseph, "You intended to harm me, but God intended it for good."

- She will always be in a one-up position over the infidel spouse ("At least *I've* never had an affair").
- She will never be able to develop intimacy in this relationship because the affair is an unresolved issue that will obstruct closeness.
- She will never be able to understand the message of the infidelity; and, as a result, the couple is always at risk of going through it again.
- She will always feel insecure and uncertain as to why the infidel chose to remain in the marriage. In later years she will often wonder whether she should have gotten out when she could have.
- The children will rarely ever respect her again (they sense that the pain and anger are still alive and unresolved). Believe it or not, the children commonly side with the infidel in later years. Why? My guess is that they instinctively know that the spouse needed to get good and angry and move toward forgiveness. Yet they didn't see that happen, and they tend to hold that against the spouse.
- She will never grow beyond where she is at the time of the trauma; she runs the risk of being emotionally "stuck" forever—or at least until she properly processes the betrayal.

THE BACKWARD BENEFITS OF EASY FORGIVENESS

Why would anyone forgive an infidel mate too quickly? Well, there are reasons a spouse does this, though not healthy ones.

Here are some of the payoffs the spouse receives for forgiving the infidel too easily.

- It maintains your innocence. You win admiration from friends and neighbors who appreciate the fact that you stayed with the straying infidel. You can feel good about yourself: *At least there is one righteous person in this family.*
- It maintains your self-image. After all, he had the affair; you were the faithful one. You don't have to look at any new information that might implicate you.
- It keeps the difficult rebuilding process at bay. It can serve as a defense mechanism that prevents you from working on potentially painful changes. It serves as a good excuse in case the infidel asks you to get involved in the process: "I've forgiven you; let's move on and forget it."

• It gives you the upper hand forever. You're the nice, forgiving spouse; he's the "no good rat who cheated." You have the power in the relationship—at least until the infidel decides to have another affair. Then you're on the hot seat again.

DISTINGUISHING BETWEEN DENIAL AND GENUINE FORGIVENESS

One of the big questions for the spouse to ask him/herself is, "How do I know if I'm actually practicing forgiveness or just denying my anger?" How can you be sure that you are actually letting go of the pain, rather than pushing it down inside, out of reach? How do you know you are becoming increasingly free of your pain and not just becoming free of its symptoms? Below is a chart that will help you sort through the difference between denial and genuine forgiveness.

Remember, forgiveness is a *process*; all the characteristics of genuine forgiveness will not always be present, but they should become increasingly apparent along the journey.

THE RECOVERY OF INTIMACY

A Class II, or entangled, affair, is always the result of an intimacy deficit in the marital relationship. Whatever personalized components there are in the message of this affair, it still boils down to a loss of intimacy before the affair occurred.

FOR THE SPOUSE

Denial of Anger Is...	Genuine Forgiveness Is...
Unawareness of feelings	Acute awareness of all feelings
No vacillations in attitude	Cyclical/seasonal vacillation in attitude
No vulnerability with mate	Complete vulnerability, at times afraid of the risk at stake
Overly predictable relationship, with tendency to gut it out, to "stay committed" (i.e., simply married) without much joy	Unpredictability at times—the normal roller coaster ride of a healthy marriage
No change in relationship style	Many changes, some of which are quite frightening
Focusing on projects outside the self	Focusing on the self and the marriage relationship
Acting out feelings, often injuring self and mate; or suppressing feelings	Ability to talk about feelings with mate
Nurturance received exclusively outside the marriage: from friends, children, job	Beginning to give and receive nurturance from mate
Emotional heaviness; nothing as good as anticipated	Freedom, exhilaration, feeling unbelievably alive at times
Never being thankful for the fallout of the affair	Gratefulness for the changes the affair has brought into the marriage and the infidel's life
Refusal to discuss the affair with others who could benefit—intense feelings of shame	Ability to discuss the affair relatively pain-free, given appropriate processing and the passage of some time
Less respect than ever for the infidel; carries cloaked disdain for him/her	Greater appreciation developing for mate
Mental accusations of multiple infidelities	Healthy, biblical sexuality; children benefit from new levels of family intimacy
Continually placing sole responsibility for condition of marriage on infidel	Growing awareness of his/her own shortcomings that contributed to the affair; shared responsibility
Victimized feelings ("one down") or superior feelings ("one up")	Healthy sense of wholeness without comparing self to infidel—growing mutual self-respect

Part of the lure of the affair for the infidel was the opportunity to be himself (herself) in his own little private world that he constructed with the partner. He desperately needed that freedom to be himself and be accepted and appreciated. He didn't feel that he had to pretend or stay within a certain mold, since it was a brand-new world with no rules except those he chose to create with the partner.

Part of the recovery process is to identify what was missing in the marital relationship and repair that loss. You need to rebuild that own special world you had when you were dating and in the early days of the marriage. Everybody needs this special set-apart world—it's a big part of what makes marriage special.

To continue to rebuild the trust and intimacy in the relationship you will need to integrate the "message" of the affair into your new way of relating. Following is a four-part integrating process designed to reestablish the intimacy that was crushed by the infidelity. Take each step as you both can handle it, adapting it to your own situation.

REVIEW CONTRIBUTING FACTORS

Factors both inside and outside the marriage combined to cause the affair, and it's helpful to review them. I examined many of them in chapters 4 and 5, and it might be good to review those, finding out which affected your marriage union.

A special factor to review is the family tree. "Rats don't have mice" goes a popular saying, and affairs do tend to run in families. I'd wager a guess that there have either been full-blown affairs in your family tree or at least "close calls." It is imperative that you go back to your parents and grandparents to find out your history.

That "historical research" doesn't excuse you or your mate's behavior; it just helps you understand the setting in which it occurred. Knowing your family heritage can help you change it in your generation so that you do not pass it on to your kids. If teenagers (who are beginning to understand adult feelings) can see their parents grieve and rebuild their marriage following the infidelity, that will help them not repeat the cycle when they get married.

Once you've surfaced the information (it may take some digging), talk it over with each other. How does the infidel feel about it? The spouse? What attitudes were modeled to your young soul as a child that you can identify? Make it a matter of prayer together, and keep talking about it. Make the information yours, not just something you read in a book!

REHEARSE WHAT DREW YOU TOGETHER ORIGINALLY

This is a time to focus on the two of you, on your special history. It's time to get nostalgic, to remember "the good old days."

The two of you did not *have* to choose each other; you were attracted to each other initially for many reasons. Explore that collection of reasons, and identify the various components. Talk about those initial experiences together—the dates you had, the places you went, the things you enjoyed. Review those, because it was during that initial dating stage that you began to trust in each other in the first place.

As you begin to rehearse and redo similar trust-building experiences (I recommend you even go on some of the old jaunts again), you will find that your feelings of trust will start to return. You will find that, even though the infidel and partner built their own experience together, there is still an overwhelming amount of history that only the two of you share. This is your story.

Many things can help you get in touch with those important memories:

- old pictures, photo albums, and scrapbooks
- time lines (charts where you list things chronologically)
- date lists (write out all the things you did that you both recall)
- revisiting the old places—even journeying across the country is helpful (you can take pictures of old haunts and develop your scrapbook, which may have been neglected for a while; in fact, further developing that old book may become a metaphor for this stage of recovery: putting time and energy back into your marriage exclusively)

One of the traumas of recovering from an affair is that the spouse often thinks about the new history that the infidel and partner have built together. Even though that is true, the memories of that illicit history will dissipate over the course of time, especially as you begin to reinvest in your relationship. That is exactly why the reconciling couple needs to rehearse and remember what drew them together.

DOING IT DIFFERENTLY: REBUILDING
YOUR OWN SPECIAL WORLD

It's difficult, especially for the spouse, to admit that her husband (or wife) started to build a special world that excluded her. It's so repulsive that sometimes the spouse tries to ignore the infidel's need for that world. But it's better to look at this need squarely and take positive steps toward rebuilding your world together.

Start going out on dates again—find a baby-sitter if you need one and go romance each other again! You'll both love it, you both need it, and you can make it fun. Try to cast off some of the old patterns (e.g., he never wanted to go to the symphony, or she never went hiking), and try doing it differently. Remember, this is a world of your own making, and you can find new freedom as you put your relationship back together again.

Surprise each other with little gifts or notes hidden in the dresser drawer or on the dashboard of the car. You can make these new ways of relating deep (late-night heartfelt talks) or playful (taking your mate on a surprise hot-air balloon ride at dawn) or sexy (fill in the blank here—this is a Christian book!)—anything you two might enjoy. Keep in mind your mate's love language.

The idea is to rekindle the flame that you once had. With God's help, your own creativity, and the other suggestions for rebuilding, you can rebuild that special world.

SHARE YOUR INTIMATE SELF

New identities: the red sports car and other changes

It's standard fare for stand-up comedians, but it's sad when you really think about it. The guy who, for thirty years of marriage would never think of doing anything but drive the same car slowly and deliberately to work and back for thirty years, suddenly begins to tool around town with sexy young blondes in a new red Porsche!

Yet caricature differs only slightly from real life: one of the common reports from the spouse in an affair is the complete change in behavior in the infidel as expressed with the partner. For example, with the spouse, the infidel never talked; with the partner, he talked for hours. With the spouse, he never read poetry; with the partner, he not only reads it—he writes it! There are dozens of examples: with the spouse, he never took walks, never had barbeques in the park, never spent lazy afternoons in a motel, never bought shiny trinkets for gifts, or planned rendezvous, but with the partner, he does all those things. It's comical in one way but sad in another.

Usually the illicit partner sees a very different person in the infidel than the spouse had come to see over the many years in the marriage. Yet that side of the infidel's personality needs to be revealed. It is a part of his psyche and of the marriage relationship that the couple has allowed to atrophy.

It is true that different people bring out different sides of our personalities, but an affair so opens up a marriage and the individuals in the marriage that there is almost unlimited access to the psyche of both mates. In affair recovery, we need to take advantage of that unique view into the other's needs and turn something bad into a growth opportunity.

Reveal yourself

One of the ways to reveal who you are and how you became that way is to talk nonstop about yourself for twenty minutes. This self-revealing exercise is usually nonexistent in marriages but extremely frequent in affairs. Talking about who you are is part of the central fascination on which the friendship builds in an affair.

At first, individuals are afraid to initiate this kind of activity with their marital partner. They think it's boring, selfish, or even narcissistic, but it doesn't have to be. They also may be uncertain about how they will be accepted, or they may suspect that what they say will be used against them.

Resist those fears and try it. Remember, lack of deep communication is usually part of the message of the affair. We all want to reveal who we are, and we all want to be known by someone who loves us and accepts us unconditionally.

Choose some safe topics. The following list might be helpful.

- Your earliest set of memories
- Grade by grade in elementary school
- My first boyfriend/girlfriend or first date
- My happy childhood memories
- My birthdays—happy and unhappy
- My favorite teacher and all of my memories about him/her
- The first time I drove a car
- My first car accident or traffic ticket
- My first kiss, job, and so on
- The favorite child in my family, why he or she was the favorite, how I felt about that, experiences and feelings I shared with him/her
- My favorite parent, grandparent, aunt, uncle, cousin
- All the houses I lived in; my craziest neighborhood friends

- All the schools I attended
- The longest walk I ever took
- The ways I always spent my allowance as a kid
- My parents' favorite sayings and how they used them; which ones I liked and didn't like
- Things that I would have changed if I had been the parent in my family of origin
- The favorite year of my life
- The age I would like to remain forever
- Any others you think of

All of those experiences have feelings attached to them. Share with your mate how those subjects made you feel. That is the part that is important to tell at this point in your relationship. Facts are helpful; perceptions are important; but feelings are crucial to reestablishing intimacy. Feelings form the core of intimacy—that special closeness that assures you that, although your mate knows you and sees inside of you, he/she still loves you and accepts you completely.

One of the best ways to do this exercise is for each mate to take turns on successive days talking about himself/herself. The wife might do it one day; the husband the next.

Regarding the proper sequence of the above four steps, only the first one is really important to do first—exploring your family history. The other three can be done more loosely. You might rehearse some of your history together, then share some of your intimate self, all the while working to restore your special little world. Whatever helps the two of you to reconnect is the thing you need to do. The order isn't important, just that you cover these four areas.

FINAL WORDS TO THE SPOUSE

On many days following disclosure, you might wish that your infidel spouse had not disclosed his ugly secret. You might hate your spouse more for telling you than you hate him for actually having the affair! You might wish that you were still in denial and didn't know the truth—after all, ignorance is bliss.

Those reactions are common, so don't let such illogical feelings throw you; they're part of the normal roller coaster ride at this point. In one of your more serene moments, consider the following truths regarding your mate. They may take a while to assimilate, but eventually, as your anger subsides and reattachment begins, you will be able to embrace them. They'll help you move toward forgiveness. If the infidel is starting to express true sorrow for his actions and isn't just playing games by suggesting he wants to repair the marriage, the following truisms will apply.

THE INFIDEL HAS PAID FOR THIS LONG ENOUGH

It's true, even though you might not believe it right now: if the infidel wants to return to the marriage, his pain is unbelievably excruciating.

You can't make him pay for this any more than he already has. He has risked all that he is and has to disclose his secret to you; now is your opportunity to repair things. Resist the temptation to flog him emotionally beyond normal and healthy expressions of anger.

REMEMBER THE INFIDEL'S COURAGE

This is the greatest risk any person could take in a relationship: to have actually betrayed the relationship and then both admit it and say that he wants to return to the relationship. It's the most courageous thing a person in his circumstances could do.

Few people have that kind of courage. Most of us hate pain so much that we opt for secrecy over honesty and transparency; your mate hasn't. That shows how badly he wants you and the relationship back. Sure, he's guilty, but he's showing you the value he places on his relationship with you by disclosing it and expressing his desire to come back.

THE MESSAGE HAS CHANGED

As discussed in chapter 8, every affair has a message to it, and that usually includes some kind of intimacy deficit. Realize that by disclosing the affair, your infidel spouse is telling you that the message of the marriage has changed. He is saying by his actions that he wants to regain intimacy with you. He wants to get back to where you were when you two got married. That is a major message, and you need to give it your full attention.

TAKE YOUR TIME

You have every right to feel overwhelmed, out of control, enraged, and practically crazy when the affair is disclosed. Don't put the pain away too quickly; take your time to finish the process as outlined in these pages.

Remember that Jesus in the Garden of Gethsemane took all the time that was available between the Last Supper and His arrest to work on the terrible emotional upheaval He was experiencing.

Taking time is healthy. You don't want to make decisions relating to others until you have worked through your own turmoil in this most important of crises.

Now that the affair has been disclosed, you know the truth. For the first time, your relationship has the potential for genuine intimacy. You will have to work through the entire recovery process whether or not you stay in the marriage. So get started. You might be pleasantly surprised.

HANG IN THERE; YOU WILL MAKE IT

As you and your mate restructure the intimacy in your marriage, realize that it's going to be two-steps-forward, one-step-backward progress. Much turmoil will remain to be dealt with.

Difficult days still lie ahead. But keep this thought firmly in mind: you are in *the process* of recovery. It won't happen overnight; in an ultimate sense you'll never be completely over the affair. Trauma always changes people, and it should.

The affair and recovery will change both of you, and as a result will change your relationship. One infidel husband had this to say upon looking back at his recovery:

> I never thought Carole could forgive me. But today our relationship is stronger than ever. I thank God for pulling us through, using Christian counseling and supporting friends to help us restore our precious relationship. I'm especially grateful for the difficult circumstances that made me face something ugly in myself: that I was seeking personal fulfillment in sex. What a foolish strategy that was. I didn't need a change in partners; I needed to change myself! As a result of my realization and her forgiveness, today Carole and I enjoy a closeness I would have thought impossible before the affair.

The fact that that husband can give such a testimony after suffering through months of uncertainty and turmoil in his marriage warms my heart like no other words.

GO AHEAD, WADE THE DEEP WATERS

More than any other message, I want to communicate hope to you. If you're willing to wade into the deep waters, God will help you put the pieces of your broken relationship back together. You can survive—even thrive—in the wake of infidelity. And I pray that you'll try, starting today.

SECTION 3:
SPECIAL CIRCUMSTANCES

12

TO TELL OR NOT TO TELL? THE SECRET AFFAIR

Remember the story of Bill and Gwen from the beginning of chapter 2? Bill was the business traveler who met a fellow traveler one night on the road in an empty restaurant. Bill's was a one-night stand, and, as you remember, he could not bring himself to disclose it to his spouse, Gwen. As a result, their relationship drifted off into the sunset of mediocrity, with a cool distance dominating their interactions with one another.

Years later, Bill found himself sinking into a strange depression, something he couldn't shake. His performance at work was suffering dangerously, and as he tried to get closer to Gwen during his "down" times, she pulled away, losing herself in increasing busyness, which served to keep her away from Bill's seeming bottomless pit of need.

Why can't Bill just snap out of his blues? Gwen would think angrily. *He's acting just like a great big baby. And it's spoiling our later years together—now that the kids have moved out, these should be the best years of our lives. Instead, it's just one big pity party.*

Worse, Gwen found herself strongly attracted to the vice president at the bank where she worked. It didn't burst into an affair, but she found herself asking for consultations with him more often than necessary. She also found herself fantasizing about him, and that worried her.

Bill sought counseling for his depression. As he and I worked on uncovering the roots of his emotional slump, we found that his first hints of depression seemed to have occurred immediately following his one-night stand. He had long since almost forgotten about the sexual slip-up and in no way had connected the depression with it. But as we continued to talk, the light began to dawn in his mind. He came to understand that his decision to cover it up with Gwen had created an emotional distance between him and his spouse that, taken with other factors, was coloring his world blue.

But even as Bill got excited as he found the roots of his depression, he got depressed about the obvious conclusion: he needed to tell Gwen about his affair. He couldn't face telling her right now, and therefore he felt trapped. He couldn't tell her, yet not to tell would mean more years of depression. For some time he agonized over his decision.

Finally, Bill resolved to tell Gwen about the affair. The conflicting emotions were just too much for him; he had to get his dark secret off his chest and "come clean" with his mate.

Gwen wasn't sure how she felt about the revelation. At first, she wished he hadn't told her, then she revealed that she had often suspected Bill of fooling around. That comment floored Bill, who thought he had covered up so well that no one could suspect him.

When his wife revealed her attraction to the vice president at work, Bill really got worried. He was glad it hadn't blossomed into an affair, but began to see the wisdom of coming clean. In fact, he felt that they were now on common ground, having both experienced that emotional entanglement that precedes sexual involvement with illicit partners.

Counseling sessions included both Bill and Gwen, and we worked through the affair as outlined in this book. They risked the truth with each other, cried together, felt anger and grief, and today are stronger than ever in their marriage.

But Bill definitely had to work through the pain of all those "lost years" when he had hidden his past from himself and his spouse. They could have built their relationship so much during those years; instead they both suffered lost opportunities for intimacy with each other and with their children. The tinge of deceit had colored those years, and Bill felt terrible about not having been honest with Gwen before now.

WHO NEEDS THIS MATERIAL?

This segment is designed for both infidels and spouses whose situation is different from the one assumed throughout this book. In the main part of the book, the spouse knows of the affair at one point or another. In this section, the spouse does not know.

- It's for the infidel who has never told his spouse but wants to.
- It's for the infidel who does not want to tell his spouse but needs to.
- It's for the infidel who thinks he can just go on pretending it doesn't matter if he tells or not, who thinks he's doing fine by hiding the secret.
- It's for the infidel who still has his illicit relationship going on the side (whether it's steady or on-and-off), who thinks he can't end it but wants to.
- It's for the spouse who has suspected her mate of infidelity for many years to one degree or another but has never confirmed that suspicion.

KINDS OF SECRET AFFAIRS

FROM THE INFIDEL'S VIEWPOINT

"Trapped" in an ongoing affair

In some cases the infidel would like to be extricated from the affair, but, due to many possible factors, feels that he "just can't." He feels "trapped," even though objectively he isn't. He may fear blackmail by the partner should he break it off; he may feel an obligation to the partner since he's carried on for so long or if the partner especially needs him; he may be deathly afraid of the fallout of admitting it to his usually explosive spouse, and so on.

Physical symptoms in the infidel are common: nervousness, ulcers, and migraine headaches. He will often try to medicate the pain by beginning to drink (or increasing his intake), abusing drugs (prescription or recreational), or requiring sleeping pills to fall asleep. The infidel, in other words, is caught between a rock and a hard place, from his viewpoint.

He may try strategies other than the "medicating the pain" route; it's not uncommon for the infidel to actually begin another affair with a new partner, just to get out of the current one!

Or he may be so miserable that he returns to the spouse (without disclosing the affair), who becomes the source of nurturance and affirmation he so desperately needs now. In fact, the spouse may become that exciting "other woman," effectively flip-flopping the roles. It is in this kind of setting, where one (i.e., the infidel) wants out and the other (i.e., the partner) desperately wants to stay that the "fatal attraction" syndrome develops. That term is taken from the movie of the same name in which the partner tries to murder the infidel when he seeks to drop her and reunite with his wife. The partner in essence attempts to take the infidel down with her, thinking, *If I can't have you, neither will anybody else.*

It's a miserable time for this infidel, and sometimes he will seek counseling at this point, even without disclosing the affair. That's a healthy response, as it can serve as an intermediate step that can help him move toward disclosure and full recovery.

If you are an infidel reading this section and are in the midst of this process, I encourage you to seek assistance soon. A serious split is developing in your personality as you continue your illicit relationship, and the longer you continue it, the more your partner will be able to manipulate and control you, prolonging your agony.

In remission but with occasional relapses

A long-term secret affair may run for years, on and off with relapses. It occurs commonly in business circles, perhaps at an annual trade show at which the infidel and partner always meet, or in professional circles at annual conventions.

There is not much personal contact in between those occasions, since the infidel and partner often live in different cities. That makes it easier for the infidel to minimize the significance in his/her mind. It's almost as if the affair doesn't even exist for long stretches at a time.

But such a pattern in no less destructive. The smoldering embers are still burning; it's just that the smoke diminishes with regularity. That's why firemen continue to hose down a structure, even toppling charred walls, after the fire's "out"—they want to find the hidden pockets of embers and put them out 100 percent!

In some ways the off-and-on pattern resembles the "destabilization" portion of the normal infidel's curve (see phase 3 of the chart on page 107), but there is an important difference. In that phase both parties (infidel and partner) alternate between wanting to maintain the relationship and wanting out of it. In this pattern, however, both parties don't bother anymore with thinking about getting out; they have an unspoken agreement to maintain the affair. The secret is then insulated by the thinking *This fire is almost out, This relationship is not a problem,* or, *I could leave it whenever I want to.* The infidel wrongly thinks he's in total control of his passions and actions.

Affair secretly terminated but never processed

Sometimes both the infidel and partner accept the ending of the affair, but it's still secret from the spouse. The tryst becomes encapsulated within the infidel, often with detrimental results.

If you are the infidel and find yourself in this position, you need a good reason to refuse to disclose the affair to your spouse. For example, if you are a female infidel and you fear abuse or a similar violent reaction upon disclosure that could threaten you or your children, then it might be wise not to reveal this secret without further counsel and direction.

Another extenuating circumstance that might (but only in very rare cases) require the old affair to remain secret is if it would destroy your spouse's career. But beware of thinking, *I need to protect my spouse; he (she) can't deal with reality.* That is often an excuse to protect yourself from painful interactions. Make sure that you have worked through the issue appropriately before you decide not to disclose. In almost all cases (I'm talking more than 99 percent here) it's better to come clean. Otherwise marital health is practically unattainable, and you'll be at risk for another affair.

FROM THE SPOUSE'S VIEWPOINT

Suspected but unconfirmed

Maybe you aren't wondering whether your mate is cheating on you now, but you do wonder whether he ever did in the past. You have lingering doubts that periodically surface and then fade. You have long periods without any doubts, then an event or combination of events triggers those nagging fears. *Did he or didn't he?* That question will, at times, cause uneasiness, sleepless nights, and create distance between you and your mate. Even when you ask your mate about it and he denies it, your nagging doubts refuse to go away.

You may want to believe the best of your spouse, but you are uncertain about what to do. You have a lot of unanswered questions. You may even begin to doubt your own perceptions—you can get to the place where you feel as if you're the one going crazy! You want to know, but you don't want to know. Many times you will generate your own (acceptable) answers to your questions, just to have some answers and a basis to continue to trust and believe in your mate. But you're never quite sure.

Three choices

If you find yourself in this category, you need to choose one of three options:

1. Do I want to pursue this and find out the truth, whatever consequences it may bring?
2. Can I honestly put this doubt away and let it go for now, with the assurance that when it surfaces again, due to my spouse's behavior, I will pursue it to the very end?
3. Am I going to remain in this unknowing state forever, turn the other cheek, and tell myself this truth: that whatever my mate is doing is his responsibility, that I cannot control him, change him, or make him do anything different?

I recommend them in the above order of preference. It's always best to deal in truth; however, options 2 and 3 are available to you.

If you should choose option 3, you will also have to make a decision about what you will do about sexual activity between you and your spouse. In this day of AIDS, marital sex with an infidel partner can be deadly. At the very least, it will make you highly susceptible to various sexually transmitted diseases, often with lifelong implications. I strongly suggest that you have your spouse tested for HIV infection and refrain from unprotected intercourse until you have the results.

You may need to choose option 3 for now, due to family circumstances, such as the age of your children, your health, your readiness to do the hard work of recovery, and so on. But that doesn't mean that you have to stay in option 3 forever. You might find that you have unknowingly exercised option 3 for a number of years, but after reading this book you have decided that you want to pursue option 1.

Don't berate yourself for not choosing option 1 sooner—you probably didn't know enough about affairs to step up to the plate and deal with it until now. Maybe you didn't have enough energy to pursue it sooner.

The difference between option 3 and option 1 can be summed up in the word *control*. In option 3, you still have some sense of control (even though you know that you'll probably have to face the truth someday). In option 1, you have none; you will pursue truth, regardless of where it leads. You will accept the consequences that it brings, knowing that the truth shall set you free.

Each spouse has to decide for himself which option to pursue; there is no right or wrong answer to this predicament.

BENEFITS AND CONSEQUENCES OF DISCLOSURE

In their heart of hearts, most infidels want to disclose their treachery but are afraid of the consequences. True, there are consequences to be borne, and they can be very difficult at times. But there are also benefits. I've developed a chart to help the infidel see the whole picture.

		AFFAIR DISCLOSED	
		YES	NO
PROCESSED	YES	RESOLUTION Protection from future affairs Beneficial changes in both mates	DISTORTION Distorted marital intimacy Ongoing disappointment with marriage
AFFAIR	NO	FORECLOSURE No benefits of disclosure Unresolved individual anger	STAGNATION High potential for future affairs

The chart has four categories, or cases:

1. *Upper Left-Hand Quadrant*—The affair has both been disclosed and processed by the couple. This is the ideal case, as the result is *resolution*.
2. *Upper Right-Hand Quadrant*—The affair has not been disclosed, but it has been processed (to a limited degree) by the infidel. The result is *distortion*. This is frequent with secret affairs. As mentioned above, the infidel is often afraid of the results if he confesses.
3. *Lower Left-Hand Quadrant*—The affair has been disclosed

but not processed. This is often the case where the infidel is discovered before he decides to confess. Unfortunately, most couples don't seek help in processing this major break in their relationship, and the result is what I call *foreclosure*. It's almost as if the curtain is going down on the marriage, with smoldering anger and resentment gradually choking the marital bond.

4. *Lower Right-Hand Quadrant*—The affair is both still secret and unprocessed. The result is *stagnation* in the marriage. It's a slow death.

CONSEQUENCES

Most infidels' fear about returning to the marriage revolves around the negative consequences of disclosure. That fear often fuels its own obsession in the infidel, hindering him/her from addressing the tough issues.

As a method for decision making, I encourage you to write down on a piece of paper any consequences of disclosure you anticipate. Think hard about it; reflect on the impact of disclosure upon every family member—in your immediate family, your family of origin, and the extended family. Consider the consequences on the job, in your social circle, among your closest friends, and so on. Leave no stone unturned.

When you think you have listed all the consequences, go back and rework the list again. You will probably have less than eight items on your list. Even though some of them might be more severe than others, none is insurmountable. Even though some might be fearful to you, there is a way to get through them.

BENEFITS

Now turn your attention to making a benefits list. To most infidels that sounds like too much to hope for, so let me help you get started. Write these down on the sheet of paper, then add additional ones that you think of that are unique to your situation.

1. You will be taking the first step toward true intimacy—real, honest-to-God intimacy—with your spouse since before you strayed, which may have been a very long time.
2. You will finally be free from the pall of deceit, with nothing left to hide.
3. The message that you have always wanted to discuss in your marital relationship can be brought out into the open.

4. You will have a renewed sense of self-respect and release from shame. You'll be able to look yourself in the mirror again, without humiliation or self-loathing. A load may be lifted from your shoulders when you finally come clean.

5. You will be free to grow—no more looking back over your shoulder, no more skewed perceptions.

Some of you are already struggling with this concept; it seems ludicrous to you that benefits could line up against (and even outweigh) negative consequences, since you've been obsessing for so long about the negatives. It's enough to make you put the book down, but before you do, here is another tool to help you sort through this process of disclosure.

Worst Case/Best Case

Look at the chart below. Here is your opportunity to look squarely at the possible outcomes of disclosing your affair, without having to go through it right now. Write in the appropriate spaces the outcomes that are actually possible and probable. They could range from "My wife will shoot me/run home to her mother/throw me into the eternal doghouse" to "My wife will be upset initially but will eventually get over it, and we can restore our lost relationship." Match the exercise to your particular situation.

If I Refuse to Reveal the Affair

BEST CASE   *WORSE CASE*

If I Do Reveal the Affair

BEST CASE   *WORSE CASE*

Adapted from discussion in Emily Brown. *Patterns of Infidelity and Their Treatment* (New York: Brunner/Mazel, 1991).

Take all that you've learned by reading this book, and go for it. Be brave and honest about both the benefits and the consequences of confession. Unless your spouse has a history of homicide, suicide threats, or physical abuse, it's always best to be honest and confess.

This exercise does not require you to go home immediately and "spill the beans." Rather, the decision to disclose your affair is one that you have to make sooner or later. It should, for your own health and for your spouse's, be sooner rather than later, but it also should be done appropriately, when there is time to process the pain.

Obviously revealing your affair shouldn't be done in a public place or just before you leave for work! It might be best accomplished with a third party present, such as your pastor, counselor, or a close friend.

Disclosure is a time of major emotional upheaval for everyone, especially for the Christian, as his conscience and the Holy Spirit convict him. It may very well compare to Christ's agony in the Garden of Gethsemane. There might be some comfort from the Scriptures or from a friend's intercessory prayer for you during this time, but don't be disappointed if there is no relief immediately. This is not the time for relief—it's a time to come clean with your spouse, with God, and with yourself. This is a time to feel the pain that will keep you from repeating the affair ever again. The benefits will follow later.

Whatever you do, don't delay in making the decision. Though there is nothing easy about confession, it never gets any easier with the passage of time.

13

EMOTIONAL AFFAIRS: HOOKED, PLAYED-OUT, AND DESPERATE FOR RELEASE

*A*uthor's note: The following is excerpted from an eight-month correspondence between the author and an infidel caught in an emotional (i.e., nonsexually consummated) affair. Allowing his heart to be exposed like this, the infidel, Don, who is a pastor, hopes that others will be able to benefit from his overwhelming pain. Don also wants the reader to realize that this kind of experience is not necessarily due to an extremely dysfunctional marriage, but rather can spring up from everyday, run-of-the-mill marriage relationships. Finally, Don wants us all to know that just like "getting involved" with the partner is a process, so also is "getting out." Both the infidel's name and his church have been changed.

. . . [In looking back, I think that] our marriage was not fraught with problems and difficulties that led to my seeking refuge or solace in another. [I asked myself,] Was it a mid-life crisis? Was it my feeling of power [resulting from my successful] pulpit ministry here at Grace Church? Was it simply the result of my pride, believing that I was untouchable in this area? Was it simply ignorance—and before I knew it, I was "hooked"? Maybe a combination of all of the above, or some other factors? It has been a mystery to me in terms of my own insensitivity to what I was doing (forsaking my wife and replacing her with another, who was more readily available every day). . . .

[Dave,] thanks again for taking the time [to respond to] my letter. I only have one last question. I realize that everybody is different and there are no hard-and-fast rules that apply to each person; however, I am having trouble with [my lack of] patience. I know your book mentions the recovery phase takes as long as the affair did, but at times I become impatient and want to be released from her (the partner). I am simply amazed at the powerful pull that this [illicit] relationship has had on me—and now that I'm pulling back, it's hard to wait for the attachment to subside. I want it to happen quickly, so I can get on with my life apart from any dependence on her. . . .

Dave, I continue to be amazed at the powerful emotional hook that has been implanted internally. My life continues. I meet my daily responsibilities at home, at work, and at church; however, the "hook" is still there. I do pray as I continue to live obediently before God that He will disengage me emotionally, because, unlike a fisherman unhooking his catch, I cannot unhook myself so easily. . . .

As I think about this emotional attachment, I have become more aware of the fact that my partner touched some part of me that [was very needy and had been denied for some time].

Because of my excellent physical relationship with my wife, I know that my response to Janice was not the "lust of the eyes"—maybe it was more the "lust of the soul." I don't know what kind of sense this makes to you, but these are my thoughts. . . .

Even adulterous partners who have made a break from their illicit affair at times find themselves in a situation (sometimes planned, sometimes not) where they rekindle the relationship. Consider the following excerpt from Don's letters.

I had been doing well here at school, keeping my comments [to Janice] few and myself physically distant [from her]. Without recognizing the danger, we both allowed ourselves to "indulge" our friendship/relationship for a period of time. As recovering alcoholics say, I fell off the wagon! Again let me stress that Janice and I have never been intimate sexually. However, a few weeks ago we were at a reception for departing administrators—and Dave, although other people were there, we "found" each other like two magnetic fields. The power/strength of the attraction was, frankly, quite scary. . . .

God has blessed me and my resolve. We exchange no notes. I keep my distance physically. I refuse to call her on weekends or evenings (when my wife is away, working), and I have decided not to attend any social functions outside of school without the company of my dear wife!

I wanted to [briefly discuss] the emotional consequences of an affair. As you know by now, Dave, my affair has not led Janice and me to the bedroom—nor do I believe it ever will, because of our Christian convictions. I have every confidence in this. Don't get me wrong, Dave, I thoroughly agree with your warning [that regardless of one's faith, one needs to be constantly vigilant of falling]—consequently I am keeping my distance. I see myself as being like Joseph with Potiphar's wife. I really can't afford to be seen with her or interacting with her outside of a simple "Good Morning" or "Good Evening." I can't afford to go back and indulge my obsession.

You speak of "emotional entanglement," and that this is generally more difficult to break away from than the physical/sexual entanglement (which must carry with it emotional entanglement as well!). Although your book started me on my road to recovery, it may have been helpful if we had all recognized the inherently powerful content of the emotional turmoil. This is what still hangs around with me these days, and it is what I deal with in prayer—every day! Here are some of the lies that Satan brings to mind: "Why are you separating yourself from Janice? Why are you denying yourself such pleasure? You know you can't live without her, so why are you even trying? How can you survive by depriving yourself of at least some daily contact? Just a little contact can't hurt! How can you be so cruel to her by ignoring her? Don't you care about her feelings?" On and on it goes. It has been very bothersome.

In this area Don has his thinking thoroughly in place. But once your heart is bonded with the partner and you seriously contemplate your sinful habit of a flirtatious affair, realizing you should cease and desist, depression usually ensues. This is normal, though not easy to deal with. Listen to Don agonize further.

I spent one entire evening unable to sleep for one second; I just kept my eyes open, looking out my bedroom window all night—trying to sleep, but unable. Not surprisingly, I contemplated suicide, feeling only blackness and despair. My wife, who slept quietly beside me that night, later asked me directly if I had slept with Janice because of my exaggerated emotional response. I was glad that I could tell her "No" then, and that I can still say that today. I guess everyone's emotional reaction will be different. Possibly mine has been so agonized because I am such a sensitive person and/or that I am an ordained minister—my conscience has been severely attacked by the realization of my sin. I hit the skids hard. I needed some antidepressant medication to help me with the shock of it all.

What I have been learning is that sin does have its consequences. My sin has been the emotional entanglement that I brought into existence and carefully nourished for almost a year. To tear yourself away from the source of pleasure, excitement, and attention is very difficult emotionally. The temptation for me now is to get back into it with her—to resolve the pain and the sense of loss I feel. However, the promise of reinstated bliss is truly an empty cup, because it only makes the permanent breaking away that much more difficult. . . .

How much time will it take for me to "get over" the affair? I have only been committed to putting this thing to death for the last three months, but am truly amazed at the incredible enduring strength of my feelings. A mutual friend told me recently that she imagines it must be difficult for me, because on several occasions she noticed Janice and me together and was very aware of the "magic," the "glow," that was evident on our faces. What amazed her was that she saw that same glow between me and my wife, on another occasion! I am truly torn between these two women in my life! I painfully realize the depth of these emotions, and I know that I cannot easily reach down inside and wrench them out of my heart.

I know I have to relax and live for Christ each day and trust that He will, in His own time, give me the emotional release I so desperately need. Crazily, there have been wonderful moments of freedom, combined with moments of agony because there is a place I long to enter, but know it is forbid-

because there is a place I long to enter, but know it is forbidden. This hurts.

And it is so surprising because, as I mentioned, I was not coming from a terribly bad marriage. I was not hurting in any sense of the term. I simply, out of ignorance and naïveté, began to relate to a woman who simply "clicked" with me in a way that only one other woman has done before in my life.

THE COMPONENTS OF CLASS II AFFAIRS

This correspondence illustrates so perfectly the innocence and genuineness that are present at the outset of most Class II affairs. It also demonstrates the bewilderment that comes with the recognition of how deep-seated the feelings have become. It's a sense of "How did this happen to me? I never started this friendship planning for this outcome." Later, the infidel does begin a cultivation process of the feelings, growing and feeding the attraction, but initially the motivation is quite different. To understand why this so intense, it is important to remember that all Class II affairs have components of emotion, time, and consequences.

EMOTION

Childhood magic

Adulterers let childhood thinking patterns infiltrate their adult reality. Childhood magic includes a place where there are no boundaries, rules, good/bad distinctions, consequences, or pain—just "heaven on earth."

Underlying this childhood magic is a need for nurturance. It is a deep longing for a sense of accommodation and of being cared for. This is especially strong if the infidel has lost an opposite-sex parent or if that parent was not there emotionally for them as a child. In the world of childhood magic, there's a sense of passion, not necessarily sexual passion, but just a feeling of being thoroughly alive; of expressive, unbelievable joy; of having immense, seemingly unlimited power.

Adolescent sexuality

All the consuming passion, the burning desire, the heightened awareness of sexual feelings that are present in the adolescent resurface in the adult involved in an affair. It's that sense of "crush" that junior high girls have for older men and that young adolescent boys often have for older women. It's an intense infatuation that many infidels report having initially felt with their spouse. It's not lust, but it does generate feelings of being more masculine/more feminine, of being more alive than normal.

Adult mobility and independence

Adult mobility brings with it the ability to drive, fly, rendezvous with, and create a special environment without the fear of getting caught and with the justification that "we're consenting adults and are therefore able to do what we want." You can see how all these factors help to grease the skids of immorality.

TIME

Few affairs can maintain all three of the above emotional components on a long-term basis. Affairs involving these three components usually can't endure beyond eighteen months. Daily contact, especially in the latter half of this time span, begins to erode the magic. Additionally, the time periods required to maintain the relationship on a regular basis disrupt the normal schedules that life demands. Affairs can be maintained long term, however, if one, or even two, of the emotional components are left out of the relationship.

For instance, after a period of intense sexual activity, the couple decides to refrain from sex so that they can maintain the friendship guilt-free. Or, because of schedules and location, they only see each other once or twice a year. Or, because of other demands in life, they lower the "magic" level to fit with reality, and the affair becomes a "bright light" instead of a "magical transport" out of a mundane life. One or two of the components has to fit with reality in order for the affair to be maintained long term.

It's usually only possible to maintain a long-term affair with all three emotional components if long periods of time exist between the togetherness experiences. Examples of these times of togetherness would be annual business conventions, periodic trade shows, or professional meetings.

CONSEQUENCES

A long-term affair can be an intense emotional attraction that has never been consummated sexually. That's Don's experience in the letters excerpted above. Since no sexual acting-out has taken place, the components of remorse, guilt, and shame are not as intense as they would be in a full-blown affair. Thus, something now has to be healed or fixed that doesn't feel "all that wrong," and this is naturally very confusing.

In fact, many times these emotional affairs can actually appear to enhance a bad marriage. How? In the emotional affair, the infidel shares, or enjoys, components of his life that he can't seem to share—or enjoy—with his spouse. An emotional affair has some attachment, interest, or appeal that is missing from or isn't tolerated in the marriage. It's a bellwether in that sense.

In the letters above, you can hear how Don tries to suppress the passion he has invested in his emotional affair. His denial is evident in varying degrees in various passages of his letters. To express his true passion for his partner would create internal dissonance, guilt, and shame—things that would be painful, given his religious beliefs. The relationship would have taken on a "wrongful" component. But as long as no touching occurs, much of the experience can remain "underground" and the individuals can assure themselves that they have "only a platonic friendship," while the opposite is actually true.

These relationships are actually supercharged with sexual tension, not simply platonic friendship. The partners are practicing the component of adult mobility, as they weave in and out of contact, both planned and unplanned, covert and overt, thinking they are not being noticed by others. And they are playing with the childhood magic component that develops deep attachment (e.g., pretending that wide-ranging and unrestrained emotional expression between them won't wreck their marriages and their lives).

GETTING "UNHOOKED"

Don asks the question "How can I get unhooked?" There is no easy way, and it will involve a process of time. In that process, several practices are important.

First of all, *separation* is important. The emphasis here is on abstinence and sobriety. You don't indulge yourself with the other person's presence. You must stop exposing yourself to this shared life experience. The contact is what keeps these feelings alive; you need to stop feeding the compulsion.

I hasten to add that you just can't bury these feelings. Therefore, the next step is *identification*. What is the "something" this person touches inside you? What unmet need does he tap into? Sometimes the infidel can process this with a spouse or a same-sex friend, but other times that will need to be done with an experienced counselor who is committed to restoring the marriage. My experience is that the longings that underlie infidelity go back to childhood; the infidel brings them with him or her into the marriage. They often were touched upon or satisfied in the initial phases of the relationship with the spouse, but over time have been buried by the crush of life's responsibilities.

The next process is *exposure*. Don't allow these longings and feelings to remain a secret. The longer an infidel allows these feelings to continue as a secret, the more he or she will idealize the person the feelings are attached to. Idealization means this partner becomes perfect, and as a result, no one else (e.g., the spouse) can measure up. The partner is beginning to be seen as "all good," and therefore the infidel will have to see the marriage as "all bad." As mentioned earlier, if you encapsulate these feelings at this point, they will only lie dormant to be triggered again later. I usually encourage the infidel to share his feelings with his spouse, after seeking counsel. After all, the spouse has been involved in this story already (in that all affairs are a triangle, even if the spouse is unaware) and might as well know the secrets that are occurring in his/her marriage.

The next concept here is to *journal*. Write down the feelings you are experiencing in this rather involved and tortuous journey. Feelings don't have to control an individual, but their influence is strongest when they are held in secret. The longings that have led to this emotional affair are a part of the childhood magic; journaling them gets them out into the open, into the adult realm.

The next practice is *displacement*. Use this process in tandem with some of the other processes. Here you do something else in lieu of focusing on the partner. You can exercise, get involved in spiritual development, or take on construction projects or hobbies. This is the "doing" part of healing.

The final idea is to *grieve*. In his letters, Don mentions his growing depression. Though this is extremely difficult for the spouse to observe, it is important and necessary. Many times this needs to start with a "good-bye" letter (written to the partner). Most infidels find this very painful to do. It seems so unnecessary initially, because (seemingly) "nothing evil has happened," since they didn't have sex. Only after thorough processing, and the passage of time, will the infidel be able to look back and to see how befuddled his/her thinking really was.

This is also a good time for the infidel to review his/her "loss history," and this leads naturally to grieving. What other significant caregivers, friends, loved ones, or pets has the infidel lost that parallel the lost feelings in giving up the affair? The infidel will probably want to do this in private and only later will be able to share the depth of the experience with his spouse. (A caution here: The depression is not about what you feel for the partner, but just what you are feeling, period. Keep the partner out of the equation—it will make it easier for your spouse to listen to your feelings, and easier for you to connect with the feelings in your heart that need processing.)

THE HEALING PROCESS

Neither your partner nor your spouse can release you from the emotional hook you've experienced. Many spouses caught in this kind of emotional affair have found portions of The Serenity Prayer helpful:

> Lord grant me the serenity
> to accept the things I cannot change,
> the courage to change the things I can,
> and the wisdom to know the difference.

Be careful of changing the components around. Don't try to change the things you cannot change—that will only lead to frustration and anger. On the other hand, don't accept the things you should be changing—that will only lead to feelings of victimization, a sense of "What's the use? I can't lick this, so I might as well give in."

Time, the healing process, always requires a backward look. Encouragement is not usually the result if you look to where you need to be, feel like you ought to be, or even want to be. You will see the feelings diminish as you look backward to where you were three, six, or nine months ago.

Rebuild and concentrate on the lost relationships that contributed to the vacuum that the emotional affair filled. That could require quite a search on your part, some intense conversations (even confrontations) with people in your life, a lot of focused reading, and even some trips/visits to significant places in your childhood.

Enjoy the process and reschedule the experiences that made your marriage good in the first place. Here I encourage couples to each identify the "eight greats" of their marital experience. Independently, each spouse should identify the eight great experiences, or highlights, of their marital history, then decide together on five that they would like to repeat. You see, shared history is a critical component of intimacy. Rare is the spouse who won't join "the almost infidel" in this endeavor and thereby experience recovery from a close call. Why, most of us have had close calls ourselves.

SOME CAUTIONS FOR THE INFIDEL

Temptations do not an identity make. Some people struggle with the same temptation for years. For instance, just because someone wants to smoke again because he's tempted doesn't mean he's a smoker. Don't let the temptation to return to the partner shame you into feeling "What's the use? I might as well give in. I'll never be free of these feelings." Don articulates those feelings so well in the letters.

Second, remember that in periods of high stress, difficult emotions, transition, and marital dullness, you will feel an increased desire to return to the partner or to renew thoughts of him/her. At times, infidels report that they have yearnings to think about this person just to see if the feelings are still "available" as in days gone by. This "testing" is common to obsessive-compulsive behaviors, and the intent is to prove to oneself how far one has come in the recovery process. Be careful—this process can begin to mimic the destabilization process of a Class II affair described in chapter 6. As mentioned there, such practices only intensify, rather than lessen, the attraction—and the hook goes much deeper.

SOME ENCOURAGEMENT FOR THE SPOUSE

First, remember that these longings were present in your spouse before you entered his or her life. You didn't create them, and you probably can't fully satisfy them.

Second, you did tap into those longings early in your relationship in some fashion. The longings were present in the initial feelings of what love is all about. For whatever reason, the infidel settled for the initial and superficial satisfaction of those longings, versus deepening and maturing them. This is not your fault. Many times it is the result of a combination of circumstances: work, school, family, and so on. But the exciting thing is now you both can go deeper in your love for each other.

Last, both of you will eventually forget the partner. The memories of this experience will fade in the same way that a widow or widower forgets about the loss of a good first marriage if the second marriage is a pleasant experience.

It is possible to rebuild after an emotional affair has been discovered. Work through these steps and you will make progress. This is the kind of stuff emotional intimacy is built on, and that is the key to any good marriage.

14

WHEN YOUR SPOUSE DOESN'T WANT YOU BACK: THE 90-DAY EXPERIMENT

Life, at times, can be messy. Very messy. That's the way it can be when, with all honesty and courage, the infidel finally admits his/her straying to the spouse. The infidel is hoping, after the initial anger and correct processing of that rage, that the spouse will have him/her back. But it doesn't always work out that way.

The following excerpts from a couple's actual letters give us some idea of what this can be like. Pam (not her real name) has had an affair with Brian and has disclosed the six-month liaison to her husband of fourteen years, Rick. There are three letters (all used with the permission of the writers, of course). The first one is from Pam to me as her counselor, after she has read this book. The second one is from the husband, Rick, to the wife, expressing his feelings after the disclosure. The last one is from the wife back to the husband, responding to his letter.

Read the excerpts below and think about what you have learned in this book and how to apply that to their (and possibly your) situation.

Dear Mr. Carder,

Thank you . . . for your excellent book, *Torn Asunder*. . . . I read the whole book the day I bought it, and now my husband is reading it. I am writing because our situation is different, and I'm stuck on what to do.

. . . I, Pam, am 42, and my husband, Rick, is 41. I am an extrovert, outgoing, love people, somewhat on the wild side. . . . Rick is an introvert, computer person, very much an intellectual. . . . We are both Spirit-filled Christians and attend church every Sunday. We have two adopted children, ages 13 and 11. We have been married going on 15 years. . . . After my first husband died, I was single for seven years, dating many men, but gave up finding anyone.

At age 28 I met Rick, and he fell for me immediately. Within a month he started asking me to marry him, and I kept telling him, "No, I don't love you." He kept asking me, saying it didn't matter, that love would come later. . . . I figured I wasn't getting younger and this man would go to church with me, didn't smoke, drink, or do drugs, had a good job, and would be a good father. In a few months I found myself looking down the church aisle, hearing "Here Comes the Bride. . . . " I turned to my maid of honor and told her, "I can't do this." She said I could and gave me a push . . . I walked down the aisle and did it. I got pregnant that week, but things were so bad [in our relationship] that we didn't have sex (again) for over a year. I planned to leave as soon as the baby was born. Well, the baby had a genetic defect and she died the day after she was born.

. . . Our marriage has *always*, always been rough. Six years ago I was ready to leave, but friends talked us into a marriage encounter weekend. That gave me some hope, so I decided to hang in some more.

. . . When Rick and I married, I weighed 190. I always fought a weight problem, but gained 25 pounds after the death of each of my babies and [first] husband, so I had 75 pounds of "dead weight." I got up to 245 and was . . . miserable, trying all kinds of diets. For years I wanted to have my stomach stapled, but Rick didn't want me to, and personally, I was afraid if I lost a lot of weight and started getting attention from other men, I might leave [Rick for one of them].

. . . I have prayed for 14 years for God to move in my heart and give me a real love for Rick, or even make me more content without love, and [able to] just stay with Rick. Two years ago I decided I couldn't stand the weight any longer—I had to take the risk. I had the surgery and have lost 70 pounds. I expected Rick to show some excitement, but it never came. I kept telling him, "I need more attention."

Well, you can guess what happened: I did get attention, from someone else.

The man is Brian; we were involved the year before I met Rick. I had not seen him in 14 years. [When I first saw him during one of Rick's out-of-town trips, Brian] kissed me passionately and I was in utter shock. I had not felt any feelings [at all toward my husband] for 15 years, and here was this man who gave me [such] a kiss and my knees buckled under me. Electric current flowed through me that I had never felt for my husband. . . . I could not push him away. After six months [of seeing Brian on the sly], I told Rick about him and he told me, "Do what you have to."

Another six months went by and my pastor found out and put an end to [the affair].

[Now] I am devastated by us being apart (it's been four months [since Brian and I broke it off]).

. . . Your book talks about working back to the love and relationship you had at the beginning . . . but what if you don't have that [original love] to try and recapture? [After so long in my marriage,] I thought I was incapable of having any feelings, but I had one year [with Brian during which] I experienced [such wonderful feelings] that I don't know if I can go back to that "dead" existence again. . . . I'm afraid Brian will be calling me again after this blows over, and I won't be able to say no.

. . . I do know that Rick does love me, and I feel guilty that I have never returned that [love] to him. . . .

Sincerely,
(Pam)

Dear Pam,

How could you let this happen? . . . Did you really want me to
divorce you? What was on your agenda? I always thought we
could talk, and that you would talk to me. . . . It seems to me
that . . . you tried to talk to me and were unsuccessful, [so]
you just let it go. You didn't search the earth over and try to
find a way to talk to me.

. . . If [I learn] nothing else in this life, I intend to learn from
this hell that I, or we, have created—and attempt to learn to
listen [to] you, Pam. Maybe you will simply stand idly by and
just let whatever [happens] happen, but I won't. I will not give
"us" up without a fight. I think [what] happened is that you
simply gave up, and I didn't [tell you about] my confusion [in
trying to understand] what . . . you were talking about.

Was I really that bad? . . . As bad as all the others that used
you, even the ones that raped, or tried to rape, you? Well, at
least you can see the joys that Satan has for women in this
world. . . . Men basically do not see the difference between
forced sex and desired sex when it comes to a woman. . . . I
can't believe I was so bad that I drove you into another's arms.
. . . I was bad, but I also believe I have been the best man in
your life in a long-term relationship. I've been with you for
almost 15 years. Who else besides your Mom and Dad can say
that? . . . I could never satisfy you totally, nor understand you
totally, nor communicate with you totally without you doing
some work on your end. If you do your part and I do my part,
we will at least have . . . everything out in the open. . . . No, I
don't think I was that bad. I think a substantial portion of the
problem is on your end. . . . Your inability to make a commitment is severely affecting your ability to stay with me and
needs to be realized, understood, and dealt with.

Couldn't you find anyone better than [Brian] to replace me? If
you have to trash me and my feelings for you, at least pick
someone that is an acceptable human being . . . with a decent
set of morals. This man is so disgusting I couldn't respect him if
I tried. . . . This man, whether you realize it or not, trespassed
on my property, my house, my wife, my marriage, and my personal feelings, and never even asked me. He didn't ask me
because he is a worm and knew he couldn't compete with me.

. . . I am tired of being understanding, both with him and with you. I don't feel patient. I don't feel understanding. . . . Fortunately, I am willing to forgive you for what you have done. Him I cannot forgive.

. . . I feel betrayed by the one person in the world that I thought I could trust. I can't trust you now. I wonder what you are doing when you are out of my sight. When I ask you about your whereabouts, you get annoyed. Well, too bad. I want some proof you are not bringing disease into our marriage. I want to believe you, I really do. But it is hard. . . . I feel so angry sometimes I cannot sleep. . . . I have wanted to display this anger to you, but when I do, it seems to drive you away. . . . Oh, woe is me.

. . . Just like you, I wonder *when* it will all end, or *if* it will end. I wonder sometimes if I can make it. . . . I feel depressed and wonder, Where is the joy I am supposed to have [as a Christian]? I have done my best to support my relationship with you. I have "died to self" as best I can, I have tried to let the Holy Spirit fill me up. And what have you done to help me? Have you supported me in my church activities? Have you offered to go out witnessing with me? I have offered to go with you and visit the sick and hurting. Have you done the same for me? Don't think that I enjoy visiting sick people, with their weakness and depression [because] . . . I don't. . . . I feel naked . . . (in fact I feel I have had to undress my life before strangers to try and straighten this mess out), I feel angry, I feel isolated, I feel alone, I feel distant, and yet somehow through it all, I feel closer to you and God, through all the pain.

Don't try this again with me. I don't feel like a failure anymore, but [if this happens again] . . . I'm [more than] willing to make others feel that way [to punish them for their transgressions].

Make up your mind: him, or me. Which of us has stood by you through thick and thin? Which of us has [raised] your children with you, worrying all the way if he would be a good father . . . ? What part in your life has this man had, anyway? . . . He has no part. The part of you that he had . . . is a cancer. It will probably eat at you the rest of your life. . . . You won't forget the freedom from responsibility this teenage pervert had in a relationship with you. . . . But this freedom is like being drunk. When you wake up . . . you come back to the original problem. The problem for all of us is us. [The cartoon character] Pogo says, "We have seen the enemy, and he is *us*." While the grammar is bad, the message is tried and true.

If you cannot make the choice between him or me, I will make it for you. Choose me or not. That is all the choice you have. . . . Choose me and the improvements . . . I have made, or choose pain, hurt, agony, defeat, and all the misery of your previous life with all the males that used you. . . . At least I never intentionally attempted to use you. Can [Brian] say that?

What kind of a man [is Brian]? . . . A rat. . . . Seek properly. Look in the rose garden of your youth, Solomon says. Remember that which is yours, given by God. Why waste time romancing a phony, when you can have a man (who, though somewhat inept, at least) . . . loves you for who you are. . . . You brought this piece of human garbage into our lives that laughed at you and me behind our backs, and lied openly to you. . . . You trusted him and didn't trust me. Don't expect me to condone it. I have very little success at feeling sorry for either one of you. You got what you deserved. . . . You are both reaping what you sowed. Why can't you get mad at this filthy, disgusting, half-empty garbage can . . . ? Okay, so I need some sincere and deep-seated body work. I am willing to do that. . . . But I need your support and your recognition.

. . . He is a vicious one, this two-legged animal. He will be back again, to feed on the carcass he has wounded. . . . He knows you can refuse him nothing. He knows that I am a mutton-head with no understanding of women, and [this] . . . makes you particularly vulnerable. He even knows that if you try to take him to court . . . his lawyer merely need mention that you have had numerous affairs. . . . But have faith, remember that God is not mocked. Sooner or later, he will reap what he sows. . . . Despite it all, and in fact because of it all, I am here for you. Come to my open arms and find rest.

. . . I do have problems, [but] some of them are the people around me. . . . Tell me that, if I change, you could fall in love with me maybe. . . . I believe you have made many mistakes with your life, as have I, but I don't believe our marriage was a mistake. I believe that both of us can come out of this whole. I believe we can take a chance on "us." I believe we can walk together, and at least be friends, even if we cannot be "as one." If I have to let you go, I will—but you must first have somewhere to go.

I tried to help you. I tried to provide . . . a safe haven of rest. I stuffed my emotions to give you space, so we could get along without arguing. How did you reward me? . . . You told me that we should go to marriage encounter . . . and things would get better for a while and then would go back to more of the same. Well, I would try the principles. You would respond at first, and then you would stop responding. I would stop doing the things and you wouldn't be disappointed. You wouldn't say anything . . . leaving me confused. . . . Later I would try to talk to you, and you would just get mad or cry. What was I supposed to do? Was I supposed to keep on changing? I read the books on what to do. I did some of the stuff. Sex got better. But why or how? I couldn't tell you. Even today, I am not sure what to do.

. . . I can't let this happen again. If it becomes a choice between me and someone else [having sex with] you, I will make the choice, even if you don't. I will kick you out of the house. I will say, "Go, and take your problems with you." I will demand your exit from my and the kids' lives. I warn you—don't press me on this. I will act. I will do what I have to. Don't force me to take control and leave you to your emotions. Let me help you, but keep me in the loop. Try to write to me every day. The things you write are beautiful and I love them. . . . Everything you write and say [is] useful, although much of it hurts.

I stand before you with open arms. Come unto me as you did Wednesday night.

Love always,
(Rick)

Dear Rick,

I want to respond to your letter to me.

. . . Has life been all that bad with you? Financially, no; physically, no; emotionally, yes. You said that you always thought we could talk . . . where did you get that idea? We HAVE talked more this past year than the previous 13 years combined.

You say it seems I just let this affair happen. . . . NO, *you* let it happen. If you had been giving me what I needed, I would never have gone somewhere else. If you feel I didn't search the world over to try and find a solution and a way to talk to you, I'm sorry, but I did a . . . lot more trying to find a way to communicate than you did. I talked, I wrote, I bought books, I signed us up for classes, I tried, I cried. YOU certainly didn't try to find [a solution].

Yes, it happened because I gave up. . . . Sorry, but for 12 years I was faithful and hung in there; I kept believing things would get better. Every year, I'd tell myself, *There's got to be something else I can do, another book I can read, another way to reach him.* And when I found books or wrote letters that I thought were so precise, I would give them to you, and it was like giving a stone wall the book and expecting that wall to read it and react [to it]. You say maybe I will stand idly by and let whatever [happens] happen, but you won't. Well it's about time you [are getting involved in our relationship]. I'm tired of [being the only one] trying and trying and trying. . . .

Were you as bad as the others who used me? Yes, you are . . . and maybe worse, in a way, than the others. Other men used me for their own purpose, yet didn't expect any commitment from me. You used me for your own purpose . . . someone to be with you [and then wanted commitment anyway,] . . . regardless of how [I] felt. . . . Once you achieve your purpose, you sit back and think that's all there is. It's like your prize goal in life was to own the Mona Lisa, you get it, hang it, look at it, but never relate to it. . . . [In fact,] once you get it, you stick it in a closet and close the door. You got me to marry you, I moved in with you, and then you think that's all you need to do. [But you need to realize that] you married a human being, not a machine. . . . You liked sitting back and doing nothing. Well, I'm sorry, but I can't stay in a relationship like that. Rather, I WON'T stay in that kind of relationship.

Furthermore, you say I need to do more work on my end. Don't you think I would have committed to a man who would act with feelings, emotions, love, etc., more than to a man who thinks and acts like a machine? Yes, I have been really drained by what has happened in my life. [My first husband's] and the babies' deaths took all I had out of me. But you know what? A computer [like you] won't help me heal those past wounds, only God and the man He gave me as my husband will be able to love me and heal me. I could not get that from you, you are so distant. . . .

Couldn't I have picked a better person with a decent set of morals? Ha, ha—that's a good one. Anyone I would have picked would never qualify . . . ! Even if it was the pastor him-self, would you think he had decent morals after having an affair? How can I respect Brian? Well, maybe I didn't, maybe I just needed him to provide me what I needed so desperately. Not that it was right, but he did give me the emotions and feelings that I forgot I ever had. Your care for me was in pro-viding a house and family, which are great. BUT you never cared for me personally.

You don't care for my actions? Well, I don't appreciate 13 years of your non-attached actions, either. You feel betrayed by me? Well, I feel betrayed by you, and Brian, and all the other "men" who have used me. You can't trust me now? Well, I've had trouble trusting things would get better for 14 years. You can't sleep? Well, join the crowd. You get tired emotionally this past year? Well, I've been tired emotionally for 14 years. You wonder where the joy is this year? I wonder where the joy has been for 14 years. No, I don't go out witnessing with you, and I don't expect you to visit the sick and elderly. God gave you your gift, He gave me a different one.

So I didn't come out and ask you if I could have an affair? Actually, I did, in a way. And your reply was, "Do what you have to do." I'll never forget those six words. I don't think I've ever been more angry or hurt over anything anyone has ever said to me. You know, I thought I was most angry at Brian between the three of us, but . . . I'm more angry at *you* than anyone. I cannot believe any man who actually loves his wife telling her to go out and do what she has to. After you fought for me to marry you, HOW could you say that? At least in the letters you write me I find that you MIGHT have some love for me somewhere.

No, I won't forget Brian. . . . Maybe, as crazy as it sounds, we should go thank Brian. If that affair didn't happen, we would still be in the same DEAD place we were in for 14 years, and I can GUARANTEE you I wouldn't have stayed too many more years in the anger and frustration of our marriage. . . . If it wasn't Brian, it would have been some other man. At the risk of sounding crude, Brian made me feel human again. He paid attention to every detail about me, and talked to me, not at me. I'm not proud about giving in to [Brian], but I'm human, not a machine.

You say I trusted Brian and not you. I only trusted him to provide me the [things] you did not give me, and he did that well. I have always trusted you in all other areas, except for your ability to express to me your love, feelings, and emotions. I have told you many times, over and over and OVER again, what I need. . . . After 20 or 100 times, I get tired and frustrated. I figure you just don't care, or don't want to bother . . . [like] I'm not worth much to you. You know how I really like certain things, and just because I don't confirm every time for years and years is no reason to stop. You are an adult. Three-year-olds need to be reminded over and over.

. . . At least now [that] we have been totally knocked down, . . . maybe we can learn how to walk all over again—properly, this time. I believe I could fall in love with you . . . or I wouldn't still be here. I'm not going to think I wasted 14 years of my life for no reason . . . but things *do* have to change.

. . . Maybe you shouldn't stuff your emotions. That just built up more walls between us. Lord knows I've built the Great Wall of China myself. You say you tried over and over to help me . . . TELL ME HOW. When you did try new ideas and things got better, didn't that give you a clue to continue on, because things did get better? Why would you want to go backwards?

. . . In ending, I've glad you won't let this happen again. I can't go through it again, either. But I won't stay in this marriage like it was, either. I can't spend the rest of my life living with someone who doesn't show me any love. I've had too many years of feeling unloved already. It's not a very good feeling to go through life feeling you don't count to anyone. [In thinking back to you convincing me to marry you], if you didn't want to come home to an empty apartment, you could have bought a dog or some kittens—that way you don't have to relate to them on a personal level.

I'm very frightened right now. I see some hope, but I've seen that before, and every time, [it has gone] back to the same hopeless existence. It may take a long time for me to breathe easy again.

(Pam)

Throughout this book the emphasis on why Class II affairs happen has been on trauma, transitions, and family history. One more issue remains: marital dullness—a complete lack of vibrancy in the relationship.

In most marriages, the breakdown is not only one spouse's fault. Rather, the causes appear to be a constellation of general life experiences. Many times, the faithful spouse is inappropriately blamed (especially if it is the wife) for "pushing" the infidel into the affair. Though I have seen cases where that was true, most of the time it's a gradual distancing between both partners that lies at the root. For men, the felt need is often loss of playfulness, a lack of flirtation, and an absence of adoration or respect from the wife. For women, it's typically the loss of tenderness, care, and concern expressed by the husband. Since most of us marry to "get more" of our new spouse—more time together, more fun together, more lovemaking—it's easy to see where disappointment can enter the picture.

As a related aside, I am convinced that these losses are major contributors to the high level of depression we have in the American culture. The depression in turn is a major contributor to the self-nurturance/addictive behaviors that are consuming the American population. The self-nurturance behaviors—doing too much of a good thing (for example, eating too much, exercising too much, always having to watch TV or listen to the radio)—have generated the obsession with larger and larger (projection- and home-theater) TV screens, a dizzying array of cable channels, and the all-day talk shows (even all-talk radio and TV networks, many of which deal with romance, affairs, and sexual perversions).

Many spouses only *give in* to infidelities after they have *given up* on trying to make their marriage work. They often feel they are the only person involved in enriching the relationship. In her letter above, Pam describes her own self-nurturing practices, as well as the resultant exhaustion and depression that followed her unrecognized efforts to get Rick involved with, and connected to her.

When an affair occurs in this setting (it doesn't make any difference which spouse acts out) there often is so much hurt and such long-buried pain that there is hardly any energy left to recover from the affair. In fact, couples in this experience compare it to the release at death after caring for someone with a long-term illness. It's an "I'm so glad it's finally over" feeling. Thus restoration efforts (one of the central goals of this book) are often fruitless, or at best extremely difficult.

If this is your situation, consider the following, especially if you have children:

- You really are not finished with each other yet. The children will require you to see and interact with each other for at least the next twenty years, even if you are divorced.
- All unprocessed pain from this relationship stays with you, and you will drag it around, like extra baggage, through life. Thus you should endeavor to process all the pain now—it's better that way.
- Unfinished business will surface in all future relationships, because an affair is a relationship issue. Another incentive to dig down deep and cover all the issues.
- In the future, if you stay out of relationships and "do life solo," you will carry a biased attitude toward members of the opposite sex and thus contaminate your children's future marriages. If you try to walk away without correctly processing the issues, many will suffer from your inability to work through this pain.

Many couples in this circumstance have found it helpful to establish some parameters regarding how much time they will spend processing the disclosure of the affair. A 90-day period of abstinence is a significant period in Alcoholics Anonymous (A.A.) for those who are attempting to achieve sobriety. I have used that same time frame for my clients and found it very helpful, especially as a program for marriages in the following circumstances:

1. Where at least one spouse is uncertain if he wants to preserve the marriage at all.
2. Where one spouse is willing to make one final attempt, but doesn't want to commit, up front, to save the marriage.
3. Where one spouse definitely wants out of the marriage.

Three conditions have to be satisfied before the 90-day program can be initiated:

1. Both spouses have to agree *not* to see an attorney, file papers, or in any other way attempt to end the marriage prematurely.
2. Both must agree to *not* ask the other person if they are going to end the marriage during the 90 days.
3. The infidel must absolutely separate from the partner during the 90 days. That means no contact whatever: no phone calls, no letters, no face-to-face visitations. Nothing! Any mementos, pictures, or gifts related to the affair must be boxed up and delivered to another party outside the home. At the end of the 90 days, the infidel can decide what he or she wants to do with the box and its contents.

Believe it or not, most partners support this process. They want the infidel, usually someone whom they love dearly, to process his/her marriage, to work through it and bring closure to this first relationship. They realize they stand a good chance of losing their affair partner, but it's better to have *all* of the person you love, as opposed to having "ghosts" from the unprocessed marriage "floating around the house."

Many infidels, on the other hand, are uncertain if they can endure this program—or they may even feel it is unfair to be asked to do it. When you, as the spouse, have explained the purpose of the 90-day program, encourage the infidel to go and ask for the partner's cooperation. (Infidels are often surprised at the response they receive from their partners.)

Now four things happen:

1. *It frees up both spouses to be honest with each other.*
2. *It forces the infidel to think clearly about the process he or she is in.* He or she no longer can return to the medication/drug of choice (e.g., secrecy, denial, childhood magic, etc.) he or she has recently been involved with.
3. *It doesn't require a commitment together for the extended/infinite future.* It only requires a commitment together to rework the past.
4. *It plants the seed for rebuilding the trust that will be absolutely necessary for life together, whether married or divorced.* It is the same trust bond they had early in the relationship, and it can—and must—be rebuilt for the sake of the children.

Should one of you decide that at the end of the 90 days that you can't continue to live with this person as husband or wife, three things will be true:

1. You'll have a clearer understanding of why you feel that way.
2. You will have built some trust between yourselves that will carry you through the many difficult times that lie ahead in the divorce process (e.g., legal hassles right away, interaction with the kids later on, etc.).
3. You will be better able to support your children in this transition period. Some marriages just can't be saved after adultery—that's why God granted a way out through divorce.

THE FIRST 45 DAYS

GOALS

1. *Stop the obsession on both spouses' part.* Rather than get angry at each other, many couples have found an exercise mentioned in chapter 9 helpful: to "beat out" their anger by using individual plastic (or foam rubber) Wiffle ball bats to strike against an inanimate object. The spouse often uses a picture of the partner, and in some cases has even used a picture of the infidel as well. You lay the pictures on the bed, shut the windows, send the kids to the neighbor's house or to Grandma's, and then you "beat the tar out of" the picture(s)! You beat those pictures until you cry. You work that anger out.

2. Talk about and agree upon *the style of this marriage* that predisposed it to infidelity. Remember: the key is not to lay the blame on someone for the direction the marriage has taken. Rather, focus on the pattern the two of you have developed over the years. The material in chapter 3 will be helpful here.

3. *Contribution/loss list.* Each mate begins writing his own list over the period of several weeks. The spouse writes a contributions list (what he or she has contributed to the marriage that allowed it to deteriorate to the level it did and predisposed it toward infidelity). The infidel writes a list of losses (what he or she has lost as a result of acting out this sexual behavior—see chapter 10).

4. *Forgiveness letters.* After several weeks of thinking this through, each spouse writes a direct forgiveness letter that he will read face-to-face to his mate. Each letter needs to be specific about what the writer has done and has contributed to the relationship disruption. The letters should never contain "you" or blaming statements, such as "You drove me to drinking by your messing around." Rather, the letters should use "I" statements, such as "I hurt you by (insert a hurtful or disruptive action)."

5. *Problem-solving communication.* You need to identify the three major unresolved conflicts you each feel still exist in the marriage. You do need to discuss this with each other, yet remember that these are your own perceptions. This will probably require some outside help, maybe a specialist in the area of conflict resolution (pastor, mediator, trusted levelheaded friend). Classes in conflict resolution are available in most larger cities, and several national programs are listed in the bibliography at the back of this book. It is inevitable that conflict will arise between the two of you in the future, regardless of what happens to the marriage. The less able the two of you are to resolve your own differences, the more fractured your children will be. Unresolved parental conflict causes children to take sides, a destructive pattern. Young children especially have no means to process parental differences except to side with the parent in whose presence they are. It tears the child apart.

EXERCISES

Exercises for opening up lines of communication and building trust have proven helpful to couples. Several are given here: "Ten Steps for Resolving Couple Conflict" (page 245) and "How to Get Your Point Across Without Puncturing Someone in the Process" (page 249), "Sculpting" (p.251), "Touching" (p. 251), and "Marital Satisfaction History" (p. 253).

As you progress through the first two communication exercises, keep the following in mind:

1. Set aside twenty minutes for your first effort and agree to quit after your twenty minutes—regardless of where you are—and talk about how well you've done. Use a timer that generates a fairly loud noise, or you may not hear it!

2. As talker, be sure to choose the least threatening of your three issues.

3. Stay in the role that you've accepted at the outset of this conversation. Conflict escalates when the listener assumes the role of the talker without the talker's permission.

4. Don't just focus on your differences. Do some of the exercises described later in this chapter in the second 45-day section. Though it might be possible, I've never heard of couples choosing each other because they like to fight together! I've seen many relationships end up this way though (remember the windshield-wiper pattern earlier in this book?).

Ten Steps for Resolving Couple Conflict

1. *Set a time and place for discussion.*
2. *Define the problem or issue of disagreement.*
3. *How do you contribute to the problem?*
4. *List things you have done in the past which have not been successful.*
5. *Brainstorm and list all possible solutions.*
6. *Discuss every one of these solutions.*
7. *Agree on one solution to try.*
8. *Agree on how each person will work toward the solution.*
9. *Set a time for another meeting to review your progress.*
10. *Reward each other as you each contribute toward the solution.*

Every couple has differences and disagreements, but healthy couples find ways to resolve marital disputes without turning them into marital wars. These couples accept and appreciate the fact that each person has independent opinions. They encourage open expression, and they work together to reach a settlement.

If you have difficulty resolving differences without serious arguments, try the following exercise. It will help boost your problem-solving success rate.

This is not a game. As simple as this exercise looks, it may be hard for you to complete. If you cannot finish it, try again at a future date.

1. *Schedule a specific date, time, and place for a couple meeting within the next week. Allow at least thirty minutes.*

   Meeting Date: _____

   Time: _____

   Place: _____

2. *Select one important issue you would like to resolve.*

   List the specific issue or problem for discussion:

   _____

   _____

   _____

3. *How do you each contribute to the problem?* Without blaming each other, list the things you each do that has not helped resolve the problem.

Male:

1. _____

2. _____

3. _____

Female:

1. _____

2. _____

3. . _____

4. *List things you have done in the past which have NOT been successful.*

1. _____

2. _____

3. _____

4. _____

5. _____

5. *Brainstorming:* Pool your new ideas and try to come up with *10 possible solutions* to the problem. *Do not judge or criticize any of the suggestions at this point.*

1. _____

2. _____

3. _____

4. _____

5. _____

6. _____

7. _____

8. _____

9. _____

10. _____

6. *Now discuss each of these suggestions. Be as objective as you can, and talk about how useful and appropriate each suggestion is for resolving your disagreement.*

7. *After you have expressed your feelings, select one solution that you both agree to try.*

Trial Solution: _____

_____

_____

_____

8. *Decide how much you will each work toward the solution. Be as specific as possible.*

Male: _____

_____

Female: _____

_____

9. *Set a date, time, and place within the next week for another meeting to discuss your progress.*

Meeting Date: _____

Time: _____

Place: _____

10. *Pay attention to each other as the week passes. If you notice your partner making a positive contribution toward the solution, praise his or her efforts.*

Future Weekly Meetings

At your next weekly meeting, review your progress. If no change has occurred, go back through steps 5–8 to try a different solution. If you have shown improvement, use this exercise to tackle a different problem.

Make couple meetings like these a regular part of your weekly schedule. To help remember this process of discussion and resolution, refer to the Ten Step Program.

We Wish You Much Success in Your Marriage!

"Ten Steps for Resolving Couple Conflict" developed by David H. Olson, Ph.D., Professor, Family Social Sciences, Univ. of Minnesota and President of PREPARE/ENRICH, P.O. Box 190, Minneapolis, MN 55440-0190. © 1992 PRE-PARE/ENRICH Life Innovations, Inc.

How to Get Your Point Across Without Puncturing Someone in the Process

I. OUTCOME—A sense of being understood, cared for, accepted.

II. GOALS

TALKER (Teacher)	LISTENER (Learner)
• Cannot use "You"	• Repress your own feelings and observations
• Be specific and brief	• Summarize with same emotional intensity
	• Summarize accurately even if you disagree

III. PROCESS—For each question (A-D)

A. Listener asks question
B. Talker responds
C. Listener summarizes
D Talker approves or corrects summary
E. Listener summarizes (again if needed)
F. Listener asks next question

IV. QUESTIONS—Always asked by listener.

A. "How do you see (view, etc.) this issue (problem, topic, etc.)?"
B. "When this happens, how does it make you feel?"

> LISTENER: Look for hurt, anger, or fear.

C. "Can you tell me why you feel this way?"
D. "What do you need from me when you feel like that?"

> LISTENER: Listen for specific behaviors.

> TALKER: Slow down; think through what you need from the listener when this issue arises. Make it a specific behavior.

V. CHANGE ROLES—Go through the four basic questions (A-D) again.

> TALKER: "How do you feel about what I have just said?" (This is equivalent to question B.)

VI. TROUBLESHOOTING

A. If you as talker are feeling "attacked," the listener has assumed your role and is no longer listening.

B. If you as talker are feeling "grilled," or "interrogated," summaries are not been given often enough or at all.

C. If you as listener are feeling "confused," not enough "feeling" words are being used.

D. Watch out for the talker who says "I feel . . ." but is using cognitions. If you can substitute "I think," then it is probably not a feeling.

E. If you as listener are feeling "overwhelmed," slow the conversation down; go "down" deeper into the topic instead of "across" it; limit feelings to those occurring in one issue at a time.

Sculpting

Sculpting is another exercise that has proven helpful to couples who have difficulty verbally discussing their feelings (especially for the men). It simply involves arranging you and your spouse in a pose that "shows" how you feel about the subject you are discussing. If a spouse is having difficulty identifying, clarifying, or even expressing a feeling, this is an acceptable way to act out his feelings. The spouse who is trying to express or "teach" a certain feeling arranges the other spouse in a pose. Use your imagination. Have the spouse stand, sit, or sprawl over the furniture; arrange his hands, head, and body in whatever position is necessary to get in touch with the feeling. Continue to adjust him until it feels right to you. Once he is positioned, immediately arrange yourself in the appropriate relationship that reflects what you are trying to say. Once each of you has been positioned, hold the pose (similar to the children's game of "freeze") for a period of time (up to several minutes) as each of you reflects on the feelings this particular arrangement generates. Afterward, talk about your feelings, both within and between yourselves, when you were in the "freeze" position.

Touching

You can do the following "Touching Exercises" (page 252) on an every-other-day basis during this first 45 days. Granted, many couples are so hurt and wounded they don't have the energy initially to do anything at all with each other. In fact, many couples will stay so busy during this crisis time that "they have no time" to even see or talk to each other. They speed off into their own world to forget about the pain. However, let me remind you, you'll only carry the unfinished stuff with you, so it's better to face up to it now.

As soon as I suggest these exercises many spouses revolt! However, these are not exercises you do with someone because you like him. In fact, they are done daily by many individuals who don't know each other at all. You can buy this service in upper middle-class hotels (you have to pay for it, of course). But the exercises themselves require no knowledge of the individual giving or receiving them. They will, however, help the two of you learn to trust each other— and trust is critical over the next several years of your interaction.

First of all, these exercises need to be done "in turn," meaning that one will give, the other receive on a certain day, and the next time you'll swap roles. Again, these exercises have nothing to do with sexual or erotic touch. Remember what I said about the hotel service. Each exercise has very specific boundaries. Finally, most couples find it best not to switch "giver" and "receiver" roles on a back-to-back basis. You need to separate after a session and allow the receiver to relish and enjoy the cared-for feelings this exercise inspires.

I have had some couples actually pay each other for this. They felt like it kept a better boundary between the two of them and helped them refrain from developing false hopes or misinterpretations of the behavior.

	Hand	Foot	Head
Setting	Seated beside each other, arm resting comfortably in giver's lap	Receiver sitting comfortably on a couch, giver seatedon the floor with back support	Giver sitting with back against a wall or a headboard, receiver lying between spouse's legs, with head on a small pillow
Boundary	The elbow	The knee	The shoulders
Practice	Light, slow, predictable	Massage type with lotion	Light, slow, and exploratory
Time	5 minutes on each side of hand and forearm Total 20 minutes	10 minutes per leg and foot	5 minutes right side 10 minutes face 5 minutes left side

Adapted from Cliff and Joyce Penner, *The Gift of Sex* (Waco, Tex.: Word, 1981), pp. 141-45.

Marital Satisfaction History

In the appendices is the work sheet "Marital Satisfaction Time Line." You will need one copy (enlarged) for every five years of marriage. The shaded horizontal bars at the top reflect each individual's perceived satisfaction level. The five small square boxes going across the middle of the page represent every year of marriage. You can either put the year of marriage (e.g., 1981) there, or you can put the numeral 1, representing the first year of the marriage. The larger solid boxes below are for you to make notes about what happened in that year of the marriage. The dotted lines and boxes are six-month markers.

On each page, draw a line, moving from left to right, reflecting how satisfied you were with the marriage at six months, one year, eighteen months, two years, and so on, through the first page. Then start with year six on the second page, year eleven on the third page, and so on. Tape the sheets together, lay them out on the floor, and look at how each of you sees the marital relationship over the years. Talk about your shared history: its up and downs, the differences between each of your perceptions, why each of you felt the way you did at the time, and how each of you responded to what was going on in the marriage. This is your joint story. It will never change. You can't go back and readjust it, but you do share it, and you will take it with you in the future, no matter what you do now. It is important to explore it, regardless of what you do with the marriage.

THE SECOND 45 DAYS

EXERCISES

Graduated Prayer

Even though many couples report at this point that the only prayer they're interested in is one that rains fire and brimstone on their spouses, it nevertheless is important to pray for your spouse. The following is a series of graduated prayer exercises that many couples have found helpful:

1. Prayer Request: Each of you take an index card and write three requests you would like your spouse to pray for in the next couple of weeks. Your requests cannot be about the children, your job, or anything similar—they must be

about you. By taking your spouse's card, you are promising to pray for him/her and his/her request, three times a day, briefly, for the next two weeks. This is not intended to be a long, drawn-out exercise. This prayer commitment can easily be completed in twenty seconds or less, even while you are doing other things, such as driving or walking.

2. Compliment Exercise (next two weeks): Each of you needs a little assignment notebook with a wire spiral across the top (approximately 2.5" by 5"). Each day you will use a new page, where you will write a compliment to your spouse—something you currently like (or at least used to like) about him or her. In America, usually we choose a spouse because we like him. No one forced you to get married, and it's important for you at this juncture to recognize that there is still some good in this person—regardless of your current feelings related to the affair's disclosure. Even if the marriage doesn't make it, this person is still not all bad.

   Now comes the hard part. Praying together (out loud, if possible), you thank God for this quality that you admire about your spouse. This really is much easier to do than it sounds. In most cases, both parties are able to acknowledge some good in the other, even if they are angry. It must be a different compliment every day. Most individuals find the first five or six compliments fairly easy to arrive at. It's the second week's worth that gets difficult. Remember, the more you put yourself into this exercise now, the less the negative consequences will be later. Both of you will still be involved with each other's children, whether the marriage survives or not. Should you stay together, exchange notebooks and read them—they are fun and encouraging.

3. Spousal Selected Prayer Request: This takes the most courage of all, and will only work if you both have become comfortable with thanking God for the qualities you appreciate in your spouse's life. Some couples can't bring themselves to do this exercise, and if that's your case, maybe you need to do the compliment list a little longer or let more time pass before you're able to tackle this level.

   If you are able, ask your spouse what he would like you to pray for about yourself. There is often a great deal of risk in doing this. If you feel like the compliments given during the compliment exercise were not genuine, or were superficial, or were done just because you read it in this book—you will not be sufficiently at ease to hear what your spouse wants you pray for about yourself. However, if you can risk doing this exercise as a couple, it will be very helpful during the last two weeks of your 90-day period.

One final caution here. Offer each other lots of encouragement and support in this process. Don't make this prayer request a "hoop" to jump through. If one (or both of you) is too uncomfortable doing it, give each other a break and come back to it, or spend time processing your feelings before proceeding.

Spousal Selective Monologue

This can also be a difficult exercise. Most spouses know of areas that they would like to hear their spouse talk about, but either haven't had the courage to ask about it, or were afraid of what they might hear, or were apprehensive of being too nosy. This is the time, before you decide to save or separate this marriage, to ask for this information. In a spousal selective monologue, you both agree to listen, in turn, to the other talk about a topic that has been selected for them. The topic should be a topic about self. It should not involve the listening spouse. The individual doing the talking should never have to use the word *you*. The husband can ask the wife to talk about anything he'd like to hear her talk about: her history, her perception of certain times in the marriage, anything in the past, for example, and vice versa.

Rules:
1. You cannot ask your spouse to talk about his/her future with or without you.
2. You must give him/her two or three days to prepare for this presentation.
3. Start with the most nonthreatening issue, such as the spouse's relationship with his/her parents/your parents, the spouse's attitude toward money, the opposite sex, spiritual issues, work, and career issues, for example, and how those attitudes were shaped.

Some Cautions:
1. Only do this after some stabilization has occurred in the relationship. That's why it's framed in the second 45-day period since disclosure.

2. As stated earlier, don't choose the riskiest topic possible; there will be more time to discuss other topics in the future.

3. Tell the truth. If your spouse asks, he/she really wants to know. Don't present some predigested content that really doesn't reflect how you were feeling at the time.

4. Do talk about it sometime afterward. However, no questions are allowed during the initial presentation. Let your spouse present the topic in the way he/she perceives it.

Writing Out the Message

Each spouse needs to write at least one page about what the affair says about their marriage (see chapter 8 for additional help). Ideally, after each has taken several days to compose this assignment, the couple needs to collaborate on one combined document describing the "message" of the affair. It should contain all the elements each party thinks are necessary. Content is more important than grammar or style here. The word *you* should only appear in a nonaccusatory sense, as previously noted. This project will provide you with an idea of how well you might be able to work together in the future. It is your final assignment prior to your joint decision about the future of the marriage. You might be surprised where this 90-day journey has taken you. You might feel somewhat more inclined to at least consider saving what you have invested together. If so, you might be ready to go back and do more of the exercises and suggestions in Section 2 of this book.

However, if you are still uncertain about committing long-term to the relationship, you might find it helpful to do another 90-day program. That's right, do it again! Sometimes spouses are afraid to recommit too quickly, for fear that the changes they have come to enjoy over the last few weeks (i.e., you're talking again, sharing feelings, and so on) might not last, and that the marriage will return to the former pattern that was so painful. One way to keep it moving in the right direction, for folks who feel the need to repeat the program, is to remain uncommitted (versus divorcing or getting back together), so that the spouse will continue to work on things.

This might work for a while, but this attitude can only carry the relationship for a brief period of time (i.e., it gets somewhat ridiculous to repeat the program a fifth and sixth time, and it is usually perceived as a manipulation). If the preceding paragraph describes you (i.e., you're befuddled as to whether to choose divorce or reunite), realize this: you will have to come to the place where you can risk again—for without risk, there can be no trust.

Remember: there are no guarantees in this rebuilding process following an affair. The proof you are looking for will be found in the process of rebuilding intimacy, found in Section 2 of this book.

It ain't easy, but rebuilding intimacy is possible for most couples. If you are both sincerely committed to it, God will help. Your marriage can be restored.

APPENDIX A

WHAT TO TELL THE KIDS

The question of what to tell the children in the midst of processing an affair is always difficult.

What follows is addressed to the case where children live with parents who are experiencing a first-time, ongoing entangled affair. I assume that their home life is somewhat normal—that they have not experienced molestation, physical abuse, substance abuse, or multiple affairs/marriages.

Basically the central issues that you need to address depend upon the children's ages. Up to and including about age eleven, the central issue is generally abandonment: "Who is going to be here with me?" "Who will stay here to take care of me?" The situation for the child becomes even more unsettling if the parent who stays with the child becomes increasingly overwhelmed with grief and rage while attempting to save the marriage.

It certainly is appropriate for the parent to express his or her emotions at appropriate times, but in the presence of the child, you need to verbally reassure him that

I'm not leaving you.
Yes, I'm upset, but it's not about you.
Daddy (Mommy) didn't leave because of you or your actions.

Combined with fears of abandonment, the child will almost always assume more guilt with increasing age. It often takes the

259

form of "If I had been a better girl, Mommy would not have left." So take special care to make sure the child's guilty feelings are not reinforced.

Other symptoms of childhood confusion during this difficult time are:

- regression in behavior (e.g., return to bed-wetting, thumb-sucking, nightmares, temper tantrums)
- need for increased attention and affection
- school failure and discipline problems
- confusion, forgetfulness, daydreaming
- loss of appetite
- complaints of stomachaches, unexplained crying spells, and so on

From the age of about twelve on up, adolescent reactions commonly include rage and acting out. Initially, though, denial is a common reaction. The adolescent blocks out the current experience, hoping that the infidel parent will return to the marriage. He will act as though nothing is wrong: his message to others is "Everything is fine if you will just leave me alone."

Don't push the adolescent unless you have heard something that can be interpreted as a cry for help. Then gently but firmly push into his or her world and find out what's happening. Symptoms might include:

- rapid deterioration of schoolwork and grades, increased troublemaking at school
- evidence of property damage or breakage in his room or around the house
- destruction of items that were important symbols of his attachment to the infidel parent
- picking on other siblings or even on the pets
- increased TV viewing, music listening, at a louder level than usual and accompanied by isolation
- sexual acting out, lewd or seductive dress, onset of, or increase in, masturbation or promiscuity
- development of sudden physical illnesses that are without history in the adolescent
- eating disorders, ranging from compulsive overeating to loss of appetite and refusal to eat

If the affair is an on again/off again experience, older adolescent children will begin to despise the infidel parent for his inability to commit himself to the parent who stays with the children (especially if the spouse continues to allow the infidel to return after going off with the mistress). They will also begin to lose respect for the spouse and her wishy-washy behavior. When the spouse becomes stronger and refuses to let the infidel come back, respect for both parents returns.

All children, and most adolescents, want to give the infidel a fair chance to come back to the family. But adolescents, with their newfound sense of justice and emerging sexuality, will usually draw the line first, saying "Enough is enough." They will usually see the necessity of applying tough love to the back-and-forth infidel before the spouse does!

Because an affair produces so much turmoil, it is difficult to spell out an ideal process that works for every family. The bottom line is that you are trying to make the best decision in a very bad situation. Unless you are getting advice from someone who has worked with affair recovery or who has been through it himself, be careful. It's easy for the well-intentioned but emotionally uninvolved people around you to provide simplistic answers. There is no perfect solution to every lousy situation.

Having said that, here is a list of dos and don'ts that apply to most situations:

Do

1. Answer questions honestly, without speculating on what you don't know.
2. Reassure children that you will be there for them, regardless of what happens.
3. Have the children talk to the infidel directly if they have questions about the affair.
4 Have family discussions regularly to see if everyone is doing OK.
5. Review common emotional symptoms with the child who appears to be locked up "tighter than a drum" emotionally.
6. Protect the children from seeing the infidel with the partner (for example, when the infidel moves out, don't let the partner come help him); ask the infidel to honor this commitment until either reconciliation or a divorce occurs.

DON'T

1. Tell all the details to the children; most details are only appropriate for adults, and kids aren't ready for them (in fact most adults aren't sure if they're ready!).
2. Force the children to choose between their parents; if it comes to that, you should decide as a couple.
3. Promise things you have no control over, such as visits or other favors from the infidel.
4. Speak for the infidel; it may be tough not to, especially in the face of the many questions kids ask, but encourage them to ask the infidel directly unless there's clear danger of physical violence.
5. Restrict the children from talking to whom they choose.
6. Lean on the children for advice and direction.
7. Make the children see the infidel if they don't want to.
8. Engage in character assassination of the infidel.

APPENDIX B

MATERIALS FOR USE WITH A COUPLES' SUPPORT GROUP

The following materials are presented here for use in support groups that help couples strengthen their marriages. In the group that meets at our church (First Evangelical Free Church of Fullerton, Calif.), known as New Foundation, the host couple reads the material below as a welcoming exercise to kick off each meeting. The Twelve Steps for Couples, along with the original Twelve Steps of Alcoholics Anonymous, are presented for collateral use in such a group, or for the reader's own use.

In the opening dialogue, the 1 and 2 represent alternate readers (the husband is 1, the wife, 2) who serve as coordinators/hosts for the group. They alternate reading this material as a welcoming exercise for each meeting.

1 Hi, my name is _____

2 and my name is _____

1 Welcome to New Foundation, our support group for couples willing to work toward having a healthy marriage.

2 We hope you will find this to be a safe place where together we can begin to build a solid foundation from which our relationships can continue to grow even stronger.

1 **THE PROBLEM.** We have come to the point in our relationship where we no longer feel safe with one another.

263

2   We are not able to share our anger with one another in a constructive way, and we are also afraid of sharing our deepest hurts with each other.

1   Our lives have come to be centered on blaming each other rather than sharing what is going on with ourselves.

2   When we feel blamed we tend to shut out what is being said and stop listening.

1   We struggle with forgiving one another, and it is often difficult for us to admit our part in a conflict.

2   It is much easier for us to point the finger at each other rather than to look at how we ourselves need to change.

1   Much to our dismay, we have found ourselves repeating family interactions that we witnessed in our own childhood.

2   We still carry many wounds from our past, and these get in the way of our loving each other.

1   While we long for intimacy, we are very frightened of it and sometimes unknowingly sabotage our progress when we start to get close to one another.

2   Being aware of the problem, we can allow ourselves to change through the solution.

1   **THE SOLUTION.** In the solution we find that just as it took us a long time to develop our problems, so we can allow ourselves time in the recovery process.

2   We find hope in knowing that others have traveled this path before us and have been successful.

1   We learn to focus on how we ourselves need to change and stop trying to change each other.

2   We learn to differentiate what we are responsible for and what we are not responsible for.

1   We recognize that it is not a sign of weakness, but rather a step of great courage to admit that we need help.

2   By allowing ourselves to experience healing from our past, we find a new freedom in the way we relate with each other in the present.

1   As we process with each other how hurt and angry we have felt, we find that forgiveness really is possible and we can be set free from the bitterness and rage that has been wreaking havoc in our lives.

2   As we learn how to listen and share more effectively, while experiencing our renewed faithfulness to one another, we grow to new levels of trust that we did not think would be possible.

1   By committing ourselves to God and working the twelve steps based on Scripture, we can turn our marriage into a new direction and more fully experience the kind of relationship we long to have.

2   Please stand and repeat the Serenity Prayer with us.

> God grant me the serenity
> to accept the things I cannot change,
> the courage to change the things I can,
> and the wisdom to know the difference.

This material was developed by David Osborne for use in New Foundation, a Twelve Step couple support group at the First Evangelical Free Church, Fullerton, California.

Twelve Steps for Couples

Step One We admitted we were powerless to change our spouse—that our lives had become unmanageable. "I know that nothing good lives in me, that is, in my sinful nature. For I have the desire to do what is good, but I cannot carry it out" (Romans 7:18 NIV).

Step Two Came to believe that a power greater than ourselves could restore us to sanity. "For it is God who works in you to will and to act according to his good purpose" (Philippians 2:13 NIV).

Step Three Made a decision to turn our will and our lives over to the care of God as we understood Him. "Therefore, I urge you, brothers, in view of God's mercy, to offer your bodies as living sacrifices, holy and pleasing to God—this is your spiritual act of worship" (Romans 12:1 NIV).

Step Four Made a searching and fearless moral inventory of ourselves. "Let us examine our ways and test them, and let us return to the Lord" (Lamentations 3:40 NIV).

Step Five Admitted to God, to ourselves, and to another human being the exact nature of our wrongs. "Therefore confess your sins to each other and pray for each other so that you may be healed" (James 5:16a NIV).

Step Six Were entirely ready to have God remove all these defects of character. "Humble yourselves before the Lord, and he will lift you up" (James 4:10 NIV).

Step Seven Humbly asked Him to remove our shortcomings. "If we confess our sins, he is faithful and just and will forgive us our sins and purify us from all unrighteousness" (1 John 1:9 NIV).

Step Eight Made a list of all persons we had harmed and became willing to make amends to them all. "Do to others as you would have them do to you" (Luke 6:31 NIV).

Step Nine Made direct amends to such people wherever possible, except when to do so would injure them or others. "Therefore, if you are offering your gift at the altar and there remember that your brother has something against you, leave your gift there in front of the altar. First go and be reconciled to your brother; then come and offer your gift" (Matthew 5:23-24 NIV).

Step Ten   Continued to make personal inventory and when we were wrong promptly admitted it. "So, if you think you are standing firm, be careful that you don't fall!" (1 Corinthians 10:12 NIV).

Step Eleven   Sought through prayer and meditation to improve our conscious contact with God as we understood Him, praying only for knowledge of His will for us and the power to carry that out. "Let the word of Christ dwell in you richly" (Colossians 3:16a NIV).

Step Twelve   Having had a spiritual awakening as a result of these steps, we tried to carry this message to others, and to practice these principles in all areas of our lives. "Blessed be the God and Father of our Lord Jesus Christ, the Father of all mercies and God of all comfort; who comforts us in all our affliction so that we may be able to comfort those who are in any affliction with the comfort with which we ourselves are comforted by God" (2 Corinthians 1:3-4).

For additional help in starting an Infidelity Recovery Group, please contact

WESOM, Inc.
Post Office Box #46312
Chicago, IL 60646
(312) 792-7034*

or

The First Evangelical Free Church
2801 N. Brea Blvd.
Fullerton, CA 92635
(714) 529-5544

* This is a computerized answering service. Please leave a message and your telephone number, and your call will be returned.

The Twelve Steps of Alcoholics Anonymous

1. We admitted we were powerless over alcohol—that our lives had become unmanageable.

2. Came to believe that a Power greater than ourselves could restore us to sanity.

3. Made a decision to turn our will and our lives over to the care of God *as we understood Him.*

4. Made a searching and fearless moral inventory of ourselves.

5. Admitted to God, to ourselves and to another human being the exact nature of our wrongs.

6. Were entirely ready to have God remove all these defects of character.

7. Humbly asked Him to remove our shortcomings.

8. Made a list of all persons we had harmed, and became willing to make amends to them all.

9. Made direct amends to such people wherever possible, except when to do so would injure them or others.

10. Continued to take personal inventory and when we were wrong promptly admitted it.

11. Sought through prayer and meditation to improve our conscious contact with God, *as we understood Him,* praying only for knowledge of His will for us and the power to carry that out.

12. Having had a spiritual awakening as the result of these steps, we tried to carry this message to alcoholics, and to practice these principles in all our affairs.

Appendix C

Marital Satisfaction Time Line

On the following page is a copy of the work sheet "Marital Satisfaction Time Line." Directions for using this work sheet are given in chapter 14, "The 90-Day Experiment."

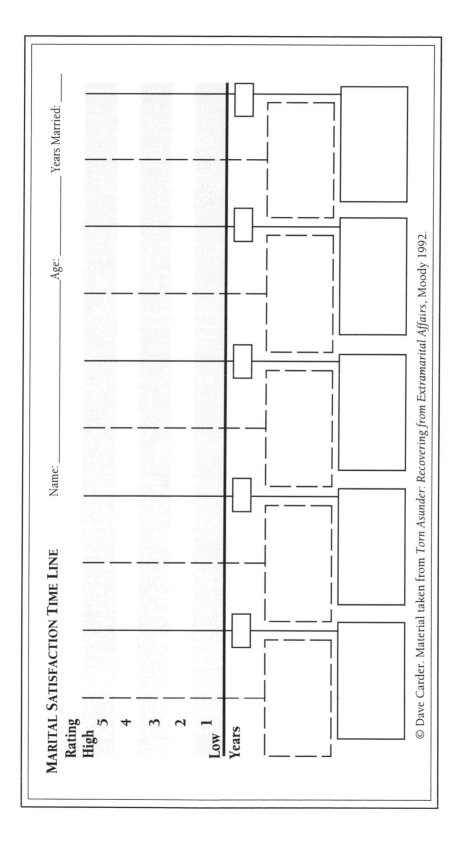

MARITAL SATISFACTION TIME LINE

Name: _____ Age: _____ Years Married: _____

Rating
High
5
4
3
2
1
Low
Years

APPENDIX D

A SELECTED BIBLIOGRAPHY

Adams, Kenneth. *Silently Seduced.* Deerfield Beach, Fla.: Health Communications, 1991.

Bradshaw, John. *Healing the Shame That Binds You.* Deerfield Beach, Fla.: Health Communications, 1988.

Brown, Emily. *Patterns of Infidelity and Their Treatment.* New York: Brunner/Mazel, 1991.

Brzeczek, Richard, and Emil Brzeczek. *Addicted to Adultery.* New York: Bantam, 1989.

Carder, Dave, Earl Henslin, John townsend, Henry Cloud, and Alice Braward. *Secrets of Your Family Tree: Healing for Adult Children of Dysfunctional Families.* Chicago: Moody, 1991.

Carnes, Patrick. *Out of the Shadows: Understanding Sexual Addiction.* Minneapolis: CompCare, 1985.

Dalbey, Gordon. *Healing the Masculine Soul.* Waco, Tex.: Word, 1991.

Dobson, James C. *Love Must Be Tough.* Waco, Tex.: Word, 1983.

Earle, Ralph, et al. *Lonely All the Time: Recognizing, Understanding and Overcoming Sex Addictions, for Addicts and Co-Dependents.* New York: Pocket Books, 1990.

Farrell, Warren. *Why Men Are the Way They Are.* New York: Berkley, 1988.

Laaser, Mark R. *The Secret Sin: Healing the Wounds of Sexual Addiction.* Grand Rapids: Zondervan, 1992.

Love, Patricia. *The Emotional Incest Syndrome.* New York: Bantam, 1990.

Rutter, Peter. *Sex in the Forbidden Zone: When Men in Power—*
      Therapists, Doctors, Clergy, Teachers, and Others—Betray
      Women's Trust. Los Angeles: J. P. Tarcher, 1989.
Schneider, Jennifer. *Back from Betrayal: Surviving His Affairs.* San
      Francisco: Harper & Row, 1988.
Swindoll, Charles R. *Strike the Original Match.* Portland, Oreg.:
      Multnomah, 1980.

Learn More about Recovering from Extramarital Affairs from Dave Carder

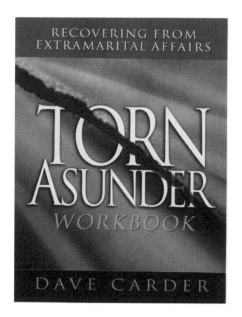

Torn Asunder (Workbook)
Recovering From Extramarital Affairs

As a companion to the *Torn Asunder* book, Dave Carder has organized a 90-day workbook with daily twenty-minute homework exercises initiated by each spouse on alternating days. The recovery process concludes with a "Final Project" consisting of bringing together what you have learned about yourself, your marriage, your future, and the family you came from in order to have closure about the situation.

ISBN #0-8024-7141-2, Paperback

Moody Press, a ministry of Moody Bible Institute,
is designed for education, evangelization, and edification.
If we may assist you in knowing more about Christ
and the Christian life, please write us without obligation:
Moody Press, c/o MLM, Chicago, Illinois 60610.